The Complete Personal Injury Practice Manual

Al J. Cone
and
Verne Lawyer

The Complete Personal Injury Practice Manual

Prentice-Hall, Inc.
Englewood Cliffs, New Jersey

Prentice-Hall International, Inc., *London*
Prentice-Hall of Australia, Pty. Ltd., *Sydney*
Prentice-Hall Canada, Inc., *Toronto*
Prentice-Hall of India Private Ltd., *New Delhi*
Prentice-Hall of Japan, Inc., *Tokyo*
Prentice-Hall of Southeast Asia Pte. Ltd., *Singapore*
Whitehall Books, Ltd., *Wellington, New Zealand*
Editora Prentice-Hall do Brasil Ltda., *Rio de Janeiro*

"This publication is designed to provide accurate and authoritative information in regard to the subject matter covered. It is sold with the understanding that the publisher is not engaged in rendering legal, accounting, or other professional service. If legal advice or other expert assistance is required, the services of a competent professional person should be sought."

—From the Declaration of Principles jointly adopted by a Committee of the American Bar Association and a Committee of Publishers and Associations.

Library of Congress Cataloging in Publication Data

Cone, Al J.
The complete personal injury practice manual.

Includes index.
1. Personal injuries—United States. 2. Actions and defenses—United States.
I. Lawyer, Verne. II. Title.
KF8925.P4C66 1983 346.7303'23 83-3166
347.306323

ISBN 0-13-162248-X

Printed in the United States of America

About the Authors

Al Cone's name is a name that needs no identification to personal injury trial lawyers.

He is a past president of the Association of Trial Lawyers of America and his firm is one of only three firms in the country that have had two presidents of that august body.

Mr. Cone was one of the founders of the Academy of Florida Trial Lawyers and its first president. He is a member of the International Academy of Trial Lawyers, the International Society of Barristers, and the American College of Trial Lawyers.

He served with distinction in World War II, winning the British Military Cross, the Silver Star, and the Bronze Star for valor in his service in France and Germany. He also received the Purple Heart.

Mr. Cone is a former associate professor of law at the University of Florida. He is the author of many legal articles and publications and has lectured in nearly every state of the union on many occasions.

He resides with his wife, Imogene, in West Palm Beach, Florida, and practices law with his firm of Cone, Wagner, Nugent, Johnson, Hazouri & Roth, P.A., in West Palm Beach.

* * *

Verne Lawyer has been an innovative leader of the trial bar for many years. Beginning as a criminal defense lawyer, he expanded his practice to the civil field and is now recognized as one of the leaders in the field of complex litigation.

His leadership and talent have been especially noteworthy in the fields of aviation law, defective products cases, and highway design and maintenance cases.

In short, he is a lawyer's lawyer.

Mr. Lawyer is one of the founders of the Iowa Academy of Trial Lawyers and has served as its longtime secretary-treasurer and as editor of its publications. He is a member of the International Academy of Trial Lawyers, the International Society of Barristers, and the American College of Trial Lawyers.

He resides with his wife, Vivian, also a lawyer, in Des Moines, Iowa.

Foreword

There are very few books available to lawyers which so completely encapsulate the span of a successful practice. This one, written by two of the masters of the trial bar who are as astute in their offices and in public as they are in court, will be worth many times its cost to any lawyer who would like to follow in such enviable footsteps. The advice contained in its pages is practical, sound, and easy to comprehend. Understanding its messages will go a long way toward avoiding mistakes in handling people and their cases. If a lawyer could have only a one-volume manual on personal injury practice in his library, this should be it.

F. Lee Bailey

A Word from the Authors

The authors' goal in this book is summed up in F. Lee Bailey's statement, "If a lawyer could have only a one-volume manual on personal injury practice in his library, this should be it."

No one book can meet such a test, but as Robert Browning said, "A man's reach should exceed his grasp, or what's a heaven for."

We believe that success in building a personal injury practice requires four ingredients:

1. Talent
2. Hard work
3. A small amount of luck
4. Successful techniques of case handling and development

We believe that if the precepts of this book are followed, the fourth ingredient will have been supplied. The techniques described in this book have worked for us and thousands of other successful lawyers. Try them.

It is our intention that if you read from cover to cover, you will find at least some ideas that will enable you to practice law better, more easily, or more comfortably. If you are a personal injury specialist, and after you have read this book you have not received at least one idea of value, the authors, with unabashed immodesty, offer to return your purchase price, but we want the book back!

If you are an experienced general practitioner, the purpose of this book is to enable you to decide with confidence to accept, refuse, or refer a personal injury case. This book will not make you an experienced personal injury specialist any more than an operator's manual would make you an experienced pilot, but if you follow the precepts of this book, you can rapidly learn to "solo," and with practice, if you have the necessary native ability, you can be an "experienced pilot."

Although this book is not intended for the neophyte lawyer, it should help the new lawyer to leave more rapidly that unlovely status for the more profitable one of "the experienced lawyer."

Philosophy of the personal injury laywer:

We believe that the practice of personal injury law, on the side of the victims of our complex and mechanized society, is the highest and best expression of the art of practicing law.

Why?

For two reasons.

First, the victims of our society are usually injured by forces beyond their control and without substantial contribution to the cause of their injury. Often their injuries stagger the imagination and strain our empathy.

Frequently, even usually, they come to the personal injury lawyer after they have exhausted the potential for help of the medical profession, and the limits of the societal largess, with their lives and the lives of their families in disarray and distress.

If the personal injury lawyer cannot help them, no one can.

It is the task of the personal injury lawyer to balance the scales of justice by forcing the element of society responsible for the injury to assume financial responsibility for that injury.

No matter what payment for damages may be made by an insurance company, rest assured that the next round of premium increases will reflect the risk.

Often the damages involve the recognition, assessment, and proof of the most subtle of human losses such as damage to human personality, loss of capacity to lead a normal life, and changes in human relationships. The transmutation of theses losses into money damages involves ingenuity in persuasion and presentation.

The fixation of responsibility on the offending tort feasors will be vigorously resisted by the honed skill of the defense bar, aided and abetted by the resources and experience of the professional defendants. Small wonder, then, that only a small percentage of the injured ever receive more than a fraction in damages for their genuine injuries, if they are not represented by competent lawyers in this complex field.

A second reason is the high quality of the calling.

The fixation of responsibility for unnecessary injury to another tends to create a safer society.

The unbridled ingenuity of statute-passers and regulation-makers can never keep pacc with the change and development in a free society. Only the general alertness and interest in safety, occasioned by self-interest in avoiding successful suit, can engender the alertness and concern necessary to create a climate of concern for safety. The personal injury lawyer should be looked upon as the guardian and enforcer of society's safety from unintentional harm.

We feel that the plaintiff's personal injury lawyer is nearly always on the side of the angels, and if an occasional client of ours should receive a little more than expected, it should be considered no more than the sting of the whip of justice on the often uncaring tort feasor.

Al J. Cone
Verne Lawyer

Contents

The Complete Personal Injury Practice Manual

1

Getting the Case off the Ground Successfully

The clue to a successful and profitable personal injury law practice hinges upon the decision whether to accept, refuse, or refer the case.

As the basis of that decision, it is extremely important that all basic facts pertaining to the incident that gave rise to the injury be obtained from the client or the referring counsel, and that the facts be accurate and confirmed, if necessary, from independent sources. Too often lawyers, young and old, engage in a process that might be called wishful thinking; in the anxiety to be helpful to an injured client, the lawyer on occasion will assume that certain facts exist when in fact they do not, and a fatal mistake can be made in failing to confirm critical facts before making the decision to undertake representation in the case.

1.1 THE MECHANICS OF PRELIMINARY INVESTIGATION

The attorney should develop a routine form for a first investigative report.

1.1.1 First investigative Report

The investigation report form should call for specific information, and should provide specific places for the investigator or attorney to ascertain whether such information was obtained. This minimizes the possibility of overlooking some information because of the pressures of a busy practice. An example of such an investigation report form used by one of the authors follows with explanatory notes.

FIRST INVESTIGATIVE REPORT

Plaintiff's name: ______________________________

Enclosures to file

1. Signed two-page statement of John Doe
2. Signed one-page statement of Jane Doe
3. Six-page copy of Police Investigation Report of Accident
4. Florida Traffic Accident Report by the Highway Patrol
5. Ten 3 × 5 black-and-white photographs taken at the scene of the accident by the police

(The list of enclosures to file at the beginning of the report permits the reviewer of the file to rapidly ascertain if all supporting data, such as statements, are attached to the report.)

Referring attorney

Smith & Jones, 268 Blank Street, Eau Gallie, Florida. (This section is desirable in order that information concerning the file may be conveyed to the referring attorney. Since the present Canon of Ethics states that fees may be shared on a basis of work done and responsibility shared, the practice of furnishing copies of all information and pleadings to the referring attorney tends to comply with this Canon of Ethics. Additionally, the referring attorney is afforded the opportunity to make suggestions or contributions concerning the preparation of the file.)

Plaintiff

This paragraph should cover, first of all, details such as age, sex, and other pertinent information concerning the client. Details of employment, or spouse's employment, as well as telephone numbers where the clients can be reached, both day and night, should be included. Any history of prior injury or related factors should be included, and if there are any impressions noted that the client should not read, they should be noted on a blind memo to the file, with no copy for the client. If at all possible, the investigator or attorney in charge of investigation should sit in on the initial interview with the client and then further interview the plaintiff, completing the data sheet and having the plaintiff sign it, as well as taking a signed statement concerning the details of the accident. In the event that the investigator is out of the office at the time of the first interview, it is desirable that at a later time he or she go over the data sheet with the plaintiff personally. This will allow the investigator to hear the plaintiff's account of the accident, to form impressions of the plaintiff and members of the family, and to acquire other background information that he or she must have in mind while proceeding with the case.

The plaintiff's statement is important in that it clearly establishes the sequence of events leading up to the accident, as well as providing the file with a short, concise account of the accident, which can often be forwarded for settlement purposes.

In preparing the data concerning the plaintiff, it should be borne in mind that unless it is otherwise designated, the client receives a copy of this report at all times. An example follows:

Deceased Plaintiff: John Doe, white male, age 43, divorced, at the time of this accident, resided at the Smith Hotel, Melbourne, Florida. Doe came to the Melbourne area late in 1978, married Jane Doe November 25, 1978, divorcing her during December, 1980. Mrs. Doe, as indicated in her statement, believes the final divorce hearing was on December 6 or 8, but she has not as yet received final papers from her attorney, John Johnson, of Melbourne. She indicated that she had not completely paid her fee for the divorce, and this is probably the answer to why the final decree papers have not been turned over to her. She indicated, however, that the decree was granted with no property settlement, alimony, or support for her two sons, now age 14 and 16, who were children of a previous marriage.

Mr. Doe worked for Commerical Cleaners, a commercial cleaning establishment, cleaning buildings and opening and closing residences, for about six or eight months in 1979. He was then employed for about one year by James Frank, and when work was slow at this point, he left and went to work for Swimming Pools, Inc. of Melbourne. He was employed by them for several months, engaged in the building and maintenance of swimming pools. At the time of the accident, he was working during the day for Builders, Inc. of Melbourne, and had run into Mr. Frank two or three days before the accident and indicated that if there was any part-time work, he was available. Mr. Frank stated that he did need a man, and on the 28th of October, 1981, contacted Mr. Doe and indicated that he should go to work that evening. Mr. Doe met Jim Smith, who worked for Mr. Frank, and with Smith driving, went to A Street and cleaned a home, beginning at about 7:00 o'clock on that evening. He also had dinner with his ex-wife that evening from about 6:00 P.M. to 7:00 P.M. and returned her to her place of employment at Eastern Auto Supply. She indicated he had nothing to drink during the dinner hour and did not appear intoxicated to her.

Smith and Doe left work about 10:00 P.M. and went to Jones Market on F Street, on Highway A1A, at which time they purchased some food, and reportedly purchased a can of beer each. Mr. Doe reportedly consumed his can of beer, and Mr. Smith drank about half of his, intending to finish it later on in the evening. At any rate, they then got into the Chevrolet truck, with Mr. Smith driving, and in pulling out onto A1A, they were struck by the defendant's 1979 Ford.

Everyone whom this writer spoke with regarding Mr. Doe stated that he is a likeable person, a reliable and conscientious worker, and gives no indication of drinking to an excessive degree.

Date, time, and place

This paragraph should include a physical description of the scene of the accident, the date, year, day of the week, and time. It should also include a description of the weather conditions as nearly as can be determined, whether or not the area was artificially lighted, if the accident occurred at night, and in some instances, factors such as the position of the sun (as in the late afternoon) oncoming traffic, etc. It should also be noted whether there were any discrepancies between the plaintiff's account of the accident and that of the police. For this purpose the traffic diagram, along with the impressions of the investigator of the scene of the accident, should be double-checked. An example follows:

Date, Time, and Place: October 28, 1981, 10:50 P.M., State Road A1A, one-tenth of a mile south of its intersection with F Street, at a location of a store known as Jones Market. Jones Market has an asphalt-paved parking lot that opens directly onto the street, along its length. The view looking north from the southern exit of the parking lot, where the accident occurred, is somewhat restricted by a concrete louvred fence; however, when the vehicle is brought to the very edge of A1A, the traffic can be seen coming from the north. The area is not artificially lit at night. At the time of this accident, it was threatening rain, it had rained earlier in that evening, and the roads were damp. Immediately after the accident, it began to rain quite heavily. A1A at this point is four driving lanes wide, divided by a broken yellow line between the northbound and southbound lanes, with a double yellow line dividing the separate lanes. The road is straight and level, slightly humped, and is 99 feet wide.

Description of the accident or defect

This paragraph should contain as concise as possible an account of the actions by all parties leading up to the accident, including the directions the automobilies were traveling prior to the accident, movements of the automobilies following the impact, final halting places, action of the police investigating the accident, a summary of the charges placed, if any, details of the removal of persons to hospitals and subsequent treatment, if known. An example follows:

Description of the accident: The plaintiff was a front seat passenger in the Chevrolet truck operated by Jim Smith, which entered into the southbound lanes of A1A, apparently intending to turn into the northbound lanes of A1A. The vehicle was struck in the left front side by a 1979 Ford, the point of impact occurring in the middle of the left-hand southbound lane. The impact caused the Chevrolet to spin around and turn over, coming to a stop on its left side, with the front end pointing southwest in the right-hand southbound lane. The Ford continued across the northbound lanes, coming to a stop in a ditch on the east side of the road, 87 feet from the point of impact.

The first person on the scene was one Arthur Jackson, whose statement has not yet been obtained. There is a bar in the market area known as Jim's Bar, and the patrons of this establishment aided in removing the plaintiff and Mr. Smith from the Chevrolet truck. Following the impact, the Ford caught fire in the hood area, and after it came to a stop, Arthur Jackson, along with several other people from the bar nearby, threw sand on the hood to put the fire out, and then removed the driver to await ambulances. Smith and the plaintiff were taken to General Hospital, where they were treated by Dr. Gold, Dr. Blank, and Dr. Johnson. The plaintiff suffered fractures of the arm and legs, and internal injuries, and died one month later, on November 30th. A statement was obtained from the plaintiff and is enclosed in the file.

(A photograph or diagram of the accident or defect described, provided or approved by your client, should be attached or included in the description of the accident or defect, if possible. See also "Photographs" and "Diagrams.")

Defendant

The details of the investigator's contact with the defendant should be included, if available: A summary of the defendant's signed statement, if such statement was obtained, investigator's impression of the defendant and how he will appear to others, the plausibility of his account, and any factors concerning the defendant's background which it is deemed advisable to learn. The investigator may also make use of local credit bureaus to substantiate information pertaining to the financial background of the defendant. A variety of approaches and methods should be used in interviewing the defendant. If the investigator is able to secure access to the insurance policy as it relates to the accident, the policy number, limits, agent, adjuster, and company should be included under this caption or set forth under a separate caption, described to the investigator by the defendant and/or the adjuster or attorney.

(See "Photographs" and "Diagrams.")

Witnesses

A brief paragraph summary of the statements of witnesses who have been contacted should be included here. The use of a negative statement should not be underrated; that is, one in which the witness states that he did not see anything, or did not hear anything, or was not in a position to observe the actions or happenings concerned. These negative statements should be taken so that at a later date the file will contain them.

A subcaption under this heading is:

Investigating Officer's Interview, covering the result of the interview with the investigating officer: the details of the accident as he recalls them, degree of intoxication and/or injuries, position of the vehicles, and other factors that can be refreshed in his mind by the investigation accident report. Photographs or diagrams of the accident, prepared by the investigator, should be included in this report.

Accident report

This caption is rarely used except when there is some possibility that the report might be in error, or when the changes listed have subsequently been changed or dropped. Immediately upon receipt of the accident report and subsequent assignment of the file, it is important to follow up on the defendant's traffic hearing so that the attorney may make an appearance and provide a court reporter if necessary. It is often important for the investigator to be at this hearing in order that any witnesses listed on the accident report may be called.

Photographs

A description of all photographs that have been taken by the police and/or public news services should be included, as well as an interpretation of them and a notation as to the feasibility of purchasing them. A description of photographs that the investigator may have made of the scene of the accident, and/or the automobiles involved, should also be included so that when the pictures are returned at a later date, the investigator will be able to refresh his memory by reviewing this report.

In photographing the automobiles concerned, it is important to take a number of photographs showing clearly all details of damage, including any damage to the interior of the car that might have been caused by the occupants, as well as objects such as containers of intoxicants within the automobile, and/or obstructing parcels. These photographs may be all that an expert witness would later have to go on in his or her analysis of the accident. As with statements, too many photographs are always better than too few.

Photographs of injuries to the plaintiff are of vital importance. The investigator must be familiar with the equipment and the techniques involved in securing proper photographs suitable for enlargement. A number of photographs should be taken at various lens settings and angles inasmuch as scars and wounds will not be available to re-photograph at a later date.

(See also "Description of the Accident or Defect," and "Defendant.")

Survey

This paragraph should be included only when it is felt that the use of an expert witness, engineer, or other specialized technician is warranted. The results of the finding of a specialist should be included briefly in this paragraph.

Diagrams

In many instances, the investigator will find that the traffic investigation report prepared by the officer at the scene is inadequate. The investigator should familiarize himself or herself with the standard procedures in diagraming an automobile accident. Possible causative factors can often best be illustrated by devices such as sequence diagrams and road profiles. Common sense should be the guide in this matter.

(See also "Description of the Accident or Defect," and "Defendant.")

Plaintiff's property damage and/or medical pay

This caption need not be used in most instances since the information can be included in the paragraph covering the plaintiff, or under the damage section. However, in some instances, the nature of the accident will be such that it may be necessary for the attorney to complete forms and act as an agent for the plaintiff in securing benefits available to him under his insurance policy or the defendant's medical insurance policy. Details of these factors may be discussed as they arise.

Investigator's analysis or summary

This area allows a synopsis or summary to be made so that the attorney reviewing the file can quickly receive an overall picture of the case as it develops. Under this paragraph should be included the investigator's impressions and recommendations for further action regarding the handling of the case in general. The investigator should voice the recommendations since often he or she is more intimately acquainted with the factors involved in the case than the attorney, and thus, the attorney must rely upon the impressions of the investigator. It will be helpful to break down this caption into three main paragraphs, as follows:

Liability: This, of course, is most important from the investigator's standpoint; hence, the paragraph should cover such factors as the degree of negligence and the possibility of contributory or comparative negligence, as well as other special factors, such as the Guest Passenger Statute, doctrine of last clear chance, and others. The possibilities of special factors concerning the defense should also be included here.

Damages: It is helpful to include any information that will allow the attorney to evaluate more clearly the damage picture as concerns the injury: the amount of special damages, the possibility of further medical treatment, and/or disability as indicated to date.

Financial Responsibility: This section will serve as a summary of those factors that constitute the essence of the file, and in this paragraph should be included confirmation of insurance coverage and/or personal assets available in the event of a recovery judgment.

Unfinished Items

In this paragraph, outlined in numerical sequence, are the uncompleted investigative steps, as well as instructions to the secretary concerning the sending of medical discovery letters, letters requesting an accident report, driving records, motor vehicle registration, letters of confirmation, and other form letters. In connection with this section, the diary (tickler) slip should be made pertaining to directions for returning the file to the attorney or to the investigator for further work.

After the attorney has obtained the basic facts—that is, the date of the incident, the location, persons involved, circumstances surrounding the incident, and injury—it is wise to conduct what may well be called a preliminary investigation to determine whether the facts, the law, and the technical aspects of the case warrant binding the attorney to representation of the injured party.

We normally advise the client that we will conduct a preliminary investigation of the facts for the purpose of determining whether the facts, the law, and the technical aspects of the case warrant further pursuit of the case by us and the client. We usually agree to conduct such a preliminary investigation at no cost to the client with the understanding that after the investigation is completed we will have a further conference with the client or referring attorney, the purpose of which is to explain our analysis of the case and whether it has merit. The factual investigation includes a review of the facts presented by the client or his referring attorney, some witness interviews, if appropriate, a review of the law applicable to the developed facts, and in the case of medical negligence, defective product liability cases, air crash cases, and the like, a review of the technical material to determine whether the client has a viable action against the particular proposed defendant.

1.1.2 Refusing the Case: One Key to Success

If the preliminary investigation reveals that the case is without merit and cannot be economically and profitably processed to the client's satisfaction, or if the case is just plain without merit, then it is incumbent upon the attorney to have a conference with the client and his or her referring attorney at an early date for the purpose of reviewing the results of the preliminary investigation and to explain why the case must be refused by the office. Our practice is to agree to make available to the client and the referring attorney, if any, the results of our preliminary investigation, together with our recommendations regarding the further pursuit of the case and with the understanding that if we do not feel it is a case that can be successfully or profitably handled by our office, agree to cooperate and make available to any other lawyer of their choice the material developed by us in the preliminary investigation.

It is imperative to be prompt in advising a client of your refusal of the case to avoid any statute of limitations problem and to maintain good client relations for the future. A brief, tactful reason for the refusal should be given.

1.1.3 Accepting the Case: Have Your Theory in Sharp Focus

If the preliminary investigation indicates that the injured party has a meritorious case against some defendant, an early conference should be held with the plaintiff and his or her referring counsel, if any, to review the evidence obtained and the results of the legal and technical research, and to discuss the terms under which the lawyer is willing to represent the client. At this stage, it is an excellent idea to advise the client not only of the terms of the relationship between client and counsel, but to explain in detail the manner in which the office processes cases such as this. It is considered highly advisable, and indeed mandatory, in some jurisdictions that a written contract of representation be executed by the parties at the inception of the actual representation and that the contract spell out in detail the respective responsibilities of counsel and the injured party. If referring counsel is involved, it is mandatory that the client be informed of the participation of referring counsel and the terms upon which referring counsel will be paid. Oral contracts are to be discouraged since they can and often do lead to misunderstandings between counsel and client and may well be unenforceable in some jurisdictions in the event of a dispute.

1.2 ACCEPTED CLIENT INTERVIEW AND CONTRACT

1.2.1 Final Factors in Decision

Early newspaper reporters were taught to look at every lead story to determine whether, in the early phases of the story, the factors of who, what, where, when, how, and sometimes why, were discussed. It is a useful mental discipline to apply this same line of thought to the ultimate decision on whether a case should be accepted, refused, or referred.

More often than not, when a case has been properly prepared, if a verdict is of a size that is different from that anticipated, and no other cause can be isolated, the personality of the plaintiff may well be an important factor. In analyzing the case, never forget to say, "How, if I were a juror, would I look on this plaintiff and his or her personality?" Ask yourself, "Would the jury subconsciously approve of this plaintiff and subconsciously desire to help?"

Ask yourself what the plaintiff was doing and how the jury would look upon the activities of the plaintiff and/or the defendant at the time the accident happened.

Before accepting the borderline case, if an attorney will quietly reflect on the factors indicated, the decision will often become manifest.

The last factor of "why" is one that attorneys should not overlook. There are cases that are likely to be unprofitable, but that nevertheless seem almost a cry for justice. These cases should not be turned down out of hand. Some of the greatest satisfaction in the practice of law is in acting as an instrument of justice.

1.2.2 Dramatic Effects of the First Interview

The first interview with the client can have an important and dramatic influence on the results obtained in a lawsuit. In this initial interview, the client must understand his or her relationship with the lawyer, the problems involved in the case, and the manner in which the lawyer can help him or her. The client can, in turn, help the lawyer by understanding something of the mechanics of a lawsuit and the amount of time necessary for the lawyer to obtain justice.

The failure to establish a relationship in which the client trusts and has confidence in a lawyer will frequently result in the client's unwillingness to follow the advice and instructions of the lawyer, and an attempt to substitute his or her opinion for that of the lawyer as to the actions that would be appropriate in the case. For these reasons, it is essential that the lawyer demonstrate to the client knowledge of some of the problems involved, including those of a medical nature. The lawyer should, moreover, demonstrate his or her competency and willingness to come to grips with these problems.

1.2.3 Recognizing and Dealing with the Client's Emotional Problems

In establishing the relationship with the client, it is important to recognize and understand the emotional problems that beset the client more often than not when he or she first comes to the office of a lawyer after having been injured. In the majority of accident cases, the normal life pattern of the client has been disrupted and the client has not been able to adjust emotionally to the disruption. This situation is often complicated by the questions of whether the client had any substantial neurotic tendencies prior to the time of trauma. One frequently encounters a client who may have a precarious adjustment to life, but nevertheless one which permitted him or her to handle the day-to-day problems of life as they arose. However, trauma added to existing neurotic tendencies may often result in total inability of the accident victim to cope with the problems besetting him or her. Where this occurs, the client is likely to be resentful not only of the tort feasor who inflicted the injury, and of the insurance company with whom he or she has been unable to conduct a satisfactory negotiation, but also, at a subconscious level, resentful of his or her own feelings of inadequacy in coping with the stress of life in general.

Frequently, too, the client has sustained some temporary or permanent change of personality resulting from a continued subjection to either physical pain or mental distress. Often the family of the injured victim fails to understand the emotional dynamics that have caused the client to be a much less pleasant person to live with, and a person who is much less considerate of the welfare of others. This lack of understanding on the part of the client's family frequently aggravates the psychic injury received by the accident victim. Thus, when the accident victim approaches an attorney, very often he or she is in great need of sympathetic reassurance, understanding, and hope that at least the immediate problems arising out of the accident will be resolved. In order to pave the way for the client's reassurance and confidence in the attorney, it is suggested that the following procedure be considered.

1.2.4 Preliminary Interview: Getting the Facts in Order

When the client first comes to the office, it is advisable to have a secretary, investigator, or other member of the staff conduct a very brief interview with him or her in which there should be obtained the name and address of the client, a general description of the accident, including the date and place, and some minor information concerning the circumstances leading to the injury. A form that may be filled out at this time by a receptionist or secretary follows:

PRELIMINARY INTERVIEW SHEET

1. Name ____________________
2. Address ____________________

3. Age ______
4. Telephone Number ______
5. Occupation ______
6. Date of Accident ______
7. Place of Accident ______
8. Referred by ______
9. Type of Accident ______
10. General Nature of Injury ______
11. Number of Dependents ______
12. Appearance and Personality of Client ______
13. Other Information ______

1.2.5 Discussing the Nature of the Injury

The attorney should consider the necessity of discussing the nature of the injury with the client. Often clients are totally ignorant of the prospects created by their injuries, even when they have been previously attended by a number of able doctors. Some doctors seem to feel that the mechanics of the patient's body are a trade secret to be jealously guarded even from the patient, and often a client cannot evaluate his or her legal position without some knowledge of the medical prospects. The lawyer need not and should not give medical advice in order to solve this problem, but he or she can serve as an agent to obtain information from the doctor in the form of medical reports and then convey it, with the doctor's permission, to the client. When the injury is of a type unfamiliar to the attorney, consulting a medical book will enable the attorney to ask relevant questions.

1.2.6 The Employment Contract

(a) Understanding the contract. It is important that in the first interview, the client understand and agree to the terms of the employment contract.

(b) Why a printed form? The employment contract should be prepared in mimeographed or printed form in order that the client may understand that this is the customary basis of representation.

SAMPLE CONTRACT

Date: ______________________

Gentlemen:

I, the undersigned, of ______________________________
______________________________________, hereby employ and engage you to represent me in connection with any and all claims which I may have against any and all persons, arising out of ______
____ .

For such professional services, I hereby agree to pay you thirty-three and one-third (33-1/3%) percent of the gross amount you recover for me or on my behalf (which term shall include the fair market value of any property which may be recovered).

In the event of an appeal, the fee will be increased by an amount to be agreed on at that time.

It is understood that I remain fully responsible for all court costs and other out-of-pocket expenses incurred by you in the investigation and prosecution of my claim.

It is understood that any payment to you for such services is entirely contingent upon your making recovery for me or on my behalf of money or property.

You are authorized to fully investigate my claim, and should you file suit or other legal proceedings on my behalf, to fully prepare for and prosecute the same. If after reasonable investigation of such claim or claims you determine that it is not feasible to prosecute such claim, upon notification to me of such fact, you may withdraw from representation under this agreement.

It is understood and agreed that neither party shall settle any claims arising out of this accident without first having obtained the consent thereto of the other.

I further agree that from the proceeds of any such recovery, whether by settlement, judgment, or otherwise, *you may deduct the attorney's fees to which you are entitled, and all costs and expenses which remain unpaid,* and I further agree that you may deduct the amount of all unpaid bills for doctors, hospitals and related items, making disbursement of such funds directly to the doctor or hospital, etc., concerned.

I understand that my case has been referred to the law firm of
____
for handling by ______________________________
and that he/they will receive ______________________

of the fee charged me by ______________________________

____.

I further understand that the referring lawyer agrees to assume the same legal responsibility to me for the performance of the service as ______________________________, that he or she will follow the course of my case with them and that he or she will be available at all times for consultation in this matter. I do, therefore, acknowledge and consent to the division of fee in my case as set forth above.

Yours very truly,

____

____

I, ______________________________,
referring attorney in the above matter,
do hereby acknowledge the contents
hereof and agree to be bound thereby.

____

Referring Lawyer

ACCEPTED AND APPROVED by us this ______ day of ______________________, 19______.

____

____

COMMENT: It is advisable to make certain that any standard form contract adopted by an attorney conforms to the rules of local practice and to the provisions of the bar association of which he or she is a member.

1.2.7 The Importance of More than One Form of Representation Contract

There is no reason why several variations of a standard form representation contract cannot be prepared and printed in advance. For example, the amount of work and problems involved in preparing and successfully prosecuting a defective products case, a "slip and fall" case, or a case involving medical negligence might justify a contract providing for a higher percentage of fee on a contingent basis than a case, for example, involving a simple rear-end collision with resulting visible injury to the client.

1.2.8 Providing for Reimbursement of Costs Advanced

The contingent fee contract should provide for a full reimbursement of the attorney for costs advanced on behalf of the client in the preparation of the case. The Canons of Ethics do not permit an attorney to actually pay the costs, nor to participate in them other than to advance them. It is also unbusinesslike for the attorney not to have a clear-cut understanding with the client in the beginning that he or she expects to be fully reimbursed for costs at the termination of the case by either settlement or judgment. Frequently, in the early stages of a case, the attorney is tempted to ask the client to advance some portion of the costs in order to avoid a substantial outlay on his or her own part. There might be circumstances in which an attorney is justified in asking a client to advance costs, but, more often than not, the client has already been financially weakened or even impoverished because of the accident. If the attorney feels that the client is financially able to advance the costs, obviously there is no reason why they should not be obtained. Frequently, however, the client simply could not advance the costs even if great pressure were brought to bear on him or her, and the request might create an obstacle to a good client-attorney relationship.

1.2.9 Agreeing to Account for Expenses

It is probably advisable to tell a client in the beginning that the attorney intends to spend everything necessary in order to prepare the client's case for trial and protect his or her interests, but that the attorney does not intend to spend anything that is not essential. The client, of course, is entitled to an absolute accounting of any funds expended on his behalf in the preparation of the case. If the client is informed of this, ordinarily he or she will not be concerned about the costs advanced.

1.2.10 Arranging to Deduct Unpaid Medical Bills from Recovery

The representation contract should contain a clause authorizing the attorney to deduct any unpaid medical bills from the settlement or judgment obtained and to remit them directly to the doctor or hospital involved. Much of the hostility on the part of the medical profession toward the legal profession is unnecessary and can be obviated by such a clause and by careful education of the medical profession to understand that the plaintiff's trial attorney is more often than not the greatest, and perhaps sole ally of the doctor in the collection of the client's bills from the reluctant insurance company. Understandably, a doctor would be displeased if he treated a patient, rendered reports to the attorney, testified in court on behalf of the patient, learned that there had been a substantial judgment or settlement, and then discovered that the money had been remitted directly to the client, who might then fail to pay the doctor.

1.2.11 Medical Authorization Forms

In the first interview with the client it is desirable to obtain medical authorization forms that would permit the doctor or hospital to furnish any information requested by the attorney. Without such a medical authorization form it would be an impropriety, and in some states illegal, for the doctor or hospital to furnish information or records. An example of a typical medical authorization form follows.

PERMISSION FOR DOCTOR AND HOSPITAL RECORDS AND REPORTS

Dated: ____________________

All Doctors who have treated ____________________

____

and all hospitals where he has been a patient are hereby authorized to give to ____________________ or any representative
(name of firm)
of that firm or ____________________ all information relative to ______________ physical condition and to permit such person to copy or photostat or have copied or photostated any record or report concerning such physical condition.
All prior medical authorizations are hereby revoked.

Signed: ____________________

Witnesses:

____

____

SWORN TO and subscribed before me
this__________ day of________ A.D. 198______

____

NOTARY PUBLIC
My commission expires: ____________________

1.2.12 Authorization for Income Tax Returns

It is also probably desirable in the first interview to receive an authorization from the client to obtain tax returns. In those parts of the country that follow a liberal discovery rule, relatively soon after the institution of suit the plaintiff should anticipate the filing of a Motion to Produce Income Tax Returns on behalf of the defendant where there has been a claim for loss of income. Securing the authorization to request income tax returns already on file with the Bureau of Internal Revenue eliminates unnecessary correspondence. A form for this purpose follows:

SAMPLE AUTHORIZATION FOR INCOME TAX RETURNS

Date: ______________________

Director of Internal Revenue

____

____

Gentlemen:

The undersigned hereby authorizes the firm of ______________
(name of

______________________, ______________________,
firm) (address)

to secure photocopies of any of my federal income tax returns.

Name: ______________________

Address: ______________________

____

Witness

1.2.13 Avoiding a Critical Omission

A form of interview sheet should be developed by each individual office suitable to its practice. In the average office, where the pressures of a law practice are as great as they are, an entire facet of a lawsuit may be overlooked by failure to acquire information from the client. A prepared interview sheet covering pertinent aspects of the plaintiff's life and every aspect of his injury obviates this possibility. It protects the attorney against the risk of later being told by the client, "Well, you never asked me that question."

Because of the length of the interview sheet and the failure of the client to understand some questions, no matter how carefully they may have been worded, simply handing the interview sheet to the client with the request that he fill it out and return it is likely to result in an incomplete form with inadequate information. Many clients who appear perfectly literate and cooperative will not, in fact, study the letter attached to the interview sheet to the extent necessary to master its contents. At the conclusion of the interview, the secretary, associate attorney, or paralegal must determine that all of the questions are properly understood and answered.

Interview information may serve as the basis for answering interrogatories. An additional advantage of a comprehensive interview sheet is that shortly after suit is filed, a series of interrogatories will probably be served on the plaintiff by the defendant's counsel. The answers to these interrogatories should be covered in the questionnaire completed by the client at the time of the first interview. With a properly completed interview sheet, it is possible to prepare a rough draft of answers to interrogatories that can then be mailed to the client with the request for corrections, additions, and modifications. Since, in Lincoln's words, "a lawyer's time is his stock in trade," the use of such an interview sheet actually makes money for the attorney by saving him time.

A sample form of the interview sheet used in the office of one of the authors follows:

OFFICE INTERVIEW SHEET

PLEASE READ THIS INTERVIEW SHEET CAREFULLY BEFORE ANSWERING THE QUESTIONS!

Enclosed are two interview sheets. One copy is for you to fill out and keep. The other is for our office and should not be completed until you have checked your own copy and made corrections.

The answers you give here are for our use only, will be held strictly CONFIDENTIAL, and will not be released to unauthorized persons. If you wish, this interview sheet will be returned to you when your claim has been concluded.

Answer every question FULLY and ACCURATELY. Success in this case depends upon mutual confidence and complete cooperation between client and attorney. It is imperative that your attorney know as much as, or more than, the defendant will know about you, your history, and activities by the time your case goes to trial. You MUST ASSUME that the defendant will then know as much about you as you know yourself.

ONE SURPRISE at the trial, produced by the defendant, because of an incorrect or incomplete answer here, CAN RUIN YOUR CASE.

That cannot happen IF your attorney knows in advance every possible move that the defendant can make, and has an opportunity to see that YOU ARE BOTH FULLY PREPARED. Do not fail to answer a question fully, even though it may be embarrassing, or you do not think it is important, or you cannot understand why it has anything to do with your case.

This interview sheet is divided into major headings. Although it may appear long and complicated, each question has some importance to your case. In each instance we have provided space for you to fill in the answer. The success of your case will be influenced by your cooperation! If it becomes necessary to file suit on your behalf, the defendant will probably send us a list of questions, called "Interrogatories," for you to answer. Your own copy of this questionnaire will help you answer those questions.

Again, answer each question fully and accurately in the space provided. If more space is needed, use the blank sheets at the end. PLEASE TYPE or PRINT ALL ANSWERS. THANK YOU.

INTERVIEW SHEET

Data for Complaint and Bill of Particulars

CASE REFERRED BY:
Attorney: ____________________
____
____
Other: ____________________
Settlement offer before referral: ____________________

DATE: ____________________
INTERVIEWED BY: ____________________
Employment contract signed? ____________________
Medical authorization form signed? ____________________
Income tax authorization form signed? ____________________

COMPLETE AS FAR AS POSSIBLE ON FIRST INTERVIEW THEN FOLLOW UP UNTIL COMPLETED

GENERAL INFORMATION

1. What is your full name? ____________________ (Age) ______
   Social Security Number: ____________________
   What is the name of your spouse? ____________________
   Present address: ____________________
   Present address of spouse: ____________________
   Telephone numbers of yourself and your spouse (Business and Residence): ____________________
   If a minor: the full name of your natural guardian: ____________________
   ____________________ (His/Her) relationship to you: ____________________
   ____________________ (His/Her) address: ____________________
   ____________________ Your age: ____, Date of birth: ____________________

2. Has either of you ever used, or been known by, any other name than that shown above? ____
If so, list here such other name(s), and state when and why you used such other name(s): ____

____

3. List the names, ages, and addresses of all those (including children) who are dependent upon you for support, and your relationship to each.

Name	Address	Age	Relationship

4. List the addresses where you have resided during the past ten years and give the period of time at each residence, including dates.

Residence	From	To

5. Are you married at the present time? ____
Date of marriage: ____ Place of marriage: ____
Are you and your spouse living together now? ____
6. Have you been divorced or legally separated at any time? ____
If so, from whom, when, and where? ____

WORK BACKGROUND

The amount of your recovery in this case will be affected by your loss of earnings and earning capacity, so please outline carefully your work background.

1. Were you employed at the time of the accident? ____
If so, state name and address of your employer: ____

____
2. What was your job title, or the type of work you were doing? ____

____
3. What was your rate of pay? ____
4. How many hours per week were you working regularly immediately prior to the accident? ____

____

5. When were you first employed by the company for which you were working at the time of the accident? ______________
6. Have you remained in the same job since the accident? ______
   If not, state the reason for the termination of your employment:
   ____
7. Have you missed any time from work as a result of your injury?
   ____
   If so, list the inclusive dates you were unable to work:
   From: ______________ To: ______________
   From: ______________ To: ______________
   From: ______________ To: ______________
   From: ______________ To: ______________
   Did you **before** this accident lose time from work due to an injury or for any other reason? ______________
   If so, give details: ______________
   ____
   ____
8. Did you lose wages for the periods of time missed from work due to this accident? ______________
   If so, state the total wages lost to date and the dates: ______
   ____
9. Have you had any increases or decreases in your pay since the accident? ______________
   If so, explain: ______________
   ____
   ____
10. If you have changed jobs since the accident, give a summary of your present job, showing name and address of employer, rate of pay, hours, type of work, etc.
    ____
    ____
    ____
11. List your employment record as far back as you can remember. Your past employment records are important in determining your disability from an occupational viewpoint.

Name and Address of Employer	Employed From	To	Reason For Leaving

12. What did you earn in the last year prior to your accident? ______

13. Have you filed federal or state income tax returns for the last three years? ______
If so, where? ______
Do you have copies of them? ______
Will the figure shown in the answer to No. 12 be the same as shown in your income tax return? ______ If not, explain:
______
______

THE ACCIDENT

1. Date of accident: ______
Day of week: ______
Time: ______
Weather: ______
Daylight, dusk, or dark: ______
2. Describe the location of the accident as to the city, county, state, and nearness to intersection, driveway, residence, fixed objects.
______
______
______
______
______
3. Describe in detail how the accident occurred. Comment, if applicable, upon the following: defects in road or car, distances, lanes, intersection, RR crossing, horn sounds, radio on, windows up (air conditioner on), brake noise, tire squeal, skid marks, turn signals, windshield, stoplights, headlights, speed or other road signs, intoxication, guard rails, stop signs, street lights, road conditions, curves, center line, curbs, hills, school zone, pedestrians, location of debris from car, brakes, speed, statements as to who was at fault.
______
______
______
______
______
______
______
______
______
______
______
______
______

____
____
____
____
____
____

(If the case is other than a vehicle accident, the statement should include sequence of events, dates, times, identification of witnesses and other specific information)

____
____
____
____
____
____
____
____
____
____
____
____

4. Name and address of defendant (specify as individual, co-partnership, all partners, or corporation): ______________
____
5. Defendant's insurance company and adjuster: ______________
____
6. If hospitalized, give names of hospitals and total charges: ______
____
____
____
7. Names and addresses of doctors, nurses, and charges (state to whom charges incurred and amount): ______________
____
____
____
____
8. Was vehicle damaged? __________ If so, what parts? ______
____
____
____
By whom was vehicle owned? ______________________
Make (and year) ________ Model ________ Tag No. ______
9. Insurance company insuring car you were in: ______________
______________________________ Address: __________

Collision coverage? ____________________
Medical pay? ____________________

____

____

ADDITIONAL BACKGROUND INFORMATION

We must know about your background because your educational background and physical history will have an important bearing upon your case.

1. Education: What education have you had, including any special employment training or training in skills? ____________________

   ____

   ____

2. Physical Examinations: List here EVERY physical examination you have ever had during the last ten years, for employment, promotion, insurance, selective service, armed forces, etc. State the date, name of the doctor and result, as fully as you recall.

   Date: ____________________
   Place: ____________________
   Name of doctor: ____________________
   Purpose of examination: ____________________
   Result: ____________________

   Date: ____________________
   Place: ____________________
   Name of doctor: ____________________
   Purpose of examination: ____________________
   Result: ____________________

   Date: ____________________
   Place: ____________________
   Name of doctor: ____________________
   Purpose of examination: ____________________
   Result: ____________________

   Date: ____________________
   Place: ____________________
   Name of doctor: ____________________
   Purpose of examination: ____________________
   Result: ____________________

3. Other Accidents and Injuries: Failure to mention other accidents or injuries can undermine your lawsuit, no matter how trivial they may seem. List here every such accident whether it resulted in a claim for damages or not, stating the date, place, nature of the accident and extent of your injuries. If none, so state.

Date: ______
Place: ______
Nature of accident or injury: ______
Extent of injury: ______

Date: ______
Place: ______
Nature of accident or injury: ______
Extent of injury: ______

Date: ______
Place: ______
Nature of accident or injury: ______
Extent of injury: ______

Date: ______
Place: ______
Nature of accident or injury: ______
Extent of injury: ______

4. Illness or Disease: No matter how trivial an illness, either before or since your accident, we must know about it. This is particularly important if there is any connection with present physical complaints. The defendant will have available at the trial, by means of medical and hospital records, veteran's records, insurance records, etc. a complete history of your past physical condition.

Date: ______
Nature of illness or disease: ______
Duration: ______
Treated by: ______
Hospitalized: ______

Date: ______
Nature of illness or disease: ______
Duration: ______
Treated by: ______
Hospitalized: ______

Date: ______
Nature of illness or disease: ______
Duration: ______
Treated by: ______
Hospitalized: ______

Have you ever had, or have you now, trouble with eyes ______ ears ______ nose ______? If so, explain: ______

______

______

Have you ever worn glasses__________ an artificial eye__________ hearing aid____________? If so, explain:____________________

____

Have you ever worn a brace, back or neck support? __________
If so, explain: ________________________________
Have you ever been denied life or health insurance because of your health? ________________________________
If so, by which company, what doctor, and why? __________

____

____

____

5. Alcoholism and Venereal Disease: If you have ever been treated for these afflictions please be sure to discuss it with your attorney, confidentially, long before your case goes to trial.
6. Claims and Lawsuits: We know that there have been many cases damaged beyond repair by a history of other claims and lawsuits which the attorney did not know about. It is NOT the fact that one has had other claims or lawsuits that is important, for he will not be penalized by a court or jury if the claims are reasonable and genuine. It is the DENIAL of previous claims and suits which damages the case. List here EVERY claim you have ever made for personal injury or property damage, and fill in the details.

Date	Against Whom	Nature of Claim	Suit Filed	Result

7. Police Record: List here every arrest, and state the date, place, charge, and result.

Date	Place	Charges	Result	Confined

8. State your driving experience with the motor vehicle involved in this accident. ________________________________
Is there any limitation on your license to operate? __________
If so, what is the limitation? ________________________
9. Activities Since the Accident: If you suffered a serious injury in the accident, it is possible the opposing side already has taken or will in the future take MOTION PICTURES OF YOU. This is done with

a telescopic lens, so that you never know it has been done until the pictures are presented in court to show that you ARE able to do something which you have either denied or neglected to mention that you are able to do. List here all your usual activities which you have NOT been able to perform since the accident, such as cutting grass, etc.

____
____
____
____
____
____
____
____

10. Military Background: Have you ever been rejected for military service because of physical, mental, or other reasons? ________
If so, explain: ______________________________
____

Have you ever had military service? ______ If so, what branch? ____________________ Please state dates: __________
____

Type of discharge: ___________________________
Any service-connected injuries? _______ If so, explain and give details: _________________________________
____
____
____

Percentage of disability: _______________________
Present condition of service-connected injury or disability: ____
____

Do you receive payments for service-connected injuries or disabilities?
____
____

If so, give VA Claim No. _______________________

11. Regarding this accident, please answer the following: Were pictures taken at the scene of the accident? __________ By whom? ____________________ When? __________________
Where? ______________________________________
Were you questioned by the police? __________ If so, what was officer's name and of what police department was he a member?
____
____

Did you give or sign a statement? __________ For whom? ____ ____________________ When? __________________

Do you have a copy? ______________________
Have you been questioned by an adjuster or investigator? ______
When? ______________ Where? ______________
Name of person who interrogated you: ______________
Was anyone else present? ______________
Did you sign papers? ________ Were you given a copy? ________
____

12. How did you leave the scene of the accident? ______________
____

13. Were other people in your car? ________ If so, list their names, addresses, and where seated in car.
Name Address Seated
____
____
____
____

14. Name and address of driver (defendant) of other vehicle: ______
____
Owner of other vehicle: ______________________

15. How did defendant's vehicle leave the scene? (If towed, state by whom and where taken.) ______________________
____

16. Was defendant's vehicle damaged? ______________________
If so, what parts? ______________________
____

17. Witnesses: List the names, addresses, and telephone numbers of all witnesses to the accident (persons who saw or may have seen the accident), and any other person who may be of assistance in testifying about your case, your injuries, or changes in your activities since the accident.
Name Address Telephone Number
____
____
____
____
____
____
____
____
____
____

DAMAGES

The amount of recovery in this case will be affected by, among other things, the damages or expenses actually incurred as a direct result of the accident, such as hospital, doctor, and drug expenses; damage to your automobile; aggravation of your injuries by doctor's erroneous treatment; loss of property, such as glasses, watches, tools; and loss of wages. These are items of special damage as contrasted with compensatory or general damages such as pain and suffering, loss of future earnings, impairment of your earning capacity, etc.

1. State, in full detail, all injuries received as a result of this accident: ____

____

____

____

____

____

____

____

____

State your present physical condition—scars, deformities, headaches, pains, etc., due to injuries received in this accident:

____

____

____

____

____

____

____

____

____

____

____

2. List here all of your usual activities which you have NOT been able to perform or can only perform with difficulty since the accident, such as climbing stairs, ironing, cutting grass, dancing, lifting children, etc.

____

____

____

____

____

____

____

____

____

____

____

3. Hospitalization: List all hospitals in which you were examined or treated or to which you were admitted as a patient as a result of the injuries sustained in the accident, the dates, and the total costs.

Hospital: ______________________________
Address: ______________________________
From: ______________ To: ______________
Total Costs: ______________________________

Hospital: ______________________________
Address: ______________________________
From: ______________ To: ______________
Total Costs: ______________________________

Hospital: ______________________________
Address: ______________________________
From: ______________ To: ______________
Total Costs: ______________________________

Hospital: ______________________________
Address: ______________________________
From: ______________ To: ______________
Total Costs: ______________________________

4. Physicians and Surgeons: List the full name, address and telephone number of each physician or surgeon who has examined or treated you for your injuries as a result of the accident, as well as the type, duration, and place of treatment or care:

Doctor's Name: ______________________________
Address: ______________________________
Telephone Number: ______________________________
Type of Treatment: ______________________________
Place of Treatment: ______________________________
Dates of Treatment: ______________________________
Total Costs: ______________________________

Doctor's Name: ______________________________
Address: ______________________________
Telephone Number: ______________________________
Type of Treatment: ______________________________
Place of Treatment: ______________________________
Dates of Treatment: ______________________________
Total Costs: ______________________________

Doctor's Name: ______________________________
Address: ______________________________

Telephone Number: ______________________
Type of Treatment: ______________________
Place of Treatment: ______________________
Dates of Treatment: ______________________
Total Costs: ______________________

5. Drugs and Medicines: State the total cost to date of all drugs and medicines used and purchased by you, as a result of the accident, and from whom purchased.

____
____
____
____

6. X-rays: Where taken, date, and by whom: ______________________

____
____

7. Hire of Nurse (Do not state lump sum, but itemize as to name of nurse, address, number of days or weeks, dates, and amount paid weekly):

____
____
____
____

Total amount spent for nursing care: ______________________

8. The cost of domestic help hired as a direct result of the accident constitutes an item of special damage. For example, in the case of an injured homemaker or mother, the cost of a baby sitter, the cost of washing, ironing, etc., which you have hired someone to do, should be listed. A father or husband would list the cost of home repairs, yard work, etc.
   State here the full names and addresses of all domestic help hired as a result of the accident, the type of work done, the number of days or weeks employed, the dates, the amount paid weekly, and the total amount paid to date.

____
____
____
____
____
____
____

Total amount spent for domestic help: ______________________

9. Special damages (other than medical) and source of proof (i.e, personal property which was damaged, lost or destroyed as a

result of the accident, and any items not previously listed, such as crutches, clothing, watches, glasses, false teeth, aggravation of injuries by doctor's erroneous treatment, etc.). State the cost of the item:

____

____

____

____

____

____

____

____

10. Convalescent Expenses: In the event that you have been confined to a nursing home or other such place as a result of the accident, list here the full name of every such place, the address, the dates so confined and the total cost.

Convalescent Places: ______________________________
Address: ______________________________
From: ______________ To: ______________
Total Cost: ______________________________

Convalescent Places: ______________________________
Address: ______________________________
From: ______________ To: ______________
Total Cost: ______________________________

Convalescent Places: ______________________________
Address: ______________________________
From: ______________ To: ______________
Total Cost: ______________________________

11. Loss of Earnings: State the length of time confined to bed as a result of the accident, including hospital confinement:

____

____

Confinement thereafter to house:

____

____

____

____

State the time lost from work (in case of breadwinner or person employed outside of the home):

____

____

____

____

Time lost from work in case of homemaker or mother: ________
____
____

State time partially lost or time partially disabled: ________
____
____
____
____

State time lost from school in case of pupil: ________
____
____

12. Insurance: Your own insurance will sometimes compensate you for your injuries and property damage and will often pay all or a portion of your medical expenses. However, most insurance companies require that they be given notice of the accident or claim within a limited time, usually thirty days. Therefore, in order that we may be of the utmost service to you, it is vitally important that we know the number and types of your policies.
Please list them below:

Name of Company: ________
Address: ________
Type of Insurance: ________

Name of Company: ________
Address: ________
Type of Insurance: ________

Name of Company: ________
Address: ________
Type of Insurance: ________

Copies of the "face sheet" of all insurance policies should be obtained (Where "No-fault" insurance exists, the lawyer may have all medical and related bills submitted through him to the insurance company in order to keep track of such bills.)

13. In completing this questionnaire have you thought of any information which we have not asked which MAY be of some assistance to us in serving you? If so, please state it here, no matter how silly, trivial, or embarrassing it may seem.
____
____
____
____

1.2.14 Example of an Initial Interview

The first interview with the client often falls into a pattern.

Put the Client at Ease:

"Come right in, Mr. and Mrs. Jones. Would you like a cup of coffee before we begin talking?" After coffee is brought, when the client appears comfortably settled, the attorney may begin:

Let the Client Know You Are Already Working:

"While we were waiting for your appointment after you called last Thursday, we had one of our investigators get a copy of the accident report. We have a little preliminary information as to how the police officer, at least, felt the accident occurred. We also know a little bit about the general nature of your injury. We understand that you had stopped your automobile at the intersection of Blue Heron Boulevard and U.S. Highway 1, waiting for a light to change, and had been there for several seconds when an automobile approaching from the rear slammed into the back of your car. We also know that in the accident, your head and neck were snapped violently to the rear and then thrown forward, and that you were momentarily knocked unconscious, or at least dazed."

Importance of Avoiding Interruptions:

"We would like to talk to you for about five minutes, without interruption, and tell you some of the things that we know about this type of accident from experience with previous cases. Then, we would like to ask you a few questions. Afterwards, you may ask us any questions which you might have."

General Information Needed by Client:

"First, let us say this is the most frequent type of automobile accident. It is a type we have handled many times before. Consequently, we know what to expect. We would like to tell you how you can help us do a better job for you. We would also like to tell you what to expect from us. There are a few general principles of law and ground rules for lawsuits you need to know. We may tell you something you already know, but that will not hurt anything. It would be harmful if we omit telling you something you should know, so we will risk telling you too much rather than too little.

Our first step is to begin an investigation for you and to develop information necessary to prove your case. It is not enough for you and me to know what happened. We must be prepared to prove it. This means that we will have to obtain medical records, take pictures of the scene and your injuries, obtain signed or recorded statements from witnesses and, in general, be certain that we have overlooked nothing. We must prepare ourselves to prove everything necessary to win your case for you."

The Three Essential Factors in Every Case:

"There are three factors in every case, and all of them must be present before we are able to effect a recovery on behalf of a client."

1. Liability: "The first and obvious factor is that we must have somebody who has negligently or intentionally injured somebody without a sufficient excuse. Certainly in your case this factor would appear to exist since, except for an unavoidable brake failure, or a sudden heart attack, or something else beyond the control of the defendant, the law ordinarily does not excuse a defendant's driving into the rear of a plaintiff's automobile."

2. Responsibility: "The defendant must be able to pay. The second important factor in a lawsuit is that we must have someone who is financially responsible, or who is insured. It would do us absolutely no good to get a judgment for a million dollars against a pauper if he had no insurance since we would then have an empty and uncollectable judgment. As a matter of fact, it might even harm the client if this occurred because in obtaining the judgment we would expend funds that we would be unable to recover. In your case, the police officer has noted on his police report that the defendant was covered by State Farm Mutual Insurance Company. Assuming that this information given to the police officer by the defendant is correct, we know that there is at least some insurance coverage on the part of the defendant."

3. Damages. "The third factor is that we must have someone who has sustained injuries or damage from the accident. This is one of the factors that determines what amount is fair compensation for a particular injury. If a person has lost a finger, he is usually not entitled to as much as a person who lost an arm. At this stage, of course, it is not possible for us to know exactly how much you are injured and the long-term effect of that injury on you."

Sample Discussion of Injury:

"You are still having trouble with your neck and are still going to the doctor. The best doctor in the world would be unable to tell us, with certainty, what the future holds for you. The type of injury that has been sustained by you may be one of relatively minor importance, and one from which a client will recover in a relatively short period of time, or it may constitute a very severe and continuing injury. The initial x-rays taken by the doctor are helpful, but are not diagnostic or conclusive. Without additional medical observation, no one can tell for certain the nature and extent of your injury.

There are varying degrees of injuries of this type.

In many cases of this type, the client has sustained a simple neck strain and will be well in a few days or weeks. We hope this is true in your case since your health is more important than your money.

However, in other cases of this type, the patient has actually had some of the soft tissue in the neck torn. This is, of course, below the skin and cannot usually be seen by the naked eye. X-rays do not always help since the common x-ray is designed to show bones rather than soft tissue. Where there has been actual tearing of the soft tissue, often as part of the healing process, scar tissue will be formed. Scar tissue is seldom as good as the original tissue. Sometimes it will form in such a manner as to drag or push or pull on nerve roots in the vicinity, and this can produce pain, discomfort, and sometimes disability.

You should understand that the spinal cord comes down from the brain largely encased in the spine. Little nerve roots emerge from the spine at intervals through little holes in the spine called foramina. These nerve roots then spread out in patterns across the scalp, over the shoulders, and down the arms. Of course, as you go down the body, other nerve roots may be involved. Pressure on these nerve roots can cause pain along the entire route of the nerve root involved, or such pressure can produce numbness and tingling.

Prior existing injury need not bar recovery. Many people have had backs that were previously weak in some manner. Often these backs would not bother them excessively if they were careful.

Sometimes, these weak back problems can be aggravated by an accident. The fact that the back was weak prior to the accident will not bar recovery. We must simply tell the truth about the back and show the extent of the aggravation. If a judge or jury cannot separate the aggravation from the previously existing condition, you may even sometimes recover for the whole condition.

Most people over forty have some osteoarthritis in their spines. Frequently, an accident such as this may aggravate the condition. This means that you must have adequate supervision so that your doctor has an opportunity to diagnose the developing arthritis by taking x-rays, or otherwise.

Some people have a very serious injury from this type of accident involving damage to an intervertebral disc. The intervertebral discs are similar to shock absorbers and occupy spaces between the bony bodies of the spine. When one of these discs is injured, it may press on one or more of the nerve roots, producing severe pain and discomfort. It can be very disabling.

It is difficult for a doctor to tell on the first few visits exactly what the extent of your injury is and what is its effect on you. This is why you must continue to see the doctor as long as you suffer from your back or neck condition in order to give him or her a fair chance to diagnose and treat your condition. If you continue to hurt, but do not see your doctor, the doctor will naturally assume you have gotten better or well.

Usually, the doctor can give you something that will help your pain and discomfort while continuing to see you in order to diagnose you. It may not be possible for him or her to completely eliminate some of the headaches, dizzy spells, or other discomforts you may be having.

The doctor will wish to test your sensation in various parts of your arm, as well as your grip and your ability to move your arm, in the event that you are having any trouble of this kind. It is important that you be as precise and accurate and truthful with the doctor as possible in relating your symptoms. The diagnosis will largely depend on what you tell him or her about your symptoms. You can easily mislead a doctor as to the nature and extent of your injuries and even cause a doctor to treat you for the wrong injury if you are careless in describing what parts of your body hurt, where numbness exists, and what occasions pain. The doctor will also wish to see whether you have any muscle spasm in your neck. This is an involuntary tightening of muscles, somewhat similar to a charley-horse, which many of us have had from high school sports. When a trained physician examines and 'palpates' your neck, he or she can actually feel the muscle spasm and it is, of course, something which you cannot control. Tell the doctor at this time something about the location of the pain you are having in the neck. The doctor will also wish to look at a series of x-rays to see whether the normal curvature of the spine has been disturbed because of muscle spasms and the injury. In some individuals who have severe muscle spasm, there will be an alteration in the normal curvature of the spine, which is visible on x-ray and furnishes some evidence to the doctor of the nature and extent of the injury.

Why is continuing medical treatment important? This kind of observation and medical diagnosis frequently takes some time. The doctor must observe you on a number of different occasions in order to reach a conclusion about the type of injury you have and the severity of it. Thus, it is important that you go to a good doctor, that you continue to see that doctor as long as there is anything legitimately wrong with you, and that you tell him or her the truth about every sensation that you have as a result of this accident.

Items of damage for which you are entitled to be paid: There are a number of items of damage that you are entitled to recover, if we are able to prove that the other party was to blame for your injuries and that you were not guilty of any negligence that contributed to the accident. For example, we are entitled to recover for your doctor bills, hospital bills, and medical bills of every kind.

We will need a medical authorization form from you in order to have your doctor furnish us with information and, before you leave, we would like to have you sign this since doctors are not supposed to furnish information concerning a patient without the written permission of that patient. Once we have this permission, we will obtain the doctor bills from the doctor and, at the time of settlement of your case, we will assist you by making certain that these doctor bills are paid. When doctors find that we wish to cooperate with them, they tend to cooperate with us in furnishing us with information."

Importance of Copies of Bills:

"We will also want copies of drug bills from your drugstore and any other places where you purchase medication. It will be important that we keep the bills resulting from the accident separate from any other drugstore bills. For example, we must see to it that the bill we obtain from the drugstore does not contain any charges for items such as talcum powder or other household supplies. If any of these were inadvertently included on the drugstore bill, you could expect that the insurance company would take advantage of this and attempt to make it look to the jury as though you were trying to recover for something you are not entitled to recover for. Not only must we keep these items separate, but we must also obtain separate receipts. If the medication is paid for by checks, we must have the cancelled checks. In the event that you take non-prescription drugs such as aspirin, it would probably be wise if you saved the bottles or containers in order that we may have some evidence to show a jury of the quantity and type of medication you have been taking."

Household Expense—Not to Be Overlooked:

"In the event that you are unable to do your housework or yard work, and it becomes necessary for you to hire a maid or a yard man whom you have not employed before, we must see to it that we are able to prove this either through receipts given you by such person or through cancelled checks."

Vehicle Damage—Subrogation:

"We, of course, are entitled to recover for the property damage to your car, but if you carry insurance covering property damage, it will be necessary that we reimburse your insurance company for any sums that have been paid to you."

Loss of Income:

"Should you lose time from your job, we are entitled to recover for any loss of income resulting from injuries sustained in the accident. However, we must, of course, be prepared to show through your testimony or the testimony of others, that the loss of time was caused by the injuries received in the accident."

Pain and Discomfort:

"We are entitled to recover not only for physical pain and suffering, but also for any mental distress that you may have as a result of the accident."

Diminished Capacity to Lead a Normal Life:

"In the event that your ability to lead a normal life has been impaired, and your normal life pattern altered by the accident, we have a right to recover for this item of damage."

Loss of Consortium:

"Since Mrs. Jones is injured and Mr. Jones is her husband, we also have a right to recover for what is called 'loss of consortium.' This is an old common law English term meaning loss of the wife's services such as those of housekeeper, companion, cook, sexual partner, or any other types of services which the wife customarily rendered to her husband and which were diminished or eliminated because of the accident."

Why We File Suit:

"The first important step we take is investigation. We obtain statements from various witnesses, pictures, and preliminary doctor's reports, and we start to accumulate the various bills, or copies of them, that are received. When the preliminary investigation is completed, if you are still suffering pain and discomfort and there is no accurate way of estimating how much longer you are likely to be ill, we will ordinarily file suit and expect to prepare the case for trial. If we attempted to settle the case at that time, we would be doing you a tremendous disservice because of the fact that we would not be able to determine how much you are hurt. If we attempted to wait until you were well, which might conceivably be from six months to a year, and then started to negotiate with the insurance company, we might find ourselves unable to negotiate a settlement. We would then still face the necessity of filing your suit and bringing it to trial. This would involve another delay of eight months to a year. Also, there are some methods of discovery that are available to us after suit is filed, because we can then subpoena witnesses and take their depositions."

Why We Cannot Evaluate Now:

"At this time, of course, it is impossible for us to tell you what your lawsuit is worth. Any lawyer who attempted to do so would certainly not be doing a very good job for his client. It is impossible for us to know how soon you will get well, or exactly what will be revealed by the investigation. There are many factors that are not yet ascertained. Often clients ask us at this time what their case is worth, and they will have their own ideas. These ideas are usually wrong. They are frequently based on what the client heard somebody else received in a lawsuit, which might be more or less than what the client is entitled to."

How to Evaluate:

"However, at a later date, when we know what your doctors say about your condition and we have had a chance to observe you and complete our investigation, we will have some idea as to what the lawsuit is worth. At that time, we will want you to come in to the office so that we may discuss every aspect of your case with you. We will then tell you what we believe a jury would assess your damages to be. In our first step in evaluation, we would ignore the possibility of losing or having your verdict reduced because of comparative negligence. We will tell you what we think the range of jury verdict would probably be, and what our best estimate of a jury verdict would be. Then we would consider the possibility of losing your case or having the verdict reduced by comparative negligence. For example, if we thought the possibility of losing was fifty percent, we would reduce the evaluation for settlement purposes by fifty percent. Similarly, if we thought the verdict would be reduced by comparative negligence, we would make an evaluation that took that into consideration."

How to Negotiate—Explaining the Negotiation Process:

"Once we are agreed as to the proper settlement value of your case, we can then begin negotiations with the insurance company. At this point, we should tell you that from a practical standpoint, we can never offer to settle with the insurance company for the amount that we have decided the case is worth. We must ask an amount slightly in excess of this and the insurance company will offer an amount less than that which they are willing to pay. Eventually, through the process of negotiation, we will arrive at an amount that we can agree to. In the event that we are unable to reach a settlement because the insurance company is not willing to pay us what we believe the case to be worth, we should then be prepared to try the case."

Factors in Evaluation:

"There are many intangible factors involved in our evaluation of this case, such as how we think the jury will react to you, how they will react to opposing counsel, what your doctors have to say, how the witnesses appear in general, and also what the makeup of the jury panel is likely to be at the time of trial. Thus, it is possible for us to be wrong in our evaluation of the case, but because of our experience over a number of years, we are more likely to be right than wrong."

Obtaining Authority to Settle:

"We, of course, will accept no offers of settlement without your approval, and you, of course, are not expected to have us do so. In the final analysis, the decision as to whether or not a given settlement offer should be taken rests with you, since it is your lawsuit; however, we expect you to listen closely to our advice. Most of our clients end up taking that advice since we have had much more experience in these matters than the client is likely to have had. What we will be concerned with at that time is not what you or we would hope to get from the lawsuit, or, for that matter, what your claim is actually worth. From a practical point of view, we will be specifically concerned with what we can get you from a jury and whether that figure is more or less than the injury is worth."

When You Can Expect Settlement:

"We do not expect to have very much success in settling your lawsuit, if it turns out that you have any substantial injuries, until we are approaching trial. Not until that time, very often, does the insurance carrier have full information. Without that information, the carrier is not in a position to evaluate the case. More important, the insurance companies are more likely to get down to the actual business of evaluating a case and settling it at the time that they are approaching trial. There are, of course, exceptions to this, but you should anticipate that, in all probability, we will not succeed in settling your case until we are approaching trial."

Explaining Expense of Preparation:

"We will expect to spend whatever money is necessary to prepare your case, and we advance those funds. We expect to be reimbursed out of any settlement we ultimately obtain. We will, of course, at that time give you an itemized breakdown of costs. We do not expect to waste any money, but on the other hand, we do expect to spend whatever is necessary to properly prepare your case. We have at stake not only your lawsuit, but our reputation as well. We do not expect to sacrifice either because of a reluctance to spend, for example, five dollars more for additional photographs, if necessary."

Copies of Correspondence and Pleadings:

"In the course of preparing your case for trial, we will wish to send you copies of all pleadings and all correspondence in order that you may be kept fully informed. Most of these will require no action on your part. You can either file them away or throw them away, as you see fit, although we would advise you to file them for future reference should you ever wish to look at them. The purpose of sending such correspondence and pleadings to you is solely to inform you about the progress of your lawsuit and to let you know that we are doing something for you. Few things are as frustrating to a client as taking a case to a lawyer's office and then having a number of months pass without any knowledge as to what is being done. The lawyer may be doing a great deal, but if the client does not know about this, he may be greatly concerned."

Who Will Work on Your File?

"Your file will be assigned jointly to two lawyers in the office and one investigator. In the event that one of us is not available, in all probability, the other will be available to answer your questions. Do not hesitate to ask the secretaries also questions about your file, since many of our secretaries have been here for a long period of time. While they cannot give you legal advice, they certainly can give you information pertaining to the progress of your case and specific items of information that would be contained in your file."

Why We Furnish an Information Booklet:

"Here is a little booklet that we have prepared for all of our clients, telling them how they can help us in preparing their case and making a proper presentation of it to a jury. We would appreciate it if you would carefully read it. If you have any questions about any part of the booklet after you have read it, please do not hesitate to tell us. There are certain questions that we know from past experience are asked by clients in this first interview, and we will run over these briefly with you and answer some of them in advance.

Some clients want to know how much the advanced costs will amount to. We cannot at this time, of course, specifically answer this except to tell you the cost to file a lawsuit, and the amount of money necessary to obtain service on the defendant. In addition, we will want to subpoena witnesses, obtain pictures, and obtain photostats of hospital records. We will have some expense for mileage as the investigators go out on your case. There may be long distance calls that we will want to make. We may want to take depositions and that will result in court reporters' expenses."

Signing the Contract:

"Here is our standard form representation contract. We would like you to read it over and to know if you have any questions about it."

Making a Full Disclosure of Referral Fees:

"As you, of course, know, you were referred to our office by attorney Jack Smith of Boynton Beach. You may wonder what our relationship is. We share some of the work and responsibility, and we share the fee with him. The fact that he is involved in the case with us does not increase the expense to you, it simply means that he must share some of the responsibility and work with us and also share the fee."

Reserving the Right to Withdraw:

"We reserve the right to return your contract to you, if we care to do so, after we have made a preliminary investigation of the case. You are then at liberty to obtain another lawyer if you wish to do so. In your case, we think that this is unlikely, but it is a right that we reserve with every client because, once we start to prepare a lawsuit, not only is much time involved, but we are emotionally involved as well. As a result, it is not possible for us to take all of the cases that are offered to us by clients and other attorneys.

These are the forms that we would like to have you sign. The first is a medical authorization form. This is a form that permits your doctors to furnish us with information. The second is a representation contract. We would like you to read it and ask any questions you may have about it at the present time. Now is the time to clear up any misunderstandings and not after we have spent literally hundreds of hours in preparation of your case."

After the client has read and signed the medical authorization form and the representation contract, the attorney may continue:

"Here is a client interview form which we would like to have you fill out. Because there are a number of questions in this form, we will want you to go over it with one of our secretaries, who will help you fill it out. After you have filled out this form, we would like you to come back and talk with us a little longer, but before you leave with the secretary, are there any questions that you would like to ask us?"

Client's Questions:

At this point, the client will occasionally have other questions, but more frequently will say, "No, you have answered all of the questions that I had, but if I think of any after I have gone over the forms, I will come back and talk to you." One of the other questions which sometimes arises is, "How long will it take to prepare and try my case?" This, it can be explained, depends upon the local jurisdiction.

When the Client Has Had an Offer:

Occasionally, the attorney will have a client who has been dealing directly with the insurance company and who has received an offer. Usually the offer received is not satisfactory, or the client would not be in the attorney's office. Perhaps he has received an offer of $5,000 or $6,000 and is concerned as to how much he would net if he retained the attorney. It may be perfectly apparent to the lawyer that the case, in fact, is worth $15,000 to $20,000. However, a wise lawyer would almost never be willing to tell a client this or to guarantee any kind of recovery since the lawyer would risk a great deal of criticism and a very poor relationship with the client in the event that he or she was wrong in the appraisal of the case. If the attorney thinks that the case is probably worth more than the sum offered by the insurance company, he should tell the client that this is his opinion, and that the client is at liberty to attempt to negotiate a settlement, but if he wants the attorney to handle the case, to come back again. Some attorneys tell the client, "All right, we will represent you for one third of the gross of your recovery, or one half of any amount in excess of the offer which the insurance company has made you, whichever is less, provided that the fact that such an offer has been made you is verified by the insurance company itself and the memoranda in their file." (This precaution is necessary, since many adjusters will hint that they might make a settlement of a given amount when, in fact, no authority for such an offer exists, and no such offer is ever made. The client will sometimes misinterpret these statements and believe that an actual offer has been made.)

At the conclusion of the initial interview, the client should be told the importance of keeping the lawyer informed in case he moves or leaves town for any reason so that the lawyer knows where to contact him at all times.

1.2.15 Investigation

After the employment contract has been executed, it is imperative that the attorney continue the investigation expeditiously. Most attorneys make it a point to go view the scene of the accident. Statements of witnesses should be obtained as early as possible and if a criminal prosecution has been processed against any of the parties, transcripts of the testimony of such action should be ordered and obtained.

1.2.16 Personal Limitations (Geography and Expertise)

The preliminary investigation will sometimes reveal that the venue of the suit must be in a geographical location far from the headquarters of the lawyer involved. In most cases, an injustice is done the client if the attorney attempts to settle the case but has no real intention of filing and trying the suit or of referring it. Too often we see the circumstance where a lawyer is representing a client who may have genuine injuries of a substantial nature. The liability may be clear or highly probable. Seldom, however, can the attorney settle the case for the full value of the claim unless suit is filed and the existing evidence is produced in a form usable at trial. Claims supervisors are sufficiently sophisticated in negotiating with claimant's attorneys that they will nearly always offer less than the true value of the claim, hoping that the avarice of the attorney who first received the case will overcome his concern for the client's welfare, and that he will settle for less than possible in order to avoid paying a referral fee. Better practice would indicate a clear-cut decision either to accept the case and process it personally as vigorously as is necessary, regardless of time and distance factors, or to promptly refer the case to the best available attorney in the locality in which the case must be tried.

There are, of course, cases and circumstances in which an attorney might be willing to try a case anywhere if his or her competence and skill are sufficient. Even under these circumstances, the attorney is ordinarily better advised to associate local counsel because of the necessity of dealing with judges, local rules of court, and local customs.

If the attorney decides to refer the case or to associate additional counsel, what are some practical ways to select the attorney to whom the case should be referred or who should be associated? One way is to call an attorney in the area in which the case must be tried who obviously does not do personal injury work; for example, a distinguished firm that might be principally involved in the representation of banks or in real estate practice. The telephone conversation might go something like this:

"Mr. Jones, I see from Martindale-Hubbell and have learned from other sources that you do an extensive bank practice, is that true?"

The attorney will say, "Yes," expecting perhaps that a case will be referred to him of the type to which he is accustomed.

You then say, "I see from Martindale-Hubbell and a look at your representative clients that you do not do very much personal injury work. What I am calling for is to ask you to give me the names of the three attorneys in your area whom you consider the most proficient in the handling of personal injury cases."

At this point, you have boxed the attorney you have called into a position where he cannot modestly admit that he does personal injury work also, and he is likely to give you the names of two or three other lawyers in the community or area who are competent in the handling of personal injury cases. If you make one or two calls of this nature and the lawyers who are contacted name the same two or three lawyers, you are well on the way to having obtained the names of the most efficient laywers for your purpose. Further honing of the selection process may be carried out through examination of Martindale-Hubbell, inspection of state plaintiff's trial lawyers rosters, and directories.

Another usually satisfactory way to select a personal injury attorney in a town far from you and in an area with which you are not familiar is to call the president of the State Plaintiff's Trial Lawyers Association or the State Committeeman to The Association of Trial Lawyers of

America, or any directors of that organization from that state, and ask them which lawyers are considered the outstanding practitioners in the field of personal injury law in that part of the state in which you need assistance. You may well find that you have to select an attorney thirty to forty miles, or even substantially farther, from the area where the suit must be brought in order to get counsel of the competence desired. If the suit has sufficient merit, this should not be a deterrent. The quality of the counsel is more important that the necessity of selecting a lawyer in the precise community where the suit arose.

There are many cases in the personal injury field that involve specialized techniques and handling. Among these are aviation cases, medical malpractice cases, and many defective products cases. The personal injury lawyer, or the experienced general practitioner, would do well to closely examine the question whether he would be better advised to associate the highly skilled specialist rather than attempting the case himself.

In aviation cases, familiarity with air traffic procedure, previous litigation in this field, the technical and mechanical history of various types of planes, and the highly complicated conflict of law decisions involved in selection of the best forum from among several choices would frequently indicate that the client is likely to be better served by the referral of the case. It is often true that the lawyer referring the case may make more money from his referral fee than he would have in retaining the entire fee himself because of the increased recovery that can often be anticipated.

Similar considerations pertain in reference to cases involving medical negligence and defective products cases.

In addition, the preparation of aviation, medical negligence, and defective product cases frequently involves the expenditure of large amounts of money in preparation of the case. Unless the lawyer who first receives the case is prepared to virtually ignore the cost of preparation, the client is frequently better served by early referral of the case.

Finally, if a case is to be referred, the earlier it is referred, the better for the client. Evidence disappears, the recollection of witnesses fades. Bringing a specialist in on a "cold trail" enormously complicates his or her problem in attempting to give the client sterling representation.

2

Developing Medical Evidence: A Working System

Medical evidence, as the term is used in this chapter, is that evidence obtainable from any source whatsoever that sheds light upon the medical problem experienced by the plaintiff as a result of the trauma sustained. Since the sources of medical evidence are many and varied, and some of them are often overlooked by the occasional trial practitioner, those discussed here are by no means all-inclusive.

2.1 THE CLIENT AS A SOURCE OF MEDICAL INFORMATION

The trial lawyer's first knowledge of the plaintiff's medical problem usually comes at the first interview. The first impression which the client makes upon the lawyer is an important one. This is the opportunity that the trial lawyer has to observe the client for the purpose of determining: first, what kind of a person he or she is; and second, whether the complaints are consistent with the trauma described. These two factors are important since they assist the trial lawyer in determining whether the client is prone to exaggerate or minimize. The trial lawyer should carefully note whether the injuries are obvious or obscure, whether the injuries are readily discernible and understandable by a jury, and whether they are of such a nature that they may form a lasting impression upon the triers of the fact.

2.2 SHOULD YOU RECOMMEND ANOTHER DOCTOR?

The lawyer should consider whether a client who is being treated by a general practitioner requires evaluation or treatment by a specialist. Does the client's present physician understand medical-legal problems? A perplexing question confronted by all personal injury specialists is whether the lawyer should recommend a specific doctor for treatment, and if so, how such a recommendation should be made. It is the general consensus that the trial lawyer should not hesitate to recommend a specialist either for examination or for treatment where it appears in the best interests of the client, or where it appears that the treating physician does not understand medical-legal problems, or is so antagonistic toward the legal profession in general as to render it impossible for him or her to cooperate in the furtherance of the patient's medical-legal interests. Fortunately, such cases are rare, but in the rare case the lawyer should feel no hesitation in protecting the interests of the client and insisting that the client obtain not only proper medical care, but also proper evaluation of his or her physical problem.

2.3 MAKING THE CLIENT WORK WITH YOU

Some lawyers fail to communicate adequately with the client and fail to insist that the client maintain adequate diaries and calendars with respect to day-to-day activities. It is important that the trial lawyer instruct the client to maintain a diary of all doctor visits, including notations as to instructions given by the doctor at the time of the visit concerning self-treatment at home and on the job.

Saving the Evidence

It is equally important that the client maintain a list of drugs purchased and consumed, including copies of the drug bills received for the purchase of drugs, and that he or she be instructed to save all drug bottles, boxes, or the containers in which the drugs are delivered. Some lawyers furnish the client with an envelope designed specifically for the purpose of preserving doctor, medical, and drug bills, with printed instructions on the outside of the envelope as to the purpose of the envelope and the listing of the bills. It is apparent that the reason for saving the bottles and containers is that at trial time some containers are dramatic evidence of the consumption of considerable quantities of drugs prescribed by the treating physician.

Client's Diary

It is suggested that the client be given a calendar upon which to circle the days lost from work, and that he or she be instructed to record all days lost from work, including those days when only part of the time was lost.

It is important that the client be instructed to keep a record of the circumstances under which he or she is examined by the physician appointed by the adverse party, including a record of the conversation with the doctor and the doctor's remarks at examination time. Such notation should be made immediately upon the client's departure from the examination room if possible. The client should also be instructed to record the time that he or she was seen by the examining physician and the time of departure. Such information serves an obviously valuable purpose in later cross-examination of the physician.

2.4 THE DOCTOR'S IDIOSYNCRASIES AND RELATIONSHIP OF DOCTOR TO CLIENT

Care should be taken to determine what the relationship between the doctor and the client really is. In other words, the attorney must know whether the doctor from whom information is sought is, in fact, a treating physician or merely an examining physician. Some states permit only treating physicians to testify as to the medical history reported. In most instances testimony offered by a treating physician carries more weight than testimony offered by a physician who examined only for purposes of testimony.

It is important to determine whether the treating physician will adopt a conservative approach in his or her estimate of disabilities. Most treating physicians are inclined to be conservative because of their natural confidence in their own skill and ability to treat the patient and make him well.

If a physician from whom the information is sought is a consulting physician, the attorney should be certain that the physician is sufficiently knowledgeable about the particular injury in order to formulate valid conclusions. Often a consulting physician has limited his consultation to a very specific area, and the attorney should be familiar with the nature of the injury about which the physician has been consulted.

If the doctor has been the family physician for some time, care should be taken to go into the details of the patient's medical history with respect to prior treatment of all injuries and all other medical care rendered by the family doctor, including the question whether the plaintiff has ever suffered injury or complained of difficulty in the same general area of the body now under consideration.

In the smaller communities it is important to know whether the treating physician has a good or poor professional reputation. In smaller communities, too, where there may be a social acquaintance between the client and the doctor, an inquiry should be made to determine the extent of the social acquaintance, particularly when the case is to be tried outside of the community and the triers of the fact may be less inclined to accept the basic integrity of the doctor.

2.5 CONTACTING THE DOCTOR

In General

The almost universal rule requires written authority of the patient prior to the obtaining of information from a treating, consulting, or family physician, and it is suggested that the trial lawyer obtain or devise a written authority form for this purpose. The form should be sufficiently broad to authorize the doctor to release to the attorney any information he has concerning previous care and treatment of the client, as well as his care and treatment of the injuries that are the subject of the litigation.

A letter of transmittal should accompany every request for medical information, and should advise the doctor of the purpose of the communication and of the wishes of the lawyer with respect to the information sought.

SAMPLE LETTER OF TRANSMITTAL

Re: ____________________

Dear ____________________:

We represent ____________________ in a claim for personal injuries arising out of an accident which occurred on __________. We have been advised by our client that you examined and/or treated __________ subsequent to this accident. We are enclosing a medical authorization form signed by __________ and request that you forward us your report as to your findings and the treatment prescribed. We specifically do not request your opinion as to prognosis at this time, since we realize it is too early for a prognosis to be completely accurate. Also, please keep us up to date with subsequent progress reports and interim bills.

Our representation contract permits us to deduct at the time of settlement any unpaid medical bills and to remit payment directly to the doctor or hospital involved. Therefore, please advise us as to the amount of your bill and whether any or all of it has been paid. If your bill has not been paid, we will protect you in the event that we effect a recovery for our client in this matter.

This office hereby revokes any and all prior medical authorizations issued by our client. It is respectfully requested that before medical reports are given to any person, company, etc. this office be consulted.

Very truly yours,

Should the Attorney Call or Write?

Personal injury specialists are not in complete agreement as to whether the doctor should be telephoned at the time that the written authority form and letter of transmittal are sent to him. Some lawyers make an appointment at such time for a conference with the doctor relative to the medical problems of the client. This conference usually takes place prior to the doctor's preparation of any written communication or medical report to the lawyer.

The reasons are obvious. If the doctor prepares a medical report in a casual manner and transmits it to the trial lawyer, it may contain information that is only casually considered at best, and that may later be used by the defense attorneys to harass or embarrass the doctor at trial time. Some doctors approach the preparation of medical reports with such casualness that they even are known at times to permit their secretaries to prepare the reports from the doctors' notes. Such embarrassment may be prevented by simply telephoning the doctor in advance of his preparation of the medical report, informing him of the purpose of the written authority and letter of transmittal and that it is the desire of the trial lawyer to confer with the doctor prior to the preparation of any medical report by him.

Such a conference may be by telephone or in person. Some attorneys ask the doctors to write a preliminary report, and after receiving it, call the doctor for an appointment for the purpose of discussing the report and making any revisions or additions that may be valuable in subsequent negotiations.

2.6 CONFERENCE WITH THE DOCTOR

In General

It should be understood that the conference with the treating physician is a business conference, and that the trial lawyer expects to pay the doctor for his time. The common practice is to arrange for an interview of at least thirty minutes in the preliminary stages and, just prior to trial, for sufficient time to go over all the medical matters prior to testimony. Most trial practitioners attempt to arrange the appointment with the doctor at the close of the day, after the doctor's waiting room has been cleared of patients, because the doctor is then at greater leisure to discuss the client's medical problems, without the pressure of patients requiring his attention.

The advantage of the prereport conference with the doctor is that it helps him to understand the importance of the information required of him in order to assist the lawyer in properly marshalling the medical evidence prior to trial. The lawyer should never attempt to persuade the doctor to "go out on a limb," but many doctors, because of their busy schedules, fail to understand the importance of complete accuracy in the preparation of written medical reports.

Checklist for Interview with Doctor

It is suggested that the trial lawyer develop a checklist in preparation for the interview of the physician. The checklist should include the questions that are of particular significance in the case for trial.

Preparing for the Medical Interview

It is important that the trial lawyer have complete knowledge of the medical witness's background. He should know whether the proposed medical witness has authored books or articles, or transcribed speeches that might be of interest to the cross-examining lawyer at trial time. Counsel should never place a medical witness upon the stand without having first checked and thoroughly studied all articles and material authored by the witness. This information should be obtained from the witness himself, and, as an added precaution, a thorough check of the medical index should be made.

It is imperative that the trial lawyer adequately emphasize to the inexperienced medical witness the importance of the explanation of medical terms in lay language so that the jury may more readily understand the testimony of the witness.

2.7 IMPORTANCE OF ASSISTING THE DOCTOR

In General

Contrary to popular belief, it is rare indeed when a doctor can comply with all the demands upon his or her time. Few doctors resent the assistance that a competent trial lawyer can provide in furnishing them with preliminary helpful information with respect to the client-patient. One device currently in widespread use is the medical brief, which has been used in recent years by some of the leading law firms of the nation. The technique involved in the preparation of such a brief is much the same as that used in the preparation of the legal brief.

2.7.1 A Medical Brief for the Doctor

In the preparation of a medical brief, the lawyer is, in fact, preparing for the doctor a brief of the latest developments in the field of medicine. Three of the most common methods of preparation of such briefs are: (1) the lawyer prepares the brief by means of medical books commonly used by doctors, which may be obtained upon request from any established medical library; (2) the brief is prepared by a professional medical researchist; (3) trial counsel sometimes hires a young intern or medical student with sufficient understanding of medical-legal problems to prepare a satisfactory medical-legal brief.

Nonspecialist Briefing Technique

A technique often used by the personal injury lawyer in the briefing of a nonspecialist prior to the preparation of a medical report or the giving of testimony in court is as follows: The lawyer determines, from either the nonspecialist himself or from his colleagues, whom the nonspecialist regards as a local expert in the particular field of treatment. Most specialists have testified in similar cases, and it is a simple matter for the attorney to draw upon his own experience with respect to the testimony of the specialist, or to consult the written transcript of the testimony of such a specialist in prior cases.

This technique is sometimes known as the nonspecialist briefing technique. It is always better to prepare in advance a written medical brief, no matter how short it may be, quoting accurately previous testimony by experts, preferably well recognized local experts, thus giving the general practitioner the benefit of the local experts' opinions on the subject in question. The trial attorney should routinely include as a part of his general pretrial briefing technique a pretrial conference with the nonspecialist, advising him at that time of the position currently taken in the community by those who are specializing in the field. Rarely will a nonspecialist disagree with a man of superior knowledge in a specialty, and often the nonspecialist has as much value as, or even greater value than, the specialist in jury presentation, since the general practitioner is apt to use words or terms more readily understandable by the jury. The family doctor is accustomed to discussing medical problems in lay terminology, while the specialist more commonly discusses such problems with other doctors.

2.7.2 Contents of the Medical Brief

The medical brief should cover at least the following topics:

1. History
2. Present complaints
3. The story of the present accident, in brief, as it affects the injury
4. Results of other examinations
5. Other or previous diagnoses
6. Previous recommendations
7. Previous tests run and results
8. Hospital records should be made available to the doctor, or at least pertinent excerpts
9. The prognosis of other doctors, if such exists
10. X-rays or x-ray positives

2.7.3 Form Medical Reports Versus Narrative Reports

In General

Should a form medical report be used? There are arguments for and against. Lawyers who routinely use a form medical report for delivery to the doctor, with the request that the doctor fill out the form, argue that it has the advantages of (1) helping to organize, in logical sequence, the contents of the doctor's report; (2) assuring coverage of all the areas necessitating coverage; (3) standardizing the procedure so that the lawyer knows where the answer should be; (4) fostering good public relations, since the doctors appreciate having a form to follow.

Many attorneys routinely use a modified short form medical report that is delivered as a preliminary to the follow-up personal visit to the doctor, and as a preliminary to an extensive narrative form of report to be later prepared by the doctor. If a written questionnaire is to be forwarded to a doctor, it is a good practice to advise the doctor of such intention and to orient him or her with respect to the preparation of the report.

Those who oppose the use of the form questionnaires in the medical report argue that (1) the questionnaire relieves the doctor of the need to carefully consider the client's problem; (2) it invites the doctor's secretary or nurse to fill out the form and thus deprives the trial lawyer of a thorough, conscientious medical appraisal by the doctor; (3) it irritates some doctors and thus is bad for public relations. Many doctors prefer to dictate a narrative statement of the history, examination, diagnosis, and treatment of the plaintiff's condition, and to those who routinely treat injured persons and deal with medical-legal problems, the form questionnaire is often not acceptable. Some doctors resent forms, and some are even inclined to charge more for the completion of a form than for the dictation of a letter. Hence the doctor should always be given the option of either completing the form or writing a narrative report. A suggested practice is requesting preliminary information from a doctor in narrative form and then arranging an early interview with the treating physician for the purpose of going over present and future medical problems of the client, at which time a guide or questionnaire is carried to the conference by the plaintiff's counsel.

The Narrative Report

When the narrative report technique is used, it is advisable for counsel to confer by telephone or in person with the doctor prior to the doctor's preparation of a report. As mentioned earlier, it is a good practice to suggest to the doctor that it is undesirable to make a prognosis at the early stages of treatment, since to prognosticate prematurely may later make it difficult to appraise the client's medical future fairly. Some doctors are prone to inject their personal feelings into narrative reports, and when a report is submitted containing such statements as "he is a very disagreeable person," or other such statements of unnecessary opinion, which have nothing to do with the medical situation, the trial lawyer should, as diplomatically as possible, attempt to persuade the doctor to delete such damaging remarks from the report.

Discussing the Report with the Doctor

After obtaining a preliminary medical report, the attorney should secure an appointment with the doctor and discuss with him or her the medical problems of the client prior to the drafting of the final report. This is recommended particularly where the lawyer intends to make available to opposing counsel copies of the medical report. The doctor appreciates being advised of the importance of a well-written report. Tell the doctor that the report should be written in such a way as to cause him or her no embarrassment at the time of trial. One of the areas of difficulty in the doctor-lawyer relationship occurs when the doctor has unthinkingly or ill-advisedly reported irrelevant matters that may be later used to embarrass him or her on cross-examination. When this occurs the doctor feels let down by the plaintiff's lawyer.

2.8 HOSPITAL CHARTS OR PATIENT'S RECORDS

2.8.1 Importance of Hospital Charts

Hospital records are ordinarily admissible as records kept in the course of business in the hospital, and contain written medical testimony by witnesses who sometimes cannot or will not be called to trial. The trial lawyer processing only the occasional personal injury case may fail to recognize the importance of such documents. The patient's chart, sometimes known as the hospital record or clinical record, is, in fact, usually the only written history of the plaintiff's experience with pain and discomfort. The hospital chart can be a virtual gold mine for the plaintiff's lawyer in the preparation of a client's case. It contains not only expressions of opinions by the doctors as to the plaintiff's difficulty and treatment, but also graphic evidence of the client's pain during the hospital stay.

2.8.2 What You Should Expect to Find in Hospital Charts

The lawyer should make a careful study of the list of contents of the common hospital charts, examining the forms in use in his or her locality to be completely familiar with the hospital chart and what it contains or should contain.

Mr. Blaine Briggs, owner and operator of Briggs Printing Company, Des Moines, Iowa, the largest distributor of hospital record forms in the world, states that there are literally hundreds of forms in use throughout the nation. He states, further, that forms produced by his company or similar ones are used in all major hospitals in the country, and that although they vary to some extent in appearance and content, most hospital charts contain approximately nineteen forms as follows:

(1) Admission—Summary Sheet
(2) Emergency Room Report
(3) Personal History and Physical Sheet
(4) Graphic Chart
(5) Doctor's Orders Sheet
(6) Laboratory Reports
(7) Consultation Record
(8) Progress Notes
(9) X-Ray Report
(10) Patient's Narcotic Record
(11) Report of Autopsy
(12) Operation Report
(13) Anesthesia Report
(14) Tissue Report
(15) Recovery Room Record
(16) Electrocardiographic Record
(17) Nurse's Medication Record
(18) Nurse's Record
(19) Physical Therapy Treatments

Admission—Summary Sheet. The Admission or Summary Sheet ordinarily contains the following information:

(1) Family name
(2) First name
(3) Middle name
(4) Home telephone
(5) Room number
(6) Hospital number
(7) Address—city, state, zone
(8) Sex
(9) Civil status
(10) Religion
(11) Church
(12) Age
(13) Birthdate—month, day, and year
(14) Birthplace
(15) Nationality
(16) Number of years in city
(17) Number of years in county
(18) Number of years in state
(19) Number of years in U.S.
(20) Military service
(21) Social Security Number
(22) Occupation
(23) Employer, or employer of spouse
(24) Address of employer
(25) Telephone number of employer
(26) Name of husband, or maiden name of wife
(27) Address, if other than above
(28) Birthplace
(29) Person to be notified in case of emergency
(30) Relationship
(31) Address
(32) Telephone
(33) Name of father
(34) Birthplace
(35) Maiden name of mother
(36) Name of mother
(37) Birthplace
(38) Hospital insurance
(39) Contract
(40) Referring physician
(41) Admitting service
(42) Attending physician
(43) Date of last admission
(44) Admission date
(45) Discharge date
(46) Provisional diagnosis "to be completed within twenty-four hours after admission"
(47) Final diagnosis
(48) Secondary diagnosis or complications
(49) Operation
(50) Consultation and results
(51) Results (recovered, improved, not improved, not treated,

diagnosis only, died, released against advice)

(52) Cause of death

(53) Autopsy—Yes or No

The Admission or Summary Sheet concludes with the following statement: "I have examined and approved this complete medical record on the ________ day of ________, 19__." It is signed by the attending physician.

Ordinarily, the reverse side of the Admission or Summary Sheet contains an authorization for medical or surgical treatment to be signed by the patient if possible, or the nearest relative in the event that the patient is physically or mentally incompetent. Often the reverse side of the sheet also contains authorization to be signed by the patient or nearest relative granting authority to the hospital to release to the insurance company such information as may be necessary for the completion of hospital claims.

Emergency Room Report. The Emergency Room Report customarily contains the following information:

(1) Family name
(2) First name
(3) Middle name
(4) Home telephone
(5) Admission date
(6) Hospital number
(7) Address—city, county, state, zone
(8) Age
(9) Sex
(10) Civil status
(11) Religion
(12) If a minor, full name of parent
(13) Address of parent
(14) Telephone number of parent
(15) Responsible party
(16) Address
(17) Diagnosis
(18) Treatment
(19) T.A.T. administered—Yes or No
(20) Tetanus Toxoid—Yes or No
(21) Anesthetic
(22) Medicine
(23) Patient to return to E.R. for follow-up care—Yes or No
(24) Patient to report to attending physician's office—Yes or No
(25) Attending physician
(26) Name of intern

The Emergency Room Report also customarily contains the following information relative to compensation:

(1) Name of company
(2) Address of company
(3) Occupation
(4) Date of injury
(5) How accident occurred
(6) Remarks

An informational report as to whether the patient has been sent home or hospitalized is also provided, together with information as to whether x-rays have been made. It is then signed by the nurse and attending physician or intern on call.

Personal History and Physical. The Personal History and Physical Sheet is an important one. Since it sometimes contains original statements made by the doctor that may be harmful to the plaintiff's case, particularly if the doctor fails to understand fully what the patient is saying, it should be very carefully examined. It ordinarily contains the following information:

(1) Last name
(2) First name
(3) Attending physician
(4) Date
(5) Room number
(6) Hospital number
(7) Final diagnosis: to be recorded when determined
(8) Sex
(9) Race
(10) Admission date
(11) Discharge date
(12) Occupation
(13) General condition
(14) Temperature, height, weight

The Personal History and Physical Sheet usually contains family history as to the age and general health of the patient's father and mother, brothers, and sisters. Space is provided for the patient's past history, listing diseases from childhood to date, habits, and social data. It contains data with respect to chief complaints upon admission, including the date of onset, mode of onset, probable cause and course. The following additional information is also included:

(1) Working diagnosis after physical examination
(2) Complications
(3) Physical findings: head, neck, chest, cardiovascular, abdomen, genito-urinary, skin, bones and joints, glandular, neuromuscular
(4) Former or subsequent admissions to this or other hospitals
(5) Date
(6) Hospital Number
(7) Diagnosis

The Personal History and Physical Sheet is customarily signed by the examining physician.

Graphic Charts. The Graphic Chart is a day-by-day graph showing temperature level, pulse, and respiration, ordinarily at four-hour intervals. It contains the following information:

(1) Last and first name
(2) Attending physician
(3) Room or ward number
(4) Bed number
(5) Hospital number
(6) Date

(7) Blood pressure
(8) Fluid intake
(9) Urine
(10) Defecation
(11) Weight

Doctor's Orders Sheet. The Doctor's Orders Sheet should contain the following information:

(1) Last name
(2) First name
(3) Middle name
(4) Room or ward number
(5) Bed number
(6) Hospital number
(7) Doctor's name
(8) Intern's name
(9) Day nurse
(10) Night nurse

The sheet is provided in the record for notations to be made by the doctors as to orders given, including the date of the order, the hour of the order, and the date and hour of discontinuance of the order.

Laboratory Reports. Laboratory Reports are usually attached to the master sheet for the patient's chart. The master sheet contains the following information:

(1) Last name
(2) First name
(3) Attending physician
(4) Room number
(5) Hospital number

The following laboratory reports may appear in the patient's chart:

(1) Urinalysis
(2) Blood (morphology)
(3) Blood (chemistry)
(4) Chemistry 1
(5) Chemistry 2
(6) Chemistry A
(7) Chemistry B
(8) Blood sedimentation
(9) Serology
(10) Blood grouping
(11) Sputum
(12) Gastric analysis
(13) Feces
(14) Bacteriology
(15) Glucose tolerance
(16) Antibiotic sensitivity tests
(17) Basal metabolism
(18) Spinal fluid
(19) Tissue report
(20) Kidney function
(21) Cytology
(22) Prothrombin time
(23) X-ray report
(24) Electrocardiogram
(25) Miscellaneous

Trial counsel should become thoroughly acquainted with the purpose of each of the above laboratory tests and should carefully consult with the attending physician as to the meaning of the report.

Consultation Record. The Consultation Record primarily contains the following information:

(1) Name of patient
(2) Room or ward number
(3) Bed
(4) Doctor
(5) Hospital number assigned to patient
(6) Date

In addition, the Consultation Record ordinarily contains the name of the consulting service or physician and the attending physician's signed report of the medical inquiry. The consultant's report, containing his or her findings, diagnosis, and recommendation, customarily appears on the lower part of the consultation record, followed by his or her signature.

Progress Notes. The Progress Notes Sheet is for the attending physician's daily notes regarding the progress of the patient. It contains the usual identification data as follows:

(1) Last name
(2) First name
(3) Attending physician
(4) Room number
(5) Hospital number

X-Ray Report. The X-Ray Report customarily contains the following information:

(1) Name of patient
(2) Age
(3) Room number
(4) Hospital number
(5) Address
(6) Date
(7) X-ray number
(8) Date of x-ray
(9) Treatment
(10) Date filed
(11) Information as to the anatomical region to be x-rayed, and the signature of the attending physician

On the lower part of the x-ray report are the findings and signature of the roentgenologist.

Patient's Narcotic Record. In addition to the usual identification information about the patient (room number, name of doctor, hospital number), the patient's narcotic record commonly contains the following information:

(1) Name of drug administered
(2) Date of administration
(3) Time of administration
(4) Dosage
(5) Method of administration
(6) Name of nurse who administered the narcotic

The narcotic record is a very important one to the personal injury lawyer, and graphically portrays the doctor's efforts to keep the patient as free from pain as possible during hospital confinement. It is a written history of the patient's fight against pain.

Report of Autopsy. Where the patient has expired in the hospital, the usual identification data are provided on the autopsy report together with the following:

(1) Date of admission
(2) Physician
(3) Date of death
(4) Occupation
(5) Nationality
(6) Clinical diagnosis
(7) Autopsy restrictions
(8) Hour of autopsy
(9) Narrative report of the physician who performed the autopsy

Operation Record. The Operation Record customarily contains sufficient data to identify the patient and the attending physician, plus the following additional information:

(1) Surgeon
(2) First assistant
(3) Second assistant
(4) Third assistant
(5) Surgical nurse
(6) Circulating nurse
(7) Sponge count
(8) Drains
(9) Pack
(10) Anesthetic
(11) Date
(12) Time operation began
(13) Time operation ended

The Operation Record should also contain the following:

(1) Preoperative diagnosis
(2) Postoperative diagnosis
(3) Procedure
(4) Findings of operation
(5) Signature of surgeon

Anesthetic Record. The Anesthetic Record should contain all information relative to the anesthetic administered, including:

(1) Agents
(2) Fluids
(3) Department of anesthetic
(4) Blood pressure
(5) Pulse
(6) Time of starting anesthetic
(7) Time operation started
(8) Time anesthetic ended
(9) Temperature
(10) Suction
(11) Receiving room
(12) Respiration

The Anesthetic Record should additionally contain information as follows:

(1) Dosage
(2) Techniques
(3) Fluid summary, including notes as to the administration of dextrose, glucose, saline, plasma, blood, or any other fluid during the course of the operation

Ordinarily, the Anesthetic Record contains the following preoperative information:

(1) Diagnosis
(2) Type of operation proposed
(3) Time of operation
(4) Age
(5) Sex
(6) Height
(7) Weight
(8) Blood pressure
(9) Temperature
(10) Respiration
(11) Urinalysis
(12) Blood chemistry
(13) Respiratory function
(14) Cardiac function
(15) Notes relative to examination of neck and teeth, drug allergy, mental condition, ataraxia, history of previous anesthetics, and cortices

Space is commonly provided for the anesthesiologist to record preoperative, operative, and postoperative complications.

Tissue Report. Most modern hospitals require postoperative tissue reports prepared and signed by the hospital pathologist. The purpose, in part at least, is to discourage unnecessary surgery. The Tissue Report signed by the pathologist, contains, in addition to the customary identification data, the following:

(1) Clinical diagnosis
(2) Macroscopic examination
(3) Microscopic examination
(4) Pathological diagnosis

Recovery Room Record. The recovery room, a hospital facility of rather recent origin, is designed and prepared to receive patients directly from the operating room for care and treatment during the immediate postoperative recovery stages. The Recovery Room Record, like all other hospital chart records, contains the usual identification information and the following additional information:

(1) Operation
(2) Anesthesia
(3) Total anesthesia time
(4) Anesthetist in operating room
(5) Anesthetist in recovery room
(6) Time of arrival in recovery room
(7) Condition on arrival

(8) Nurse in recovery room
(9) Time of transfer to patient's room
(10) Condition upon transfer to patient's room
(11) Age
(12) Sex
(13) Doctor's recovery room orders, with signed information about the patient's pulse, blood pressure, and respiration, usually determined at twenty-minute intervals
(14) Patient's blood type
(15) Infusion record: type of fluid infused, blood bank number, total volume in cc's, time infusion began, time finished, notations for reactions
(16) Time patient regained consciousness
(17) Notations as to nausea, vomiting, or other miscellaneous complications, and the time of these conditions
(18) Body temperature
(19) Skin condition
(20) Therapy
(21) Oxygen
(22) Other medication administered
(23) Remarks and signature of the anesthetist

Electrocardiographic Report. The cardiologist's signed Electrocardiographic Report contains information relative to the patient's electrocardiogram: clinical interpretations, electrocardiographic diagnosis, and remarks.

Nurse's Medication Record. The Nurse's Medication Record, like the Nurse's Record, is, as a general rule, important to the plaintiff's attorney. It commonly contains the following information relative to the administration of drugs, whether they be parenteral drugs, oral drugs, suppositories, or others:

(1) Date drug administered
(2) Time
(3) Site
(4) Initials of nurse who administered drug
(5) Remarks and signature of the nurse

Nurse's Record or Nurse's Notes. The Nurse's Record is extremely useful in understanding some of the client's problems while he or she is confined in the hospital. The nurse records periodically the temperature, pulse rate, and respiration of the patient, together with medicine administered and nourishment given. A space is provided for the nurse's remarks concerning observation of the patient—urine, stools, etc.

Physical Therapy Treatments. According to Mr. Briggs, the Physical Therapy Treatment Record is one of only three new areas covered in the hospital patient's chart during the last ten years. The form usually contains information with respect to the following:

(1) Date
(2) Area treated by therapy
(3) Type of therapy administered
(4) Time in minutes
(5) Remarks
(6) Name of the technician administering such therapy

2.8.3 Terminology

In General. The modern personal injury trial lawyer must study and thoroughly understand the terminology and symbols used in the hospital charts. Although the symbols vary from locale to locale, certain symbols are standard and commonly used in all hospital charts. Assistance in reading and understanding hospital charts and symbols may be obtained from an experienced nurse, any intern or practitioner, or perhaps from the treating physician.

Hospital Chart Abbreviations and Symbols. One useful text is *Understanding Medical Terminology* by Sister Agnes Claire Frenay, S.S.M., published by Catholic Health Association (St. Louis: 1977).

3

Practical Strategies on Where, When, How, and Whom to Sue

The most important decision the lawyer must make, second only to the decision to accept or refuse the case, is the decision concerning Where, When, How, and Whom to sue. The identity of the defendant often dictates or influences the requirement to sue in a particular jurisdiction since the rule of fair play, the rule of due process under most long-arm statutes, and the sometimes harsh rule of forum non-conveniens, can leave the attorney with no viable option.

When, however, there are multiple jurisdictions available, careful consideration must be given to the choice of the most appropriate and favorable forum for the presentation of a client's case. The where, when, how, and whom to sue are critical decisions that must be made with dispatch, but only after a careful consideration of all options available with the sole question being, "What is in the best interest of my client?" not, "What would be most convenient and profitable for me?"

3.1 WHERE TO SUE

The world is full of lazy, unimaginative, and greedy lawyers. Don't be one.

When two cars collide at an intersection in Chicago, and both the plaintiff and defendant are citizens and residents of the Chicago area, the decision concerning where to file the suit is automatic—Cook County Courts, and that's it. When an aircraft departs South Bend, Indiana, with a Wisconsin-based pilot flying a Kentucky-owned and maintained aircraft, and with an Iowa citizen and a Nebraska citizen aboard, and the crash occurs in Missouri en route to a destination in Kansas, the question of where to sue is not only complex, but of vital interest to survivors who may have conflicting desires and interests, to put it mildly.

3.1.1 The Search for Jurisdiction

The primary question, and one that must be answered with clarity, is, "Where can I obtain personal and subject-matter jurisdiction over the defendant or multiple defendants against whom actions should be maintained?" After one has identified the jurisdiction or jurisdictions, and usually there are multiple jurisdictions where a suit or suits may be maintained, the next question is, "Which of the various jurisdictions where the suit may be maintained has the best climate for the prosecution of the client's cause?" The answer to this question requires a sophisticated approach.

First, all information about court personnel, particularly judges who may be assigned to hear the case, must be obtained. The identity of the most likely defense lawyers must be investigated, as well as their relationships to the court personnel and judges. A review of jury verdicts in the area must be made and in some instances, usually based upon complexity or seriousness of the case as well as dollar value, community attitude surveys should be ordered and obtained for review prior to the filing of the action.

3.1.2 Statute of Limitations

Care should be taken to examine the law of the state where the incident occurred, as well as the law of the proposed forum, to identify the appropriate statute of limitation and the applicability of the statute where the incident occurred, and the question of whether the proposed forum state will apply its own statute of limitations or adopt the limitations set by the incident state. This can be very critical. For instance, Louisiana has a one-year statute of limitation on death cases. California has a one-year statute of limitation on death cases. Other states have similar short statutes. It is imperative that the statutes of limitations of both the "incident" state and the "forum" state be researched thoroughly since, for instance, the California courts have denied access to its courts after the expiration of one year, even though the incident occurred in a state with a much longer statute. California has ruled that its statute of limitations is procedural and therefore, "incident" state statutes are meaningless if one seeks to use the California courts.

One should not assume, where an incident occurs in the State of California, but suit may be maintained in a state with a longer statute of limitations, that simply filing it in the "forum" state outside of California will solve the problem. Many states remain lex loci delicti states and will adopt the statute of limitations applicable to the incident state.

3.2 WHEN TO SUE

It is an old maxim that time favors the defendants. "Time works against the party having the burden of proof or the burden of going forward." That this is true cannot be the subject of serious debate. Witnesses get lost, witnesses forget, physical evidence disappears, and all of the things that increase the hardship of the plaintiff in carrying the burden of proof are affected by the passage of time. For these reasons alone, the action should be filed at the earliest possible moment after the attorney has completed a review to identify the appropriate forum. Extreme care must be taken to identify each appropriate defendant with exactness and if the defendant is a corporation, care must be taken to determine the principal place of business of the corporation, as well as its state of incorporation, since for purposes of removal from state court to federal court, a corporation may, and often does, maintain two distinct citizenships in different states.

Be certain to explore the possibilities of removal if the case is filed in state court. Always order and have available to you the local rules of civil procedure, both state and federal. Some such rules contain subtle traps that can be devastating to the plaintiff's chances of victory. Always, when filing a suit outside your home state, select local counsel with extreme care, with emphasis upon his or her standing in the community, knowledge of the procedures, and willingness to follow a well-defined outline of responsibility between your office and his or hers. After a judge has been assigned to your case, it is a good idea to review the whole situation to determine whether there are any deficiencies or disadvantages occasioned by your selection of local counsel. Local counsel should be initially selected with the understanding that if after the action has been filed it becomes apparent to you, in your sole discretion, that a substitution of counsel should be made for any reason, such substitution may be made after first paying original counsel for his or her work and expenses advanced. This is critical. Never let your emotions or loyalty to an individual attorney interfere with the prime objective, which must be maintained at all times; that is, your total commitment to the interests of your client and your client alone. Some lawyers have personality conflicts with a particular judge, conflicts that have arisen through past associations, that can unconsciously cause the judge to exercise discretion unfavorable to the plaintiff. This is a situation to be scrupulously avoided. The only way to avoid it is to handle the problem if it arises in a dispassionate, unemotional way, maintaining at all times that the interests of the client must prevail.

It is a good idea at the outset when employing local counsel, to advise local counsel that the arrangement may well be temporary. It is also an excellent suggestion to level with original counsel and have him explain to you a history of his relationship with each of the judges to whom the case may be assigned after filing. It is suggested that you may well want to make inquiry from other sources concerning such relationships. It has rarely been beneficial to the plaintiff to have the services of local counsel who has, by past associations, no rapport with the judge or who, indeed, may be in a posture of antagonism with the judge. Keep always in mind that the judge who tries the case has a very broad discretion which he or she may exercise without effective limitation and the exercise of such discretion, favorable or unfavorable to the plaintiff, often spells the difference between victory and defeat.

3.3 HOW TO SUE

Suit should never be filed unless and until the attorney has made a thorough review and investigation of the rules of civil procedure governing the filing of actions in the jurisdiction where the action is to be filed. A failure to follow such procedure can result in consequences fatal to the case; in short, a dismissal with no hope of reinstituting the action. Actions are usually begun by filing a petition or complaint and the issuance of summons. The federal rules and local rules in some states permit a procedure known as "notice pleading," that is to say, that the plaintiff can file a short-form complaint requiring only identification of the parties, the time and place of the incident, the statement that the defendant was negligent or breached a warranty, or placed a defective product in the channels of commerce and that plaintiff sustained the injuries as the proximate result of such negligence, breach of warranty, or defective product. Federal rules and most state rules of cival procedure permit the serving of discovery documents with the summons and they should in all instances be used as a method of launching discovery in the case in a meaningful manner. Some lawyers routinely serve interrogatories, requests for production, and requests for admissions with the summons. They should be well thought out and well drafted. Such steps are intended to serve a distinct purpose in getting the jump on the discovery process.

It is considered by some to constitute good and effective practice to serve a notice of the taking of key witness depositions with the summons, but care should be taken to fix the date well beyond the required appearance and answer date.

3.4 WHOM TO SUE—THE SEARCH FOR DEFENDANTS

Most lawyers see the obvious. If Motorist A approaching an intersection fails to stop at a stop sign and collides with Motorist B on the through street, the "fault" is obvious. But is it really? Many factors may contribute to the "cause" of an accident. Few lawyers and their investigators take the time and trouble, or have the imagination, to fully analyze such an everyday occurrence. Usually, a full analysis arises only when it is discovered that Motorist A is either uninsured or underinsured, thus the necessity for seeking other potential defendants.

The Systems Safety Analysis of Facts—an Important Tool of Success

The facts should be analyzed from the systems safety approach. Consider that in order for an injury-producing incident to occur, there must be a failure of the "system" in which all activity is conducted. Think of it this way. Accidents don't just happen, someone or something causes them. In the business of transporting people in vehicles upon a highway or street, a failure of any component of the system, that is: (1) the person (driver); (2) the machine (vehicle); and (3) the environment (roadway or street and surrounding structures) can produce injury or death. Often a failure of more than one element occurs and we find concurring negligence, thus concurrent responsibility.

An easy method of visualizing and analyzing an injury-producing event is through the establishment of the responsibility, or Systems Safety Analysis Grid, such as that reproduced on p. 96. By analyzing the occurrence block-by-block, we are able to uncover hidden or obscure culprits.

Now, let's analyze the following statement of facts and apply them to the grid:

1. Driver A fails to stop at stop sign.
2. Driver A vehicle has brakes that are inadequate due to design or manufacturing defect.

SYSTEMS SAFETY ANALYSIS GRID

	Before	During	After
1. The Person (Driver)			
2. The Machine (Vehicle)			
3. The Environment (Roadway and Surrounding Structures)			

By using the grid, we find that Driver A caused a segment of the system to fail, both before and during the event, through failure to have control, perhaps excessive speed for the braking capacity of the vehicle, and by failing to yield to Driver B. Thus, Driver A may be responsible for injuries inflicted upon Driver B.

The machine, that is, the vehicle, failed a part of the system, both before and during the event, because of the defective or inadequate brakes. It follows that the manufacturer or maintainer of the vehicle may well be in part responsible for the injuries to Driver B.

Now add another factor. Suppose Driver A did not know of the requirement to stop because he or she was given no, or inadequate, warning of the stop requirement; that is, no advance warning of the stop sign. The governmental authority that owns and maintains the street or highway owes a duty to all persons using the facility to provide adequate advance warning of the requirement to stop a vehicle. Failure to do so may be negligence. This is an example of failure of the environment aspect of the system. It follows that if an analysis of the entire system establishes that the governmental agency failed in its responsibility to provide reasonable and adequate warnings of hazards on and adjacent to the roadway, the governmental agency may well be, in part, responsible for the injuries to Motorist B and possibly to Motorist A if he or she sustained injuries.

Let's add another element. Assume that the vehicle that Driver B was operating had a defect in design such as to cause or enhance the injury to Driver B, which represents a failure of the system during the event. The automobile manufacturer may well be responsible for the injuries to Motorist B under the well-established crashworthiness doctrine.

Now we will add another fact. Assume that after the collision, the rescue personnel mishandled the victim in Auto B or Auto A—such as failing to use a spine board in a suspected cervical cord injury, and it can be established that failure to properly handle the victim, either at the time of rescue or at the hospital later, was the final act that caused the victim to be hopelessly paralyzed.

We now have an example of a failure of "The Person" after the event.

Here is an example of a failure of "The Machine" after the event—the motor vehicle gas tank ruptures and catches fire after the collision event is terminated, and the driver or passenger of the vehicle is seriously burned.

An example of failure of "The Environment" after the event is the situation where the governing authority has permitted a structure such as a utility pole, a boulder, or some other removable obstruction to remain in the right-of-way, and in a location where it is foreseeable that a vehicle may hit the structure.

The Systems Safety Analysis Grid is a handy and effective device that can be used by the attorney to search out and identify all of the possible defendants in every case. The authors recommend that it be used routinely as an investigative aid.

3.5 SAFETY ENGINEERING

Some knowledge of the principles of safety engineering can be helpful in analyzing the occurrence.

The engineering of safety into a product or a system is well known and understood by the professionals who call themselves safety engineers. Unfortunately, few lawyers understand the basic principles of safety engineering and indeed, fewer still take the time or trouble to apply the basic principles, or they do so in a haphazard way.

The purpose of this discussion is to alert the lawyer to the effects of an understanding of the basic principles of safety engineering and the way in which those principles can be applied in almost every case to enhance the prospects of victory.

Hazard: We have taken the depositions and testimony of many so-called experts who are concerned daily with the identification of hazards and are charged with the responsibility of either eliminating the hazard or instructing or warning as to its presence. Yet with the rare exception has any such witness been capable of providing a concise, acceptable, and meaningful definition of the word "hazard." It doesn't take a safety engineer to know that, "A hazard is an existing condition that, when coupled with human activity, can produce injury or death," the key word being *can*. That's the definition that you must start with and that's the definition that almost every engineer or person concerned with identification of hazards will accept. It is a simplified version of the technical definition of hazard, but acceptable for use in courts and in analyzing whether a condition in a product or an environment is, in fact, a hazard. You say, why it is important that I know a definition of "hazard," or that I obtain an admission from the person charged with the responsibility of hazard identification, hazard elimination, and warnings as to hazards? Here's why. Most such persons confuse hazard with danger and have a very loose concept or an inaccurate concept of the fact that the hazard is the *condition* created or maintained that, when coupled with human activity, can produce injury or death. Thus, a four-leg intersection of roadway, a T-intersection of roadway, any roadway, contains certain hazards, either on or adjacent to the roadway. The law universally requires the governing authority—that is, the authority that has control and ownership of the roadway—to maintain it reasonably hazard-free and to instruct and warn as to the hazards that do exist. It is obvious that a T-intersection may, at times, be a necessary hazard and incapable of elimination because of land contour, man-made structures, and the like. It is equally apparent that a T-intersection constitutes a hazard to those approaching it. What is the answer? The law requires and the exercise of reasonableness dictates that the motorist be instructed and warned of the hazard of the T-intersection and that the warning be afforded him in time to perceive, understand, react, and act in order to avoid injury or death to himself or the occupants of his vehicle. Thus, one sees in a well-signed environment an advance warning of a T-intersection, usually seven hundred feet or more from the end of the terminating leg, a series of rumble strips to alert the driver aurally and a yield or stop sign halting traffic on the terminating leg of the T-intersection before entry onto the throughway.

In the business of hazard and risk recognition, one must be cognizant of the fact that risk is defined as the *chance* that a hazard *will* produce injury or death and it is directly affected by exposure.

3.6 SUMMARY

The attorney should never assume that because his client appears to have a "good case," Where, When, How, and Whom to sue is relatively unimportant. An otherwise good case can be reduced to little or nothing because the attorney has failed in his obligation to his client to make good judgments concerning these factors. Truly successful lawyers leave little to chance. In the answers to the questions regarding where, when, how, and whom to sue lies the secret to almost every successful case.

3.6.1 How Not to Be Caught Short in Pleadings

Plead broadly, to include every possible theory of the case. Many facts may be unknown to you at the beginning of the case and may not be ascertainable until discovery procedure is available. For example, if you have neglected to plead the theory of "design negligence" in a defective products case, relying on "defective manufacture" alone, subsequent revelation of design negligence may necessitate an amendent to the pleading or, if you have not done that, cause exclusion of evidence of design negligence. Before you start to prepare your Complaint, make a list of all possible theories of negligence that could apply in your case. For example, simple negligence, gross negligence, breach of express warranty, breach of warranty of merchantability, violation of a state or federal statute, code or regulation, and strict liability where applicable. In pleading damages, plead broadly also. If there has not been enough time to determine that a previous condition has been aggravated, plead it regardless. You can always drop or abandon a plea, but there are times when you may have difficultly in adding one.

Do not fail to amend pleadings should new facts justify or necessitate doing so. Often, the addition of parties may become desirable as the investigation and discovery proceed.

3.6.2 Form Complaints

The creation of a file of form Complaints can be very useful, but in each instance, thought should be given to possible necessary individual variation.

4

Effective Research and Discovery: Purposes and Methods

4.1 NECESSITY OF A TECHNICAL LIBRARY

Every successful plaintiff's personal injury lawyer has a well-developed technical library at least in the areas of his technical interests.

What is a technical library?

A technical library is a library that contains books, treatises, documents, reports, and journals concerning the technical aspects of the particular field.

Example: Lawyers who acquire an expertise in the preparation and trial of highway signing cases, roadside environment cases, and the like, must have a working knowledge of the history of highway design, roadside environment hazards, and the appropriate application and philosophy behind the use of highway signs. They must know that there are three basic types of signs; the regulatory sign, the guide, and the warning sign. They must know the purpose of each and the appropriate application of each. It is not sufficient that attorneys simply acquire a copy of the *Uniform Manual on Traffic Control Devices for Streets and Highways* now published by the Federal Highway Administration and adopted by most states as minimun signing requirements. They must, in order to adequately represent their clients, become knowledgeable and conversant in the history and philosophy behind the use of such signs. They must know, for instance, that the warning that the uniform manual prescribes is the minimum requirement for the use of highway warning signs and that often, the minimum requirements do not rise to the level of reasonable or due care under the circumstances. They must be acquainted with the American Association of State Highway Officials' publications and the fact that many such publications provide standards (that may or may not constitute due care), but standards that form a foundation and a basis for liability where such guidelines and standards are not followed. They must know and understand the purpose of highway delineators, edge-line markings, center-line markings, lane-line markings; of the use of barricades and cones; and of the significance of driver expectation in the roadway environment. Attorneys must know why it is imperative that the authority that controls the highway and its right-of-way environment have a responsibility in the interests of safety to reasonably anticipate that vehicles go out of control and leave the roadway with startling regularity (approximately thirty-five per cent of all motor vehicle accidents are single-car accidents). They must be acquainted with the contents of the "Blue Book," (*A Policy of Design for Rural Streets & Highways,* AASHO 1965), of the provisions of the "Yellow Book," (*Highway Design & Operational Practice Related to Highway Safety,* AASHO 1967), the they must have access to and regularly review the Highway Safety Literature Abstracts that are published by the Federal Highway Administration.

Lawyers who successfully prosecute air crash cases must be thoroughly acquainted with the workings, organization, and structure of the Federal Aviation Administration and the National Transportation Safety Board, and the methods by which aircraft are certified both by the United States Government, and by those who are designated or granted the authority to so certify such aircraft as airworthy in the field. They must know and understand the three basic causes for the crash of an aircraft and injury or loss of life of its occupants. They must understand that the crash may be occasioned by failure of the pilot (the person), the aircraft (the machine), and the environment. Their libraries should contain treatises, journals, magazines, and training manuals with respect to pilot activities; maintenance manuals; maintenance guides; and advisory circulars published by the Federal Aviation Administration. They need to understand that rarely, if ever, does a crash occur because of the environment, since the pilot in charge of the machine invariably directs the aircraft into the environment that may contribute in some manner to an ultimate crash. They need to know and understand the method by which aircraft are designed, developed, and manufactured, and placed in the stream of commerce by the manufacturers of the product, and the manner in which the aircraft are expected to be maintained in order to assure an airworthy condition of the flying vehicle.

The lawyer who is to be involved in the prosecution of a case involving injury because of electrical activity—that is, the transmission and distribution of electricity—must generate a technical library concerning the standards and techniques used and intended to be used in the interest of safety by the industry. This lawyer needs to know, for instance, that the *Lineman and Cableman's Handbook,* which has been published for years, has been substantially revised since the fourth edition, and has had removed from it many useful instructions and standards of care that formerly appeared before the specter of liability for injury through tort litigation arose during the 1960s.

Example: In a "fallen-line case," it would be useless to seek in the latest edition of the *Lineman and Cableman's Handbook* instructions to the lineman or cableman regarding what to do in the event he comes upon a fallen line. Everyone knows that fallen lines are dangerous. A fallen wire charged with electricity can maim and kill. There are definite and reasonable standards that must and should be followed by a lineman or cableman who comes upon a fallen wire; yet, the latest edition of the *Lineman and Cableman's Handbook,* Fifth Edition, contains no instructions or admonitions whatever regarding the conduct of a lineman or cableman in the interests of safety should he come upon a fallen wire. However, the *Lineman and Cableman's Handbook,* Fourth Edition, published in 1964, contains specific and direct admonitions with regard to such activities. They are as follows:

> Fallen wire: It shall be the duty of all employees to watch for fallen wires. When an employee finds a fallen wire carrying a high voltage in a more or less congested district, he shall stand by it so as to protect all street and highway traffic from it. He shall, as soon as possible, instruct someone else from those available in the neighborhood to telephone to headquarters either to have the wire killed or to have it raised from the ground.
>
> This employee shall not leave the fallen wire until he has been so instructed by the official in direct charge of the fallen wire.

The foregoing examples are used simply to illustrate the importance and indeed the necessity of acquiring, building, and maintaining a technical library in the attorney's field of expertise. The technical library constitutes an indispensable tool for ensuring success.

Most cases are won because of the ability of the lawyer to review and understand the literature and its application to the specific case undertaken and to recognize the value of the spoken and written word in the discovery and trial process when one is called upon or confronted with the necessity of forcing an adverse witness to admit misconduct, either upon his part, or upon the part of a colleague.

4.2 ELECTRONIC RESEARCH AS A NEW AND DEVELOPING METHOD OF INFORMATION ACQUISITION

Use electronic research—if you wish to keep up with your profession

What is it?

What is its scope?

How do you do it?

Examples of use.

The past ten years have seen the development and virtual explosion of the use of computers. Their use in the storage, classification, and retrieval of information offers a truly new and exciting tool. Lawyers who do not familiarize and equip themselves to use this tool will shortly be analogous to plumbers who do not have access to a Stillson wrench or PVC pipe.

The amount of information being stored in data banks for subsequent retrieval is nearly beyond comprehension and is increasing exponentially in volume and type.

Examination of the structure and contents of one of the larger data retrieval systems is instructive.

The DIALOG™ Information Retrieval Service of DIALOG Information Services, Inc. located in Palo Alto, California, is one of the larger systems and will serve as an example.* DIALOG Information Services, Inc., is a wholly owned subsidiary of Lockheed Corporation.

The system embraces over 150 separate files, each of which contain enormous amounts of information.

From the lawyer's point of view, it may be useful to think of this information resource as classified into four categories; legal, medical, technical/scientific, and general information.

A description of the contents of one each of the files dealing with the broad categories of law, medicine, technical/scientific data, and general information will illustrate the scope of the assistance available.

The file "Legal Resource Index" is number 150 of the DIALOG system. This one file provides cover-to-cover indexing of key law and law-related literature of a scope previously unavailable. Each article, book review, case note, president's page, column, letter to the editor, obituary, transcript, biographical piece, and editorial is indexed from over 660 law journals and 5 law newspapers. The only items not included

*© DIALOG Information Retrieval Services of DIALOG Information Services, Inc. (Trademark Reg. U.S. Pat. & Trademark Office, 1982)

BLUESHEETS
Alphabetical Listing
DIALOG INFORMATION RETRIEVAL SERVICE*

Database	File Number
ABI/INFORM	15 *
ADTRACK	43 *
AGRICOLA	10, 110 *
AIM/ARM	9 *
AMERICA: HISTORY & LIFE	38 *
APTIC	45 *
AQUACULTURE	112 *
AQUALINE	116 *
AQUATIC SCIENCES & FISHERIES ABSTRACTS	44 †
ARTBIBLIOGRAPHIES MODERN	56 *
AS!	102 *
BHRA FLUID ENGINEERING ABSTRACTS	96 *
BI/DATA FORECASTS	129
BI/DATA TIME SERIES	128 *
BIOGRAPHY MASTER INDEX	88 *
BIOSIS PREVIEWS	5, 55 *
BLS CONSUMER PRICE INDEX	175 *
BLS EMPLOYMENT, HOURS, AND EARNINGS	178 *
BLS LABOR FORCE	177 *
BLS PRODUCER PRICE INDEX	176 *
BOOK REVIEW INDEX	137 *
BOOKS IN PRINT	470 *
CA SEARCH	308, 309, 320, 310, 311
CAB ABSTRACTS	50 *
CAREER PLACEMENT REGISTRY/EXPERIENCED PERSONNEL	162 *
CAREER PLACEMENT REGISTRY/STUDENT	163 *
CHEMICAL INDUSTRY NOTES	19
CHEMICAL REGULATIONS & GUIDELINES	174 *
CHEMNAME™	31
CHEMSEARCH™	30
CHEMSIS™	328, 329, 330, 331
CHEMZERO™	300
CHILD ABUSE & NEGLECT	64 *
CHRONOLOG® NEWSLETTER-INT'L ED.	410 *
CIS	101 *
CLAIMS™/CITATION	220, 221, 222
CLAIMS™/CLASS	124 *
CLAIMS™ Patent Files	23, 24, 25, 125, 223, 224, 225
COFFEELINE℠	164 *
COMPENDEX	8 *
COMPREHENSIVE DISSERTATION INDEX	35 *
CONFERENCE PAPERS INDEX	77 *
CRIMINAL JUSTICE PERIOD INDEX	171 *
CRIS/USDA	60 *
DAILINDEX™	411
DIALOG PUBLICATIONS	200 *
DISCLOSURE II	100 *
DOE ENERGY	103 #
DUN'S MARKET IDENTIFIERS® 10+	516 * #
ECONOMICS ABSTRACTS INT'L	90
EIS INDUSTRIAL PLANTS	22 *
EIS NONMANUFACTURING ESTAB	92 *
ELECTRIC POWER DATABASE	241 *
ELECTRONIC YELLOW PAGES -	
CONSTRUCTION	507 *
FINANCIAL SERVICES DIRECTORY	501 *
PROFESSIONAL DIRECTORY	502 *
RETAILERS DIRECTORY	504, 505, 506 *
WHOLESALERS DIRECTORY	503 *
ENCYCLOPEDIA OF ASSOCIATIONS	114 *
ENERGYLINE®	69 *
ENERGYNET	169 *
ENVIROLINE®	40 *
ENVIRONMENTAL BIBLIOGRAPHY	68 *
ERIC	1 *
EXCERPTA MEDICA	72, 73, 172 *
EXCEPTIONAL CHILD EDUCATION RES	54 *
FEDERAL INDEX	20 *
FEDERAL REGISTER ABSTRACTS	136 *
FIND/SVP REPORTS AND STUDIES INDEX	196 *
FOOD SCIENCE & TECHNOLOGY ABS	51 *
FOODS ADLIBRA	79 *
FOREIGN TRADERS INDEX	105 #
FOUNDATION DIRECTORY	26 *
FOUNDATION GRANTS INDEX	27 *
FROST & SULLIVAN DM	59 *
GEOARCHIVE	58 *
GEOREF	89 *
GPO MONTHLY CATALOG	66 *
GPO PUBLICATIONS REFERENCE FILE	166 *
GRANTS	85 *
HARFAX	189 *
HEALTH PLANNING AND ADMINISTRATION	151 *
HISTORICAL ABSTRACTS	39 *
INPADOC	123 §
INSPEC	12, 13 *
INSURANCE ABSTRACTS	168 *
INT'L PHARMACEUTICAL ABSTRACTS	74 *
IRIS	53 *
ISMEC	14 *
LABORLAW	244 *
LANGUAGE & LANG BEHAVIOR ABSTRACTS	36 *
LEGAL RESOURCE INDEX	150 *
LIFE SCIENCES COLLECTION	76 *
LISA	61
MAGAZINE INDEX	47 *
MANAGEMENT CONTENTS	75 *
MEDLINE	152, 153, 154 *
METADEX	32 *
METEOR/GEOASTROPHYSICAL ABSTRACTS	29 *
MILLION DOLLAR DIRECTORY®	517 * #
MLA BIBLIOGRAPHY	71 *
NATIONAL FOUNDATIONS	78
NATIONAL NEWSPAPER INDEX	111 *
NCJRS	21 *
NEWSEARCH	211 *
NICEM	46
NICSEM/NIMIS	70
NONFERROUS METALS ABSTRACTS	118 *
NTIS	6 *
OCEANIC ABSTRACTS	28 *
ONLINE CHRONICLE	170 *
ONTAP® CA SEARCH	204 *
ONTAP® CHEMNAME	231 *
ONTAP® DIALINDEX	290 *
ONTAP® ERIC	201 *
ONTAP® PTS PROMT	216 *
PAIS INTERNATIONAL	49 *
PAPERCHEM	240 *

*Reprinted by permission of DIALOG Information Retrieval Service.

* Databases available under the Classroom Instruction Program.
# Available to U.S. users only.
Available only in U.S. and Canada.
† Not available in Canada.
§ Not available in Japan.

(September 1982) B-1

Database	File Number	Database	File Number
PATLAW	243 *	SSIE CURRENT RESEARCH	65 *
PHARMACEUTICAL NEWS INDEX	42 *	STANDARD & POOR'S NEWS	132, 133 *
PHILOSOPHER'S INDEX	57 *	STANDANDS & SPECIFICATIONS	113 *
PIRA	48 *	SURFACE COATINGS ABSTRACTS	115 *
POLLUTION ABSTRACTS	41 *	TELEGEN	238 *
POPULATION BIBLIOGRAPHY	91 *	TRADE & INDUSTRY INDEX	148 *
PSYCINFO	11 *	TRADE OPPORTUNITIES	106, 107 #
PTS F&S INDEXES	18, 98 *	TRIS	63 # #
PTS FORECASTS	81, 83 *	TSCA INITIAL INVENTORY	52 *
PTS PROMT	16 *	U.S. EXPORTS	126 *
PTS TIME SERIES	82, 84 *	U.S. POLITICAL SCIENCE DOCUMENTS	93 *
RAPRA ABSTRACTS	95	U.S. PUBLIC SCHOOL DIRECTORY	120 *
RILM ABSTRACTS	97 *	WATER RESOURCES ABSTRACTS	117 *
SCISEARCH®	34, 94 *	WATERNET™	245 *
SOCIAL SCISEARCH®	7 *	WELDASEARCH	99 *
SOCIOLOGICAL ABSTRACTS	37 *	WORLD ALUMINUM ABSTRACTS	33 *
SPIN	62 *	WORLD TEXTILES	67 *

are nonanalytical case digests and case reports, minor personnel notes, brief bulletins, and other ephemera.

The files entitled "Excerpta Medica" are numbered 72, 73, and 172.

The file description and subject coverage of File 72, 73, and 172 is as follows:

DIALOG INFORMATION RETRIEVAL SERVICE* (Excerpta Medica)

File Description:

Excerpta Medica has long been recognized as an important, comprehensive index of the world's literature on human medicine and related disciplines. About 230,000 records are added annually, over 60 percent of which contain abstracts. Each record is classified and indexed by medical research specialists who assign terms and codes in accordance with a highly developed classification schedule and controlled vocabulary. In-process records are placed initially in File 73. As processing is completed by Excerpta Medica, records are periodically transferred to File 72. The backfile of Excerpta Medica for records created from June 1974 through December 1979 is File 172.

The Excerpta Medica database is used to produce 43 printed abstract bulletins and 2 printed drug literature bibliographies. The on-line database contains a large proportion of additional citations (approximately 40 percent more) not announced in any of the printed Excerpta Medica journals.

Subject Coverage:

Nearly every aspect of human medicine, including topics in the basic biological sciences with some relevance to human medicine, is covered.

*Reprinted by permission of DIALOG Information Retrieval Service.

Nursing, dentistry, psychology, and the paramedical professions, such as podiatry, optometry, and chiropractic, are normally excluded, but there is much information relevant to these topics in the database. An outstanding feature of Excerpta Medica is its unusually complete coverage of articles on drugs and potential drugs. Some of the specific areas covered are:

* Anatomy
* Anthropology
* Anesthesiology
* Bioengineering
* Dermatology
* Drug Dependence
* Environmental Health and Pollution Control
* Forensic Science
* Genetics
* Hematology
* Immunology
* Microbiology
* Neurology
* Nuclear Medicine
* Occupational Health and Industrial Medicine
* Pathology
* Pediatrics
* Pharmacology and Toxicology
* Physiology
* Psychiatry
* Public Health
* Radiology
* Surgery
* Urology

In the technical/scientific field, an example of one file is "Scisearch," file numbers 34 and 94.

The file description and subject coverage of File 34 and 94 is as follows:

DIALOG INFORMATION RETRIEVAL SERVICE* (Scisearch)

File Description:

Scisearch is a multidisciplinary index to the literature of science and technology prepared by the Institute for Scientific Information® (ISI®). It contains all the records published in Science Citation Index (SCI®) and additional records from the Current Contents series of publications that are not included in the printed version of SCI. Scisearch is distinguished by two important and unique characteristics. First, journals indexed are carefully selected on the basis of several criteria, including citation analysis, resulting in the inclusion of 90 percent of the world's significant scientific and technical literature. Second, citation indexing is provided, which allows retrieval of newly published articles through the subject relationships established by an author's reference to prior articles. File 94 is the backfile containing records from 1974 through 1977; File 34 includes records from 1978 to the present.

Subject Coverage:

* Acoustics
* Aeronautics
* Agriculture
* Astrophysics
* Behavioral Sciences
* Biochemistry

---

*Reprinted by permission of DIALOG Information Retrieval Service.

* Biology
* Biophysics
* Botany
* Cardiology
* Chemistry
* Dermatology
* Electronics
* Engineering
* Environmental Science
* Geology
* Mathematics
* Medicine
* Microbiology
* Pharmacology
* Physics
* Physiology
* Psychiatry
* Psychology
* Surgery
* Virology
* Zoology

In the general information field, one file named "Newsearch," numbered as file 211, is instructive. Its file description and coverage is as follows:

DIALOG INFORMATION RETRIEVAL SERVICE* (Newsearch)

File Description:

Newsearch is the daily update of Magazine Index (File 47), National Newspaper Index (File 111), and Legal Resource Index (File 150). It provides front-page-to-back-page indexing of *The Christian Science Monitor*†, *The New York Times*†, and *The Wall Street Journal*†, as well as cover-to-cover indexing of over 370 popular American magazines, 660 law journals, and 6 law newspapers. All articles, news reports, editorials, letters to the editor, obituaries, product evaluations, biographical pieces, poetry, recipes, columns, cartoons, illustrations, and reviews are included. The only items *not* included are minor personnel notes, brief bulletins, stock market tables, weather charts, horoscopes, and other ephemera. Newsearch provides an extensive and current source for answering general reference questions. Its greatest value lies in its currency, for it can be used with the Search† Save feature to produce a customized SDI service.

Subject Coverage:

* Current Affairs, National and International
* Business and Economics
* Education, Cultural Events
* Health, Medicine
* Consumer Product Evaluation
* Society and the Individual
* Law
* Environmental Issues
* House and Home Activities
* Performing Arts, Literature
* Regional News
* Science, Technology, Agriculture
* Travel, Sports, Leisure

---

*Reprinted by permission of DIALOG Information Retrieval Service.
†Trademarks of the respective organizations.

Each of the files described above is only an example of a number of files that contain and index information in the board fields of legal, medical, technical, and general information fields.

How can you access and utilize these resources? There are three methods of which we are aware.

First, you may purchase or lease the necessary computer and software and subscribe to or join one of the great data retrieval systems such as DIALOG. This is a fascinating approach. However, it necessitates acquiring the knowledge and skill to utilize the equipment and the system. The expense is mitigated at the present time by the fact that if the equipment is utilized strictly in a business activity, there may be the opportunity to take an investment tax credit on the investment. (So our accountants tell us. Check with your own. We are not tax lawyers.)

DIALOG conducts schools periodically at various places in the country where instruction in accessing the system can be obtained, as well as instruction in the use of specific files, such as "Medline," or "Excerpta Medica."

A second method of accessing the system is by requesting research from various companies that specialize in information acquisition and retrieval.

After subscribing to their service, call them on the phone. Explain your problem, in detail. They will design the search, access the system, and furnish your choice of lists of articles, abstracts of articles, or the full articles. They can also furnish information concerning authors, their writings, and their location. This often furnishes an excellent beginning in the search for qualified experts in the field of information needed by you.

You put a budget limitation on what you wish to expand and it will be honored. It is not expensive, but the terms are ten days/cash.

Third, if you have already located articles or information that you need, usually in addition to the above, you can obtain copies of the articles from some or all of the suppliers listed hereafter:

DIALOG INFORMATION RETRIEVAL SERVICE*
DIALORDER™ SUPPLIERS
(as of September 1982)

ORDER ACRONYM	DATE OF MOST RECENT YELLOWSHEET	SUPPLIER
ACCESS	July 1982	Associated Information Consultants (Ann Arbor, MI)
ACQUIRE	June 1982	Tracor Jitco, Inc. (Rockville, MD)
ADS	Apr. 1982	Information Specialists (Cleveland Heights, OH)
ADTRACK	Jan. 1982	Corporate Intelligence, Inc. (St. Paul, MN)

*Trademark Reg. U.S. Pat. & Trademark Office

.ORDER ACRONYM	DATE OF MOST RECENT YELLOWSHEET	SUPPLIER
All	Nov. 1981	Access Innovations, Inc. (Albuquerque, NM)
APLSD	June 1980	Pelner Library Service (West Los Angeles, CA)
AQUA	June 1981	Water Research Centre (Medmenham, Marlow, Buckinghamshire, U.K.)
ASAP	Apr. 1982	Information Consultants (Chicago, IL)
ATLINFO	Apr. 1981	Atlanta Information Services (Decatur, GA)
BBA	May 1982	Bogart-Brociner Associates, Inc. (Annapolis, MD)
BLLD	May 1982	British Library Lending Division (Boston Spa, West Yorkshire, U.K.)
BNF	Apr. 1982	British Non-Ferrous Metals Technology Centre (Wantage, Oxon., U.K.)
CAB	June 1981	Commonwealth Agricultural Bureaux (Farnham Royal, Slough, U.K.)
CANDOCS	Jan. 1980	Micromedia Limited (Toronto, Ontario, Canada)
CAROLIB	July 1982	Carolina Library Services (Chapel Hill, NC)
CASDDS	Feb. 1981	Chemical Abstracts Service Document Delivery Service (Columbus, OH)
CDUMI	Apr. 1982	University Microfilms International (Ann Arbor, MI)
CHALDOC	July 1982	Chalmers University of Technology Library (Gothenburg, Sweden)
CIS	Oct. 1981	Congressional Information Serivce (Bethesda, MD)
CPR	Nov. 1981	Career Placement Registry (Wilmington, DE)
CRC	Jan. 1982	Clearinghouse for Regulatory Material on Chemicals (Fairfax, VA)
CTRC	Apr. 1980	Colorado Technical Reference Center (Boulder, CO)
DATA	July 1982	DATA-SEARCH (Pittsboro, NC)
DATAQUE	Apr. 1980	DataQuest International, Inc. (Chicago, IL)
DELFTLIB	July 1982	Library of Delft University of Technology (Delft, The Netherlands)
DIALOG	Nov. 1980	DIALOG Information Retrieval Service (Palo Alto, CA)
DISCLO	July 1981	Disclosure, Inc. (Washington, DC)
DYNAMIC	Aug. 1981	Dynamic Services (Menlo Park, CA)
EIC	Nov. 1979	Environment Information Center, Inc. (New York, NY)
ERIC	Nov. 1979	ERIC Document Reproduction Service (EDRS) (Arlington, VA)
ESL	Oct. 1981	Engineering Societies Library (New York, NY)
EUROSERV	Jan. 1982	Mikro-Cerid (Boulogne, France)
FINDIT	June 1981	FIND/SVP (New York, NY)
GEOARCHS	Nov. 1979	Geosystems (London, United Kingdom)
GPOPRF	Mar. 1982	U.S. Government Printing Office (Washington, DC)
HIRS	Feb. 1982	Harkers Information Retrieval Systems (Australia)
IFIPATS	Nov. 1979	IFI Plenum Data Company (Arlington, VA)
IIIAZ	Aug. 1981	Information Intelligence, Inc. (Phoenix, AZ)
INFO	Nov. 1981	Information on Demand (Berkeley, CA)
INFODOC	Nov. 1979	INFO/DOC - Information Documentation (Washington, DC)
INFORM	Jan. 1982	Data Courier, Inc. (Louisville, KY)
INFOSRCH	June 1982	Info-Search (Bloomfield Hills, MI)
INFOSTOR	Nov. 1981	Information Store (San Francisco, CA)
IPDNY	June 1981	Information Processing and Delivery (New York, NY)
KINOUSA	June 1982	Kinokuniya Company, Ltd. (Tokyo, Japan)
KNAWLIB	July 1982	Library of the Royal Netherlands Academy of Arts and Sciences (Amsterdam, The Netherlands)
LAWINFO	May 1982	Information Store (San Francisco, CA)
MASIS	Oct. 1980	Maruzen MASIS Center (Tokyo, Japan)
MEDLIT	June 1982	Medical Literature Retrieval (Seattle, WA)
METALS	Aug. 1980	American Society for Metals (Metals Park, OH)
MGMT	Apr. 1982	Management Contents, Inc. (Skokie, IL)
MITS	June 1981	Michigan Information Transfer Source (Ann Arbor, MI)
NTHBINFO	Aug. 1981	Norwegian Institute of Technology (Trondheim, Norway)
NTIS	Mar. 1982	National Technical Information Service (Springfield, VA)
NTISJPN	Apr. 1982	Mitsubishi Research Institute (Tokyo, Japan)
NTISUK	Sept. 1980	NTIS, United Kingdom Service Center (United Kingdom)
OATS	Mar. 1982	Institute for Scientific Information (Philadelphia, PA)
PATA	June 1982	The PATA Group (Washington, DC)
PHARMACY	Jan. 1982	American Society of Hospital Pharmacists (Washington, DC)
PTS	Feb. 1982	Predicasts, Inc. (Cleveland, OH)
QUEST	Nov. 1981	InfoQuest (Kensington, MD)
RAPRA	Feb. 1980	Rubber and Plastics Research Association of Great Britain (Shawbury, Shrewsbury, U.K.)
RPIPAT	Mar. 1981	Research Publications, Inc. (Arlington, VA)
RSPD	May 1982	Bureau of National Affairs (Washington, DC)
SCANINFO	June 1982	Business Information International (Copenhagen, Denmark)
SISINFO	June 1982	Savage Information Services (Rolling Hills Estates, CA)
SPECS	Aug. 1981	National Standards Association (Washington, DC)
TIBORDER	Jan. 1982	Technische Informationsbibliothek, Universitatsbibliothek (Hanover, Germany)
WATERNET	Sept. 1982	American Water Works Association (Denver, CO)
WEA	July 1982	Warner-Eddison Associates (Cambridge, MA)
TRAIN		Training Acronym. No Yellowsheet

ORDER TRAIN can be used to practice use of DIALORDER or for training and demonstrations to others. All orders entered using ORDER TRAIN or ORDERITEM TRAIN are ignored.

Reprinted by permission of DIALOG Information Retrieval Service

A useful book listing sources for development retrieval is *Document Retrieval, Sources and Services,* copyrighted by the "Information Store," 235 Montgomery Street, 800 Russ Building, San Francisco, California 94104, telephone number (415) 421-9376.

EXAMPLE OF USE OF ELECTRONIC RESEARCH

A crop damage case

The crop: bell peppers

Damages: $600,000.00

Cause of damages: Substitution, under false labels, of a genetically different but similar pepper seed for the one ordered. The seed variety ordered was well established and certified by years of experience as suitable for use in the particular environment.

Problem: The defendant seed company furnished the names of two purported experts in response to court order who were prepared to testify that the crop damage was caused by either faulty agricultural practices or weather, or that the seed furnished was, in fact, that which was ordered.

Solution: A computer search of the writings of the two experts involved showed extensive involvement with cucumbers, third-world economics, palms in central and South America—but nothing on bell peppers—followed by some interesting cross-examination.

ANOTHER EXAMPLE OF USE OF ELECTRONIC RESEARCH

A need for an expert on chemical burns to humans

Solution: A computer author search for information on who has written in this field.

The utility of electronic research is limited only by your imagination and need. It is not a substitute for common sense and diligence.

4.3 METHODS OF DISCOVERY

"Discovery" is the handmaiden of success.

Napoleon once said, "Artillery is the queen of battles." No less important to success in trial is adequate use of discovery procedure.

4.3.1 Interrogatories

Written interrogatories often serve as a means of preliminary discovery that can vastly facilitate the preparation of a case for trial. Many trial specialists feel that interrogatories should be routinely filed, as soon as permitted by the rules, in order to ascertain the identity and location of individuals who should be subsequently deposed, or to ascertain the location of evidence that should be examined by means of a Motion to Produce. Some trial specialists develop standard-form interrogatories for use in different circumstances, saving both the attorney's time and that of the secretary. A few examples of such standard-form interrogatories follow.

Interrogatories should accompany the Complaint for service with the Complaint in those jurisdictions where this is permitted. These should include searching questions relative to the existence of insurance.

SAMPLE INTERROGATORIES TO ACCOMPANY THE COMPLAINT

1. Please state the names and addresses of any and all persons who are believed, or known by you, your agents or attorneys, to have any personal knowledge concerning the happening of the accident described in the complaint herein.

2. Please state the name and address of any person known to you, your agents or attorneys, who has possession or control of any photographs, model, plat, map, drawing or motion pictures pertaining to any fact involved in this controversy, including pictures of the scene of the accident, persons or vehicles involved.

3. Please state the name and address of every person, other than an investigating police officer, known to you, your agents or attorneys, who has heard or is purported to have heard the plaintiff make any statement, remark, or comment concerning the incident described in the complaint.

4. Please state the name and address of any person, persons, or corporation who was the registered title owner of the motor vehicle you were driving as of the date of the accident described in plaintiff's complaint.

5. As of the date of the complaint, if any person or corporation, other than those persons or corporations named in the answer to the preceding interrogatory, had any legal or equitable ownership interest in said motor vehicle, please state the names and addresses of such person or corporation, and what interest that person or corporation had in the ownership of such motor vehicle.

6. If the motor vehicle described in the answers to the preceding interrogatories was damaged in the accident described in the

complaint, please state the cost of repairing it. If it has not been repaired, please describe any repair estimates that have been made, giving the name of the person or company making the estimate, and the amount of such estimate.

7. Describe the year, make, and model of the vehicle you were driving at the time of the accident, and state the type of transmission with which the vehicle was equipped, any power equipment on such vehicle, and the weight of such vehicle.

8. Did any mechanical defect in the motor vehicle you were driving at the time of the accident contribute to the occurrence of the accident? If your answer is in the affirmative, please state the nature of such defect.

9. If you are claiming this accident happened as a result of any mechanical defect in your vehicle, please state the nature of said defect and the length of time it existed.

10. If you are so claiming a defect, please state the last time the vehicle was inspected by the State of Florida, and the location of said inspection.

11. If you are so claiming a defect, please state the name and address of the person who last worked on this portion of the vehicle that was alleged to be defective at the time of the accident, and the place and date of such work.

12. If you were suffering from physical infirmity, disability, or sickness at the time of the occurrence of the accident described in the complaint, please describe the nature of such infirmity, sickness, or disability.

13. Please state whether or not you had consumed any alcoholic beverages, or taken any drugs or medications, within 12 hours before the occurrence of the accident described in the complaint. If the answer to this interrogatory is in the affirmative, please state the type and amount of alcoholic beverages consumed and when and where you had consumed them, or the amount and nature of the drugs or medications you had taken and when you had taken them.

14. Please state whether or not you have ever been convicted of a crime. If so, state the number of times you have been convicted of a crime, the date and place of each conviction, and the nature of the crime of which you were convicted.

15. Do you wear glasses? If so, who prescribed them, when were they prescribed, and when were your eyes last examined, and by whom?

16. Do you wear a hearing aid? If so, please state who last examined your ears.

17. If you are currently employed, please state the name and address of your employer, and the type of work you do.

18. Had you ever traveled the highway on which the accident

occurred, prior to the time of the accident? If your answer is in the affirmative, please state the period of time prior to the accident when you had traveled that highway.

19. Did you plead guilty to any charge placed against you arising out of the accident described in the complaint? If your answer is in the affirmative, please state the charge to which you pleaded guilty.

20. Please state whether you, your agents, servants, or employees have possession, custody, or control of any movies of any of the parties to this lawsuit.

21. If the answer to the above interrogatory is in the affirmative, please state, with respect to *each* such movie:

a. The name and address of each party who was the subject of the movie.
b. The date the movie was taken.
c. The name and address of the individual who took the movie.

22. Please state whether you, your agents, servants, or employees have possession, custody, or control of any photographs of any of the parties to this lawsuit.

23. If the answer to the above interrogatory is in the affirmative, please state the number of such photographs and state, with respect to *each* such photograph:

a. The name and address of each party who was the subject of the photograph.
b. The date the photograph was taken.
c. The name and address of the individual who took the photograph.

24. Have you, your agents, attorneys, servants, or employees retained any individuals to perform any surveillance of any of the parties in this lawsuit?

25. If the answer to the above interrogatory is in the affirmative, please state:

a. The name and address of the person or firm you retained.
b. The name and address of the party who is or was the subject of the surveillance.
c. Whether such surveillance has already been performed, and if so, the dates of surveillance.

26. Please state whether you, your agents, attorneys, servants, or employees have any information indicating whether any of the parties has been convicted of a crime.

27. If the answer to the above interrogatory is in the affirmative, please describe the information you have and what your information reveals about the number of convictions.

28. Please state the name and address of each individual known to you, your agents, or attorneys who will or may testify as to the past or present physical capabilities of the plaintiff (or plaintiffs).

29. Please state the name and address of each individual known to you, your agents, or attorneys who will or may testify to what the plaintiff(s) said concerning the injuries sustained by the plaintiff(s) as a result of the incident described in the complaint.

30. Have you, your agents, attorneys, insurance company, or anyone on your behalf requested, ordered, and/or received any information from any computer information center concerning the plaintiff(s) named in this suit? If so, please state:

a. The name, address, and job title of the person(s) having custody and control of this information.
b. The date the information was ordered and the name, address, and job title of the person(s) so ordering the information.

31. State whether you have made any statement or statements in any form to any person regarding any of the events or happenings referred to in the complaint. If so, state, with respect to *each* such statement:

a. The name and address of the person or persons to whom such statement was made.
b. The date the statement was made.
c. The form of the statement, whether written, oral, by recording device, or to a stenographer.
d. Whether the statement, if written, was signed.
e. The names and addresses of all persons presently having custody of the statement.
f. Whether you received a copy of said statement.

32. State whether you, your attorneys, your insurance carrier, or anyone acting on your or their behalf obtained statements in any form from any persons regarding any of the events or happenings that occurred at the scene of the incident referred to in the complaint immediately before, at the time of, or immediately after said incident. If so, state, with respect to *each* such statement:

a. The name and address of the person from whom the statement was taken.
b. The date on which the statement was taken.
c. The name(s) and address(es) of the person(s) and employer(s) of such person(s) who took the statement.
d. The name(s) and address(es) of all person(s) having custody of the statement.
e. Whether the statement was written, by recording device, by court reporter, or by stenographer.
f. Which of the statements mentioned in subparagraph (a) above are signed by the person giving them.

33. State whether there is or was in existence any policy of liability insurance that would or might inure to the benefit of the plaintiff(s) herein, by providing for payment of a part of or all of any judgment

rendered in favor of the plaintiff(s) against any defendant or against any other person, firm or corporation who is or may be liable to the plaintiff(s) by reason of the incident described in the complaint, and if the answer is in the affirmative, state as follows *as to each* such policy of insurance known or believed to exist by you or your attorneys:

a. The name and address of the insurer on each such policy.
b. The name and address of *each* named insured on each such policy.
c. The relationship, if any, between each named insured on each such policy and any named defendant(s) in this cause.
d. The policy number of each such policy.
e. The name and address of any person, firm, or corporation who is or may be an "additional insured" under such policy by reason of the incident described in the complaint, and the relationship, if any, between such "additional insured" and any named defendant(s) in this cause.
f. The limits of liability in such policy as might be applied to any one plaintiff by reason of any one incident and the total limits of liability to all persons by reason of any one incident.
g. Whether or not any insurer has notified any insured that said insurer or any other person, firm, or corporation must pay a part of or all of any judgment before the insurer must make any payment; if so, what payment must be made and by whom before the insurer must make payment.
h. Whether any insurer has notified any insured that said insurer claims that there is or may be no coverage under the terms of the policy of insurance involved.

   (1) If the answer to subparagraph (h) is in the affirmative, describe the reason given for the claimed lack of coverage or failure thereof as stated by said insurer (identifying same) to said insured (identifying same), and state the date of such notice. [*NOTE:* If such policy defense is withdrawn or waived, this subparagraph need not be answered.]

i. The exact name and address of the resident agent of each insurance company.

34. Are you protected against the type of risk sued hereon by any:

a. Reinsurance?
b. Excess insurance?

35. If your answer to either of the subdivisions of the preceding interrogatory is in the affirmative, for each such coverage, state:

a. The name and address of the insurer.
b. The number of the policy.

c. The form of insurance.
d. The effective dates of coverage.
e. The amount of coverage.
f. The name and address of the named insured.
g. The name, address and telephone number of the person or entity who has possession of the policy and the reinsurance or excess insurance clauses.

36. Do any of the policies which protect you against the type of risk sued hereon have a provision for medical payments?

37. If so, for each such policy, state:
a. The name and address of the insurer.
b. The number of the policy.
c. Who is covered by the medical payment clause.
d. The amount of medical coverage per person.
e. The total overall amount of medical coverage.

38. Are immediate medical payments available under the terms of any policy?

39. If so, identify each policy that provides for immediate medical payments.

SAMPLE INTERROGATORIES TO INSURANCE CARRIER TO ACCOMPANY THE COMPLAINT

---

1. State whether there is or was in existence any policy of liability insurance that would or might inure to the benefit of the plaintiff(s) herein, by providing for payment of a part of or all of any judgment rendered in favor of the plaintiff(s) against any defendant or against any other person, firm, or corporation who is or may be liable to the plaintiff(s) by reason of the incident described in the complaint, and if the answer is in the affirmative, state as follows *as to each* such policy of insurance known or believed to exist by you or your attorneys:
a. The name and address of the insurer on each such policy.
b. The name and address of *each* insured on each such policy.
c. The relationship, if any, between each named insured on each such policy and any named defendant(s) in this cause.
d. The policy number of each such policy.
e. The name and address of any person, firm, or corporation who is or may be an "additional insured" under such policy by reason of the incident described in the complaint, and the relationship, if any, between such "additional insured" and any named defendant(s) in this cause.
f. The limits of liability in such policy as might be applied to

any one plaintiff by reason of any one incident and the total limits of liability to all persons by reason of any one incident.

g. Whether or not any insurer has notified any insured that said insured or any other person, firm, or corporation must pay a part of or all of any judgment before the insurer must make any payment; if so, what payment must be made and by whom before the insurer must make payment.

h. Whether or not any insurer has notified any insured that said insurer claims that there is or may be no coverage under the terms of the policy of insurance involved.

(1) If the answer to subparagraph (h) is in the affirmative, describe the reason given for the claimed lack of coverage or failure thereof as stated by said insurer (identifying same) to said insured (identifying same), and state the date of such notice. [*NOTE:* If such policy defense is withdrawn or waived, this subparagraph need not be answered.]

i. The exact name and address of the resident agent of each insurance company.

2. Are you protected against the type of risk sued hereon by any:

a. Reinsurance?

b. Excess insurance?

3. If your answer to either of the subdivisions of the preceding interrogatory is in the affirmative, for each such coverage, state:

a. The name and address of the insurer.

b. The number of the policy.

c. The form of insurance.

d. The effective dates of coverage.

e. The amount of coverage.

f. The name and address of the named insured.

g. The name, address and telephone number of the person or entity who has possession of the policy and the reinsurance or excess insurance clauses.

4. Do any of the policies that protect you against the type of risk sued hereon have a provision for medical payments?

5. If so, for each such policy, state:

a. The name and address of the insurer.

b. The number of the policy.

c. Who is covered by the medical payment clause.

d. The amount of medical coverage per person.

e. The total overall amount of medical coverage.

6. Are immediate medical payments available under the terms of any policy?

7. If so, identify each policy that provides for immediate medical payments.

OTHER INTERROGATORIES WILL PROBABLY BE NECESSARY AT A LATER DATE, INCLUDING "EXPERT INTERROGATORIES."

---

1. State the name, profession, and professional address of each person whom you or your attorneys will or may call to testify as an expert witness at the trial of this matter.
2. State the education and experience of each expert that allegedly qualifies him or her to render opinions in this case.
3. State, in detail, the subject matter about which each such person named in the answer to the foregoing interrogatory is expected to testify.
4. State the opinions that each such person will testify to at trial.
5. State the factual basis for each opinion.
6. State the specific documents and authorities relied on by each expert in forming each opinion.
7. If any person named in answer to the foregoing Interrogatories has submitted a written report or opinion relative to the subject matter of this case, state:
   a. The name of the person submitting such written report or opinion.
   b. The date or dates of such written report or opinion.
   c. The name and address of the person to whom such written report or opinion was submitted.
8. As to each expert consulted by you or your attorneys relative to the subject matter of this case, but whom you do not expect to call to testify at trial, state:
   a. The name, profession and professional address.
   b. The subject matter about which he or she was consulted.
   c. If expert has submitted any written reports or opinions relative to the subject matter about which he or she was consulted, indicate the date (or dates) of such report, and the name and address of the person to whom submitted.
9. As to each expert consulted by you or your attorneys relative to the subject matter of this case, about whom you are undecided as to whether or not to call to testify at trial, state:
   a. The name, profession and professional address.
   b. The subject matter about which he or she was consulted.
   c. The opinions stated either orally or in writing of such person relative to the subject matter of this case.
   d. The facts relied on in forming each opinion.
   e. The specific documents and authorities relied on in forming each opinion.
   f. If expert has submitted any written reports or opinions relative to the subject matter about which he or she was

consulted, indicate the date (or dates) of such report and the name and address of the person to whom submitted

---

TYPICAL WRITTEN INTERROGATORIES THAT MIGHT BE UTILIZED IN A TRAIN CROSSING ACCIDENT

---

1. Do your records indicate that Engineer ________ had any physical defect or any impairment of any sensory faculty?

2. Who is the manufacturer of, and what is the model number of Engine No. _____, the engine that struck the car occupied by the plaintiff?

3. Please describe in detail the braking equipment on Engine No. _______, the engine that struck the car occupied by the plaintiff, stating the make and model number of such component.

4. What distance did the train travel from the point of impact to the point at which it stopped?

5. Please describe in detail the operation of Train No. _____ for the distance of two miles before the accident to the point of rest, stating the throttle settings and brake-valve positions for each one-hundred-year interval.

6. Was the train air-coupled through all cars in the train?

7. Please state whether any other person or corporation, not an employee of the defendant, was under obligation to maintain any part of the track, or right-of-way, or rolling stock involved in this accident. If so, name such person or corporation and describe the relationship with the defendant.

8. Please state the names and addresses and job assignments of the train crew and other persons riding on the train, as well as are known to you, at the time and place of the accident giving rise to this cause of action.

9. Please state the names and addresses of all persons known to you to be at or near the scene of the accident, described in the complaint herein, just before, during, or after the accident.

10. Please state the names and addresses of all persons known to you to have knowledge of the facts and circumstances described in the complaint, or of the conditions surrounding the site of the accident described in the complaint.

11. Are accident reports filed as a part of the normal course of operation of the Universal Transport Railroad Company?

12. If the answer to the preceding interrogatory is in the affirmative, are such records part of the routine, normal records kept by the defendant after the occurrence of an accident?

13. If the answer to either or both of the preceding interrogatories is in the affirmative, please state the name and address of the custodian of each of the accident reports.

14. Were photographs made of the scene of the accident at the time of the accident or since the accident?

15. If the answer to the preceding interrogatory is in the affirmative, please state the name and address of the person making these photographs, and the names and addresses of the persons, if any, under whose supervision such photographs were made.

16. Have you made, since the accident, any repairs or changes at the site of the accident involved in this cause of action?

17. Are records kept relative to the maintenance and repair of the various engines and equipment operated by your railroad system?

18. If the answer to the preceding interrogatory is in the affirmative, please state the name and address of the custodian of such records.

19. Please state the engine number of the train involved in the accident described in the complaint.

20. Did the engine involved in the accident have a speed tape or other recording device showing the speed of the train at the time of the accident?

21. If the answer to the preceding interrogatory is in the affirmative, please state the name and address of the custodian of the tape or record.

22. Please state if there have been any other accidents involving railroad trains and automobiles at this particular crossing described in the complaint.

23. If the answer to the preceding interrogatory is in the affirmative, please state whether records were kept of these accidents.

24. If the answer to the preceding interrogatory is in the affirmative, please state the name and address of the custodian of such records.

25. Please state the name and address of the person actually operating the railroad train at the time of the accident described in the complaint.

26. Please state the age of the person named in the preceding answer, and the number of years that he has been in your employment.

27. Please state the length of time that the above named person has been on this particular run.

28. Was there a train order filed on this particular train as identified in the complaint?

29. If the answer to the preceding interrogatory is in the affirmative, please state the name and address of the custodian of such an order.

30. Please state the location of the blow post or whistle board for the approaches to the site of the accident as described in the complaint.

31. Please state whether there are any engineering drawings available showing the railroad right-of-way at the site of the accident described in the complaint.

32. If the answer to the preceding interrogatory is in the affirmative, please state the name and address of the custodian of these drawings.

33. Please state if the brakes on the locomotive involved in the accident, as specifically described in the complaint, were inspected, repaired, and/or adjusted within one month prior to the accident.

34. If the answer to the preceding interrogatory is in the affirmative, please state the dates of same.

35. If the answer to the above is in the affirmative, please state the name, address, and job title of the person or persons making this inspection, repair, and/or adjustment.

36. Please state the name and address of the custodian of the records pertaining to the above.

37. Please state the number of railroad cars that made up the train involved in the accident as alleged in the complaint.

38. Please state the types of railroad cars, and the number of each, that constituted the aforesaid train.

39. Please state the overall load weight of the aforesaid train.

40. Please state the speed of the aforesaid train at the time of the accident.

41. Please state the number of feet it would have taken this particular train to come to a complete stop while traveling at the speed indicated in the preceding answer.

42. Please state the posted speed limit of the defendant's train throughout the immediate area of the accident as alleged in the complaint.

43. Please state if the speed limit indicated in the preceding answer was in force at the time of the aforesaid accident.

44. Please state the following as to the locomotive involved in the accident alleged in the complaint:

a. Type of horn.

b. Name of the manufacturer of this horn.

c. Date of the manufacture of this horn.

d. The exact location of said horn on the locomotive.

45. Please state the average number of trains that pass this crossing in a twenty-four hour period during the twelve months prior to the incident.

4.3.2 Discovery by Request for Admissions of Fact and Genuineness of Documents

The rules of practice of many states and the Federal Courts provide that at the commencement of an action, a party may serve on any other party a written request for the admissions by the latter of the genuineness of any relevant documents described and exhibited, as well as the truth of any relevant matters of fact specified in the request. This rule serves the useful purpose of avoiding much time and expense in proving the genuineness of documents or truth of matters of fact which the adverse party does not intend to contest. For example, many doctors' bills may be admitted to be reasonable and incurred as a result of the injury, thus obviating the necessity of bringing the doctor to the trial when his testimony is not sufficiently useful to justify the trouble and expense involved.

Often early Requests for Admissions of Fact will obviate the necessity of expensive preparation or discovery.

Ordinarily, inadequate reasons for either admitting or denying are the equivalent of an admission, although the Federal Court decisions, under the Federal Rule, which also pertains in most states, are in disagreement as to whether a party is required to supplement his personal knowledge by obtaining the necessary information from a third party. The view set forth in the recent decisions, and the one held by most text writers, is that the rule requires that the party answer, even though he has no personal knowledge, if the means of information are within his reach. *Baldwin v. Hartford Accident Indemnity Co.* (DC Neb, 1954) 15 FRD 84. If the statements of fact are denied, the party making the request may be required to produce evidence toward proof. Where proof is shown, the opponent may be required to pay the costs of obtaining such proof.

REQUEST FOR ADMISSIONS OF FACT (SAMPLE)

The plaintiff, ____________________, requests that the defendant, ____________________________, on or before the _____ day of ______, 19____, to make the following admissions of fact for the purpose of this action only and subject to such pertinent objections to admissibility as may be interposed at the trial:

1. The copy of the hospital records attached hereto and made a part hereof by reference is a true and correct copy of the same.
2. The said hospital record was made and recorded as part of the

usual business of the hospital and in the course and scope of that business.

3. The persons recording things therein were required to make the said record and to record the items of information contained therein correctly.

4. The events recorded in the said record were recorded contemporaneously with the happening thereof.

5. The parties who made the entries in the said hospital records have no interest in the pending litigation.

6. If the originals of the said hospital records were produced at the trial of this cause, they would correspond to the copy attached hereto in every material aspect.

(Certificate of Service)

4.3.3 Discovery by Production of Books or Documents

In general

The rules of practice in most states permit filing of a Motion to Produce, for inspection, copying, or photographing, any designated documents, papers, books, accounts, letters, photographs, objects or tangible things, not privileged, which constitute or contain evidence relating to any of the matters within the scope of examination permitted by oral discovery, and which are in the possession, custody, or control of the adverse party.

Pursuant to this rule, an adverse party may be compelled to permit entry upon designated land or other property in his possession or control if the matter is within the scope of the examination, permitted by oral discovery of parties and witnesses in the pending action. Land or other property upon which entry has been made, as well as any designated objects or operations thereupon, may be inspected, measured, surveyed, or photographed.

Limitations of Rule

The rule is limited in its scope to parties to the action. If it is desired to inspect documents in the possession of a person who is not a party to the action, including a party's attorney, the proper instruments to accomplish this are a deposition of the person involved and a subpoena duces tecum. This rule has great utility, particularly in the preparation of products liability cases. In order to derive the maximum benefit from this rule, however, it is often necessary to do preliminary discovery and to consult with experts in order to know what to look for when the object or place is viewed. Frequently it is desirable to have the attorney's own experts present at the time of the inspection in order to make maximum use of the opportunity and prepare them for the giving of their testimony at the trial.

SAMPLE MOTION TO PRODUCE

[Court and Cause]

MOTION FOR PRODUCTION, INSPECTION AND COPYING OF DOCUMENTS, AND INSPECTION AND PHOTOGRAPHING OF THINGS AND REAL PROPERTY

The plaintiff, ________________, moves the Court for entry of an order requiring the defendant, ____________, to:

1. Produce and permit plaintiff to inspect and copy each of the following documents: ______________________________.
(List documents and describe each of them)
2. Produce and permit plaintiff to inspect and photograph each of the following objects: ______________________________
(Here list objects and describe them)

For grounds for the said motion plaintiff shows unto the Court that the defendant has the possession, custody, and control of the foregoing documents and objects or the places where the same are contained. Each of the documents constitutes or contains evidence relevant or material to a matter involved in the above entitled action or tending to lead to the production of evidence.

____
Attorney

(Certificate of Service)

Protection against abuse—in general

The party through whom such discovery is sought may obtain protection against a request that is too broad by an order prohibiting

SAMPLE MOTION TO QUASH SUBPOENA

[Court and Cause]

MOTION TO QUASH SUBPOENA
FOR THE PRODUCTION OF DOCUMENTS

The defendant moves the court to quash the subpoena, issued at the request of the plaintiff, whereby ______________ is directed to appear at ______________.

The following grounds are submitted in support of this motion:

____

(List in separate, numbered paragraphs the reasons for the motion)

____
Attorney

(Certificate of Service)

---

discovery of secret processes, developments, or research; by requiring the information or documents to be enclosed in sealed envelopes to be filed with the court and opened upon the direction of the court; or upon such other orders which justice requires to protect the party from annoyance, embarrassment, or oppression. Memoranda and other documents that constitute work product may also be protected from discovery under this rule.

When discovery is sought through the taking of a deposition accompanied by subpoena duces tecum, the proper method to protect against unwarranted discovery is a Motion to Quash the subpoena for the purpose of protection of documents. The same form could be modified to cover the instances where the subpoena is oppressive in some manner.

Suggestions for Railroad Crossing Cases

The following items, pertaining to train crossing accidents, might warrant discovery by means of a Motion to Produce for examination or copying:

1. Personnel record of Engineer ________ and Fireman ______

2. Engineer's work reports on Engine No. ______ from (date 30 days before accident) to (31 days after)

3. Speed tape from the speed recorder on Engine No. ______ for day of accident.

4. Accident reports made by each employee at time of accident (on S.P. Form 2611).

5. Copy of Rules of the Transportation Department of __________ Railroad and of any other rules applied at the time and place of the accident, including safety rules, notices, bulletins, and circular letters posted, issued, or circulated by Road Foremen of Engines, trainmasters, or other supervisory employees.

6. The timetable in effect at the time and place of the accident.

7. Timetable bulletins in effect at the time and place of the accident.

8. The special instructions in effect at the time and place of the accident.

9. Copy of the rules and instructions for the inspection, adjustment, repair, maintenance, and cleaning of braking equipment on all units and cars involved in the accident.

10. Copy of the rules and instruction for the inspection, adjustment, maintenance, repair, and cleaning of crossing warning devices of the ______________ Railroad.

11. All train orders, clearances, and messages addressed to the engine crew of Train No. ______ on the day of the accident.

12. Train sheets or operator's reports from all stations passed by Train No. ______, showing time of departure on day of the accident.

13. All switch lists, spot lists, and messages conveyed to the crew of Train/Engine No. __________

14. All correspondence received from individuals and from public or private agencies concerning the maintenance of the crossing and its warning devices, or concerning the operation or trains over the crossing, including reports from the defendant's employees.

15. Graph or tape from control console of centralized traffic control.

16. Conductor's telegraphic report of accident.

17. Blueprint of tract and appurtenances at scene of accident and one mile east (or ________) thereof.

18. Wiring diagram of crossing warning devices, and blueprint series showing changes made in wiring during the past ten years.

4.3.4 Oral Discovery Depositions

In general

In its simplest form, an oral discovery deposition is the oral testimony of a witness—usually, but not always, the adverse party—which is taken under oath before trial, and at which time most of the objections permissible at trial do not apply, the basic rule being that the question must concern itself only with information that is relevant to the case, or that will lead to the discovery of relevant facts.

How effective the deposition may be for later use depends to a large extent upon the proper preparation of the lawyer taking the deposition, and the preparation of the witness who is giving the deposition.

The time to take oral discovery depositions

The discovery deposition should always be taken, if possible, prior to the expiration of the Statute of Limitations in order to permit the complaint or petition to be amended to include additional defendants discovered through the discovery deposition technique. In those states where it is not permissible to amend the complaint and to change the theory of the lawsuit after the expiration of the Statute of Limitations, there is an additional advantage in taking early depositions.

Purpose of oral discovery depositions—in general

The basic purpose of the oral discovery deposition is to determine from the witness all of the facts which he may have in his possession which may assist the trial lawyer in the preparation and settlement or trial of the lawsuit. The deposition may be used effectively in three important ways:

1. To assist the lawyer in the investigation and preparation of the case for trial.
2. To assist the lawyer in evaluating the case and in settlement negotiations.
3. As substantive proof or admissions, or for impeachment or other purposes during the trial.

Oral discovery as an aid in investigation

Most well-prepared cases are built upon a base of adequate investigation, making full use of the discovery deposition technique. At deposition time the interrogator may discover the names and location of witnesses, the existence of photographs or other possible exhibits that may be used at trial, new leads for further independent investigation, any hidden or unthought-of defenses, and often the existence of additional defendants. The discovery deposition may also provide the foundation for later expert testimony in support of the plaintiff's case.

Use of oral discovery in the settlement process

An interesting time to use discovery depositions is during the settlement process. The defendant's deposition actually gives the plaintiff's lawyer the best opportunity he or she has to see and appraise the defendant. It gives the lawyer a chance to observe the type of individual that the defendant really is, and to determine what sort of witness the defendant will make: whether he or she will become angry easily, or will be subject to a particular type of cross-examination, or will be evasive. It is also possible to determine whether the defendant is defending the case reluctantly, under the pressure of the insurance company, or appears to have a good defense and is acting in good faith.

Perhaps most important of all, the defendant's deposition affords the trial lawyer the opportunity to observe whether the defendant has what is sometimes known as "jury appeal." It is well known that a defendant who creates a good impression is usually a good defendant, as jurors are reluctant to return a sizable verdict against a likeable defendant. The appearance, manner, and conduct of the defendant should therefore be carefully noted by the trial lawyer at the time of the discovery deposition.

The plaintiff's deposition is the plaintiff's lawyer's first opportunity to present the client to the opposition, and this can be particularly important when the plaintiff is attractive and possesses jury appeal. If the plaintiff has disfiguring injuries or other injuries which are readily observable, very often his appearing at discovery deposition time is a long stride toward serious settlement negotiations by the defendant's attorney. The impression that the plaintiff makes often influences defense counsel to expedite settlement negotiations. An important fact to remember is this: The defendant's attorney, the busy insurance lawyer, has many files in his or her office, and in most instances the client's case does not really come alive to the defense lawyer until that lawyer sees the plaintiff. Usually this is at discovery deposition time.

Preparing the client for deposition

Offering the plaintiff for discovery deposition presents certain hazards, but these may be minimized by proper preparation of the witness prior to the deposition. An interesting feature of the plaintiff's discovery deposition is that it is in a way a "trial run" for the plaintiff's lawyer, the first chance to see what kind of witness his or her own client will make while testifying. It is always well to instruct the client, prior to the giving of a discovery deposition, as to conduct in the deposition room. The plaintiff who has confidence in the lawyer and who will accept such suggestions is not as rare as one might suppose. Some trial specialists use a prepared pamphlet of instructions which is mailed to the client at the time he or she is advised about giving the discovery deposition. One such pamphlet, entitled *Your Discovery Deposition*, prepared by one of the authors, and in general use throughout the country, instructs the witness with respect to conduct and appearance at discovery deposition time. The material contained in the pamphlet is as follows:

> Under the rules of practice in this state, each side in the lawsuit has the right to take the discovery deposition of the opposing party. Thus, when you become a plaintiff or defendant in any litigation, the opposing party may require you to appear at a specified time and place and give your oral testimony under oath, which testimony is taken down by shorthand or mechanical means and transcribed for future use in the lawsuit.
>
> Your deposition, properly given, can go a long way toward assisting your lawyer in handling your litigation either by way of settlement or at the trial. What YOU do at the deposition can help you or hurt you, depending upon your attitude, truthfulness, and appearance.
>
> The following information and instructions are offered in an effort to better acquaint you with what is expected of you and how you can be an effective witness at discovery deposition time:
>
> **Physical Appearance**
>
> You should remember that usually the first opportunity that the opposing counsel has to see you is at the time of the giving of your discovery deposition. It is important that you make a good impression upon opposing counsel and client, and you should appear at deposition time dressed as you would expect to dress if you were actually going to court to appear before the jury, in clean, neat clothing.
>
> **How to Act While Giving Testimony**
>
> A. Treat all persons in the deposition room with respect.
>
> B. Come prepared to exhibit any and all injuries which you have suffered.

C. Have with you the facts and figures with respect to your time lost from work, amount of wages lost, doctor bills, hospital bills, and all other facts with respect to the damages caused as a result of your injury.

D. Consider this an important and solemn occasion, and avoid becoming overly friendly with opposing counsel or the client.

E. Tell the truth.

F. Never lose your temper.

G. Don't be afraid of the lawyers.

H. Speak slowly and clearly.

I. If you don't understand the questions, ask that they be explained.

J. Answer all questions directly, giving concise answers to the questions, and STOP TALKING.

K. NEVER VOLUNTEER any information. Wait until the question is asked, answer it and STOP. If you can answer yes or no, do so and STOP.

L. Stick to the facts and testify only to that which you personally know.

M. Do not magnify your injuries or losses.

N. Be conservative with respect to a description of your injuries. Adopt an unexaggerated attitude toward your injuries.

O. Testify only to *basic facts,* and do not attempt to give opinions or estimates of time and distance unless you have good reason for knowing such matters.

P. If you don't know, admit it. Some witnesses think they should have an answer for every question asked. You cannot know all the facts, and you do yourself a disservice if you attempt to testify to facts with which you are not acquainted. It is IMPERATIVE that you be HONEST and STRAIGHTFORWARD in your testimony.

Q. *Don't try* to memorize your story. Justice requires only that a *witness* tell his story to the best of his ability.

REMEMBER, perhaps the most important aspect of your lawsuit is YOU and the impression that you make. If you give the impression of earnestness, fairness, and honesty, and if in giving your discovery deposition you keep in mind the suggestions made here, you will be taking a great stride toward successful completion of the litigation in which you are involved.

Use of discovery depositions at trial

Admissions. The use of portions of the depositions as admissions may be very effective at the time of trial. Very rarely does the entire deposition of the defendant lend itself to admission into evidence in support of the plaintiff's case, but because the attorney may wish to extract portions from the discovery deposition, care should be taken to word each question in such a way that it is complete in itself, does not rely upon previous questions in order to be understandable, and demands a complete answer.

Affirmative Proof. The discovery deposition may be used in support of the plaintiff's case by providing affirmative proof of the defendant's negligence. In some states this type of testimony may be extracted from the deposition and offered as admissions.

Proof of Freedom from Negligence. The discovery deposition may be helpful in proving the plaintiff's freedom from contributory negligence where such proof is required.

Proof of Essential Facts. The discovery deposition may be used to discover and prove other essential facts, such as the fact that the plaintiff was hurt and that the defendant recognized this fact at the scene of the accident.

Impeachment Purposes. These uses merely need mentioning.

Avoidance of the "Dead Man's Statute." In some instances where the witness or party dies before the trial, the deposition may be helpful in avoiding the harsh rule of the "Dead Man's Statute."

Contradiction of Allegations in the Answer. The deposition may be used to contradict allegations in the answer. For example, most defendants do not read the answer that is filed by the insurance company defense lawyer. Sometimes the defense will claim that the plaintiff failed to signal, or stopped suddenly, or otherwise acted irresponsibly. At discovery deposition time the defendant witness should be asked about these matters, and often the defendant disproves by his or her testimony the allegations in the answer which the insurance company lawyer has filed.

Foundation for Future Admissions and Expert Testimony at Trial. If the plaintiff's lawyer acts as cameraman and takes pictures for use at trial, the witness should be asked if the pictures are fair and accurate and a portrayal of that which they are intended to portray. Invariably the witness will admit that they are, and a foundation is laid for future admission at trial. This technique may also be used with the identification of other exhibits.

The discovery deposition may also be used as a foundation for later expert testimony. For instance, the defendant fixes his or her speed. The plaintiff's lawyer thinks that it has been misrepresented. An example is the interpretation of skid marks. What do they mean? The defendant witness should be asked the following questions:

1. What kind of a car were you driving?
2. What was the weight of the car?
3. What was the type of tires?
4. What was the tread on the tires?
5. What was the condition of the pavement?
6. Were the brakes on the vehicle working perfectly? (The witness will almost invariably answer that they were.)

Finally it should be determined, from the defendant witness or from other sources, what the temperature was on the day of the accident. Thus the foundation is effectively laid for the opinion of an expert—the attorney's own expert—as to whether or not the defendant's estimate of speed is accurate.

4.3.5 The Lawyer Prepares for Deposition

In general

Perhaps equally important as the preparation of the witness for giving discovery deposition is the preparation of the trial lawyer. In preparing to take the deposition of the defendant and the defendant's witnesses, it is advisable that the lawyer review the file sufficiently prior to the taking of the discovery depositions to be fully acquainted with the basic problems and determine the course to follow in the taking of the depositions.

Since well-taken discovery depositions often contain important admissions, which are later usable at the trial, and by means of which the plaintiff's counsel can often dramatically establish fault, it is imperative that the plaintiff's lawyer, in preparing for deposition, understand the law with respect to the occurrence.

Many lawyers use an outline, prepared prior to the discovery deposition, of the basic facts involved. Such a basic facts sheet should contain, together with other information, the following:

1. The date of the occurrence
2. The place of the occurrence
3. The type of occurrence
4. The time of day
5. A general description of the plaintiff's conduct, or at least a general description of the defendant's conduct.

Preliminary questions

The lawyer should include in the questions to be asked at the discovery deposition such preliminary questions as will properly place the witness upon notice that the deposing lawyer expects a response to the questions asked, but not until such time as the witness fully comprehends them, so that the witness may not later escape when caught in a misrepresentation or admission.

Suggested stock questions are as follows:

1. "Do you understand that the proceedings here today are known as a discovery deposition, and that under the rules of this state I have the right to ask you certain questions; you have a right to expect that the questions I ask will be understandable; and I, in turn, have the right to expect that when you answer my question you will have understood it fully and you will answer truthfully? Do you understand that?"

2. "Will you tell me, at this time, that if I ask you a question which you do not fully understand you will advise me that you do not understand the question and ask me to rephrase it, re-ask it, or explain it so that you may fully understand before answering? Will you tell me that?"

3. "Will you give me your assurance at this time that when you do answer a question you will have thought about it before you answer, and answer correctly and honestly?"

It is obvious that the witness must answer yes to each of the foregoing questions. The witness has been placed on notice that he or she has every right to ask that any question not understood be rephrased or explained before answering it.

Closing questions

If certain key questions are asked of the witness at the close of the interrogation, he will effectively be prevented from later claiming that he did not understand the question or know what the interrogator meant. It is suggested, therefore, that at the close of the discovery deposition the following questions be asked:

1. "Have there been any questions which I have asked you that you have not understood and that you would like to have me rephrase or re-ask?"

Usually the witness will answer no, but this gives the witness an opportunity to advise the interrogator of any questions which he did not fully understand and which he would like to have rephrased or re-asked.

2. "Do you feel that the questions which I have asked have been fair and reasonable enough, and understandable enough so that you have been able to answer them intelligently?"

Ordinarily the witness will answer yes to this question, but if he answers no, and gives some explanation for his answer, counsel should conduct further interrogation accordingly.

3. "I want you to stop and think back over the questions I have asked you and the answers you have given me, and to tell me whether there are any which you would like me to change, correct, or modify in any respect."

It isn't often that the witness at this time will be able to think back over any of the questions, let alone make any suggestions as to changes or corrections or modifications. Therefore, the question will undoubtedly be answered in the negative.

The value of the questions listed above should be apparent. Nothing is more disheartening in the trial of a lawsuit than for counsel to offer into evidence what appears to be a valuable admission, only to have the witness claim that he did not understand the question at the time it was asked.

Developing workable techniques

Many lawyers fail to develop workable oral discovery techniques. One available, commonly used technique is to state in one of the opening questions certain undisputed facts about the occurrence, and to secure the witness's acceptance of a key word, such as "collision" or "occurrence," as referring, in all subsequent questions, to the collision or occurrence described. An example follows:

"In order to save time, Mr. Witness, I want to know if we may agree to certain basic facts: first, that you were the driver of an automobile, a 1960 Pontiac automobile, belonging to you and driven by you on the first day of February, 1961, which was involved on that date in a collision with a vehicle owned by the Yellow Cab Company, which collision occurred on the corner of 6th and Grand in the city of Des Moines. May we agree to that, sir?"

Almost invariably the witness will agree, since it is an undisputed fact; or sometimes counsel will stipulate that such a fact is undisputed. The interrogator should then ask the following question:

"So that we may save a lot of words, hereafter when I refer to 'collision', will you understand that I am referring to the collision which I have just described, which occurred at the time and place stated in the previous question?"

Here again, the witness will usually answer in the affirmative, or counsel will stipulate that such be the case.

Planning the questions

In taking the adverse party's deposition, the attorney should plan the questions in advance, in logical sequence, categorizing them according to the information desired. If a damaging admission is obtained from the witness, and the attorney is certain that the witness has fully understood the question, the attorney should drop the subject immediately and go on to something else. The witness can explain why he gave the answer he did at the time of trial. The attorney should develop the habit of asking questions that are readily understood, insisting upon short and concise answers if possible. He or she should always move to strike nonresponsive answers or voluntary statements of the witness, and should re-ask the question, at the same time insisting upon a direct answer. Should an admission of the adverse party be obtained, it should be used at the trial in the most effective manner possible, and at the most dramatic moment of the trial. It is important to remember that the defendant is almost never as well prepared at discovery deposition time as at the trial, and usually neither is his or her lawyer.

Defendant's prediscovery checklist

In taking the defendant's discovery deposition, it is recommended that the plaintiff's attorney use a checklist, since it assists in organizing thoughts and prevents the possibility of overlooking important areas to be covered. The plaintiff's attorney should also have a checklist to assist in briefing the client about expected questions to be asked by opposing counsel.

The following is a checklist used by one of the authors in preparation for the defendant's discovery deposition:

BASIC OUTLINE FOR DEFENDANT'S DEPOSITION

I. PERSONAL DATA
  A. Name
  B. Address
  C. Age
  D. Occupation
  E. Driving experience
    1. General
    2. With particular vehicle
II. DRIVING HISTORY
  A. Accidents
  B. Traffic convictions
  C. Pleas of guilty
  D. Lawsuits

III. DRIVER'S LICENSE
  A. In force
  B. Ever revoked? or
  C. Suspended?
  D. If so, for what reason?
  E. By whom?

IV. PHYSICAL CONDITION
  A. Eyes
    1. Glasses fitted
    2. By whom?
    3. When?
    4. Artificial eyes
  B. Artificial limbs
V. PHYSICAL CONDITION AT TIME OF ACCIDENT
  A. Sickness
  B. Fatigue
VI. ALCOHOL, DRUGS, ETC.
  A. What?
  B. When?
  C. Where taken?
  D. Reason
VII. MENTAL CONDITION AT TIME OF ACCIDENT
  A. Worry
  B. Grief, upset, etc.
VIII. VEHICLE INVOLVED
  A. Description
    1. Make
    2. Color
    3. Model
    4. Year
  B. Ownership
    1. Name registered
    2. Title certificate
    3. Still owned
    4. Financed
  C. Prior accident with this vehicle
    1. When?
    2. Where?
IX. CONDITION OF VEHICLE AT TIME
  A. Headlights
    1. Up or down
    2. Blinding lights from other car
    3. Defendant's lights burning
    4. Both
    5. Adjusted or repaired
    6. Last checked
    7. Condition after checked
  B. Brakes
    1. Condition
    2. Power brakes
    3. Last adjustment
    4. Hand brake
  C. Tires
    1. Age
    2. When purchased?
    3. Mileage
    4. Condition
  D. Windshield
    1. Clear
    2. Obstruction
X. DRIVER OF OTHER CAR
  A. Name
  B. Physical condition
  C. See driver's license
XI. AUTHORITY FOR TRIP
  A. Permission expressed by whom?
  B. When?
  C. What?
  D. Where?
  E. Limitations
XII. TRIP
  A. Reason
  B. Mileage
  C. Passengers
    1. How many?
    2. Who?
  D. Time
    1. Time of departure
    2. Time due
    3. Hurry
  E. Route
    1. Usual
    2. Other routes
    3. Detours
XIII. SCENE OF ACCIDENT
  A. Street
    1. Type—straight, curved
    2. Traffic
    3. Width
    4. Pavement type
    5. Markings
    6. Familiarity with street

7. Before the accident
8. Since the accident
9. Last there when?
10. Who with?

B. Traffic controls
1. Lights
2. Where?
3. How many?
4. Location as to accident

C. Street lights
1. How many?
2. Where?

D. Obstructions to view
1. What?
2. Where?

XIV. TIME OF ACCIDENT
A. Date
B. Time of day
C. Light or dark
1. Sun
2. Moon

XV. WEATHER CONDITIONS
A. Rain
1. Type
2. When?
3. Amount

B. Cloudy or clear
C. Effect
1. On road
2. On vehicles
3. On windshield
4. On traction

XVI. JUST BEFORE THE ACCIDENT
A. Doing what?
1. Talking
2. Radio on
3. Smoking
4. Hands on wheel

B. Looking where?

XVII. THE ACCIDENT
A. Other traffic
1. Vehicles
2. Where?
3. Direction
4. Speed

B. Plaintiff's vehicle first seen
1. Obstruction of view
2. Speed
3. Direction
4. Lane

C. Plaintiff's vehicle next seen
1. Change in speed
2. Change in direction
3. Point of collision

D. Speed and gear
1. Speed at time of collision
2. Speedometer reading
3. Changes
4. Vehicle traveling in what gear?
5. Any shifting of gears

E. Brakes first applied
1. Where?
2. Type (hard, slow, fast)
3. Distance traveled

F. First noticed damages
1. Where?
2. What reaction?

G. Signals by plaintiff
1. Arm signal
2. Directional signals
3. Stop signals

H. Collision
1. Point of collision
2. Draw diagram
3. Which vehicle struck other?
4. Direction vehicles going in
5. Rear-end collision
6. Parts each touched
7. Damage to each
(a) Front end of defendant's car
(b) Rear end of plantiff's car
8. Violence
(a) Glass
(b) Radiator leak
(c) Frame bent
(d) Skid marks

I. Vehicle first stopped
   1. Position of defendant's car
   2. Position of plaintiff's car
   3. Distance between vehicles
   4. Forward movement as a result of accident
J. Last clear chance
   1. Condition of vehicle
   2. Realized peril
      (a) When?
      (b) Where?
      (c) Following at what distance?
   3. Could have avoided collision by
      (a) Stopping
      (b) Swerving
      (c) Not so close
   4. Distance could have stopped in
   5. What plaintiff could have done to avoid collision

XVIII. AFTER ACCIDENT
A. Location of each person
B. Condition of each person
   1. Anyone ask you if injured?
   2. Did you ask anyone if injured?
   3. Walking around
C. Position of vehicles
   1. Moved
   2. Where?
      (a) By police
      (b) By others

XIX. POLICE
A. Names
B. Previously acquainted
C. What you told police
D. What others said to police
E. Photographs taken by police
F. Measurements
G. Arrest
H. Charge

XX. LIQUOR
A. Who drinking?
B. Defendant drinking
C. Liquor in vehicle

XXI. MISCELLANEOUS
A. Conversation
   1. Talked to whom?
   2. Heard other driver or occupants
   3. Exclamation
   4. Who was present?
   5. Police present?
B. Persons taken away
   1. When?
   2. How?
   3. Why?
   4. Where?

XXII. TRACKS AND TRACES
A. Observed at scene
   1. Skid marks
      (a) Where?
      (b) Measured
      (c) By whom?
      (d) Length
      (e) Straight or curved
      (f) Left, right, or all wheels
      (g) Equal, even, or otherwise
   2. Debris
      (a) Describe
      (b) Location
   3. Other damage noticed
B. Observed later

XXIII. PARTICIPANT AND WITNESSES
A. Driver of other vehicle
B. Occupants of other vehicle
C. Persons in the area
D. Persons who came later
E. Names of such persons

XXIV. PHOTOGRAPHS
A. Who?
B. When?
C. Where?

XXV. VEHICLE DAMAGE
A. Description of damage to defendant's vehicle
B. Cost of repairs; other estimates

C. Vehicle still owned and in use
D. Vehicle sold
   1. When?
   2. Where?
   3. For what reason?
   4. To whom?

XXVI. ANY OTHER INFORMATION

4.3.6 Arranging for Depositions

Where to depose doctors

Taking the doctor's deposition in his or her office, at a time set after conferring with the doctor's nurse, has two advantages. First, the doctor is inconvenienced as little as possible, and consequently a greater degree of co-operation may be hoped for. Second, it is possible to see what textbooks the doctor may possess describing the type of injury involved in the case. If the doctor is not friendly, he or she may be interrogated as to whether these books are considered useful and authoritative, and if necessary they may be used in cross-examination.

Predeposition conference with doctor

In many instances doctors see so many patients that unless a conference is held just prior to the taking of the deposition they cannot readily recall the precise facts of the patient's case. There have even been instances of doctors giving testimony about one patient which actually pertained to another because their attention was not sufficiently focused on the case prior to the taking of the deposition. Thus, when a doctor who has been a treating physician is being deposed, a predeposition conference should routinely be arranged.

Where to depose adverse party

Taking the deposition of the adverse party at the office of that party's attorney is frequently unwise because this enables opposing counsel to confer with the client immediately prior to the taking of the deposition and to prepare the client for the questions that will be asked. Therefore when the deposition is that of some person other than a doctor, many attorneys prefer to take it in their own offices or in the court reporter's office.

Predeposition conference with client

Consultation with the attorney's own client, just prior to the giving of a deposition, is strongly recommended. The secretary should routinely arrange a predeposition conference with the client in the attorney's office, allowing sufficient time for this purpose.

Immediate preparation of the lawyer

It is often wise to have a standard operating procedure whereby the file is to be on the desk of the attorney the day before the deposition is to be taken. The attorney should routinely be interrupted one hour before the deposition, regardless of what he or she is doing, and reminded of the deposition in order to be suitably prepared.

Professional courtesy

Many offices follow the custom of checking with opposing counsel as to his or her availability at the time of the taking of the deposition. While this professional courtesy is not recognized in all parts of the country, it is, in general, a comfortable practice.

Out-of-state depositions

In General. Because of the fact that many depositions must be taken out of the state in order to conform to the Rules of Practice of the state in which the attorney resides, it is advisable to develop a standard instruction sheet to be sent to attorneys who are assisting by taking a deposition in another state. These sheets can be printed in advance at relatively little cost and save much secretarial time.

SAMPLE DIRECTIONS TO FOREIGN ATTORNEY

INSTRUCTIONS FOR TAKING DEPOSITIONS TO BE USED AT TRIAL

1. We have served notice to plaintiff's (defendant's) counsel here of the taking of the deposition of the witness.

2. We are at this time enclosing the original notice of the taking of the deposition. This is the notice that will form the first page of the deposition itself. Also enclosed you will find forms for the commencement and for the conclusion of the deposition. The commencement, as you will note, starts on the second page after the notice and after the opening portion as to time, etc. Questions will follow in regular form. The certificate is executed by the notary public, and this forms the last page of the deposition. Both the commencement and certificate are merely forms for your guidance, and will, of course, have to be rewritten in order to be placed in the actual deposition.

3. After the deposition is taken and the certificate is executed by the notary public, the notary should seal the original deposition in an envelope and address the same to the Honorable ________________,

Clerk of the Circuit Court of Palm Beach County, West Palm Beach, Florida. The style of the case, as shown in the notice, should be endorsed on the envelope, and the notary's name should be affixed across the flap.

4. When the original deposition is in the mail, we ask that you have the notary send us one copy of the same for our file. You may at that time also forward us your statement for services and the reporter's or notary's statement for services.

5. This is a deposition to be used at trial, and conducted by oral questions and answers. The usual rules of evidence apply to the proper form of questions and the admissibility of questions and answers. Of course, leading questions should be avoided, and opinions or conclusions of the witness should be avoided.

6. The act that took place on ________________ at ____________

____

(date) (time)

____

(Here describe the accident and state any relevant information needed by the attorney assisting you).

7. It is believed that opposing counsel will have someone to conduct cross-examination at the taking of this deposition. It will be satisfactory with us if you will stipulate with opposing counsel that all objections to questions and answers be reserved until the time of trial, and you are further authorized to stipulate as to the waiving of the reading and signing of the deposition by the witness.

8. If the opposing counsel wishes to set another date for the taking of this deposition, it will be satisfactory with us, provided that it is satisfactory with you, and provided, further, that it is certain that the witness will be available. We would not want a delay, however, of more than two or three days. As we have said, we do not want the deposition delayed at all if there is any question of the witness being available.

COMMENT: Samples of some of these standard forms to be forwarded to attorneys in other states should be available for the attorney's own secretary. It should not be assumed that the court reporters in other states will necessarily comply with the court requirement of the attorney's particular state, since the rules of courts sometimes vary, and additional information is nearly always welcomed by the court reporter in the other state.

SAMPLE FIRST PAGE OF A DEPOSITION

IN THE CIRCUIT COURT OF THE FIFTEENTH JUDICIAL CIRCUIT, IN AND FOR PALM BEACH COUNTY, FLORIDA.—AT LAW

JOHN M. JONES,)
Plaintiff,)
vs.) No.
LARRY SMITH, et al,)
Defendants.)
____________________)

Ann Arbor, Michigan
January 2,
9:30 o'clock A.M.

APPEARANCES:

J. Q. RUDIBAUGH, ESQ., of counsel, appearing on behalf of the plaintiff.
I.M. SKEPTIC, ESQ., of counsel, appearing on behalf of the defendants.
Deposition of JOHN M. JONES.

Deposition of JOHN M. JONES, a witness of lawful age, taken by the Defendants for the purpose of discovery and for use as evidence in the above entitled cause, wherein JOHN M. JONES is the Plaintiff, and LARRY SMITH, et al, are the Defendants, pending in the Circuit Court of the 15th Judicial Circuit in and for Palm Beach County, Florida, pursuant to notice heretofore filed, before MARIAN SCRIBET, a Notary Public in and for the State of Michigan at Large, at the offices of I. M. SKEPTIC, 405 Courthouse Square Building, 200 S.E. 6th Street, Ann Arbor, Washtenaw County, Michigan, on the day of January, A.D. commencing at o'clock .M.

Stipulation Waiving Signature. In many states it is desirable that counsel stipulate that the parties waive the reading and signing of the deposition, since nothing is accomplished by the reading and signing, and a great deal of trouble may be saved. A typical form of stipulation is as follows:

STIPULATION

It is hereby stipulated by and between counsel for the respective parties that the reading and signing of the foregoing deposition and notice of filing be, and the same are, hereby waived.
AND FURTHER DEPONENT SAITH NOT.

COMMENT: This stipulation is commonly affixed at the close of a deposition.

Notary's Certificate. The notary's certificate is a typical form for the particular state of the lawyer involved, and should be forwarded to attorneys in other states. A typical certificate follows:

CERTIFICATE OF DEPOSITION HEARING BY NOTARY

STATE OF ____________________) s.s.
COUNTY OF ___________________)

I, __________, a Notary Public for the State of _______, hereby certify that pursuant to the stipulation of counsel in the above entitled cause wherein ________________ is (are) plaintiff(s) and ____________ ____________ is (are) defendant(s), now pending in the Court of ____________ County, I sat at __________ Street in the City of __________, State of ________________, at the time stated in said notice herein above, and was attended by ____________________ and ________________ (attorneys for the defendant) and the said witness ______________, who was by me first duly cautioned and sworn to testify the whole truth and carefully examined, whereupon said witness testified as is herein above shown, and the testimony of said witness was reduced to typewriting by me and was thereafter read and subscribed by the said witness in my presence. I further certify that the said deposition was taken at the time and place specified in the aforesaid stipulation herein above or at a regular adjournment thereafter, and I further certify that the reason for the taking of the said deposition was and is that the parties reside out of the county in which the cause(s) is (are) pending and that I, neither counsel nor attorney to either of the parties in said suit, am not interested in the event of the cause.

I further certify that I have retained the said deposition for the purpose of sealing the same and directing it with my own hand to the court for which it was taken by sending it to the clerk of the said court by the United States Mail, there to remain under seal until the same shall be duly opened.

WITNESS MY HAND AND OFFICIAL SEAL in the City of ________, County of ______________, State of __________, this _____ day of ____________, A.D. 19_____.

____
Notary Public
My commission expires: _____

SAMPLE NOTICE OF TAKING DEPOSITION

IN THE CIRCUIT COURT OF THE
JUDICIAL CIRCUIT OF FLORIDA, IN AND
FOR __________ COUNTY. AT LAW.
CASE NO. __________

____________	)	
Plaintiff,	)	
vs.	)	
____________	)	NOTICE OF TAKING
Defendant	)	DEPOSITION
TO: ____________	)	
________________	)	
________________	)	

PLEASE TAKE NOTICE that on the _____ day of __________ A.D., 19____, at _____ o'clock, ____.M., at ____________________ __________ the ____________ in the above entitled cause will take the deposition of ______________ upon oral examination, before ______________________, a Notary Public, or before some other officer authorized by law to take depositions in the State of Florida. The oral examination will continue from day to day until completed. This deposition is being taken for the purpose of discovery, for use at trial, or for such other purposes as are permitted under the applicable Statutes, Rules of Civil Procedure, or Rules of Court.
You are invited to attend and cross examine.

MILLER, CONE, OWEN, WAGNER & NUGENT
P.O. Box 3411
West Palm Beach, Florida

____

Attorneys for ______________

I HEREBY CERTIFY that a copy of the above Notice was furnished to the above addressee by ______________ this ______ day of ______________, 19____.

____

Attorney

Videotape use in depositions, movies, and experiments

What is the purpose of videotaping?
How do you do it?
Evidentiary problems.
How do you use it?

It is a well-known fact of human psychology that a major part of human sensory perception is visual. In the courtroom, an abnormally high part of sensory input is aural. This fact handicaps sensory perception and frequently results in a lower curve of learning, and hence, of persuasion. The use of all demonstrative evidence is an effort to overcome this problem and the use of videotapes and movies is an extension of this effort.

Possible uses of videotaping and movies are limited only by your imagination, the nature of the case, and compliance with the rules of evidence and procedure. Some of the multiple uses are:

1. The recording of the deposition of a particularly effective or important witness whose testimony you desire to highlight;

2. The making of a movie of a typical day in the life of an injured party for the purpose of dramatically demonstrating the effects of the injury on his or her life;

3. The recording of conditions at an accident site, such as the manner in which traffic signals sequence; or

4. The faithful recording of an experiment to demonstrate a point in question.

In order to take a videotape deposition, all jurisdictions require normal "notice of taking" procedure. The fact that the deposition will be by videotape should be included in the notice. It will be necessary to have the customary certified court reporter present under the normal rules of procedure.

There are a number of organizations offering services in videotaping, frequently listed in your phone book under "recording service—sound and video." Often your court reporter can recommend one from the many, or you may contact a lawyer in the area in which the deposition is being taken for recommendations.

The deposition or movie should be carefully planned before being recorded. If you intend the expert witness to use demonstrative evidence in the deposition, be sure you have shown him or her the material or devices to be used and that he or she knows what you intend to demonstrate. Often medical doctors are more willing to cooperate in the predeposition preparation of a videotape deposition than in the more familiar aural one.

Do not blindly rely on the operator of the videotape recorder to ensure that the equipment is operating satisfactorily. Insist that the deposition be interrupted a few minutes into the recording and visually and personally check the status of the recording. To discover after an hour or more of deposition that the operator has made some simple mistake can be devastating. Be certain the operator has sufficient tape to record the whole session before you begin. The session should not be a learning experience for the operator of the videotape machine at your expense.

It is often wise to have a videotape or movie of a "day in the life" of your plaintiff, narrated by someone whom you will have testifying anyway, and whose narration is natural and not strained.

The agonizing efforts of a paraplegic to dress himself and tend to his daily needs can be brought home with breathtaking clarity to even the least empathetic juror.

The videotaping of an experiment or demonstration can put the cap of finality on a question of fact.

We remember a case in which the railroad experts had testified that the railroad crossing gates could not fail to function, but in which movies showed the gates failing to function until the train was within fifty feet of the crossing and in which the lights did not come on until the train, at full speed, was entering the immediate vicinity of the roadway.

When the videotape deposition is complete, the tape should be sent by the court reporter to the clerk of the court in which the case is pending. Occasionally, an attorney will attempt to keep the tape in his or her possession pending the pretrial or trial. No more propriety exists for this than letting the attorney keep the court reporter's notes.

At some time prior to trial, frequently at pretrial conference, the court should be asked to view the videotape and rule on its propriety and any objections. By maintaining an uncut and unaltered tape, and preparing one that conforms to the court's ruling, the presentation can be made smoothly without the interruptions of objections, rulings, etc., and yet nevertheless the objections of either party can be preserved for any appellate procedure.

Summary

Videotaping is simply an extension of the use of demonstrative evidence, but it is one that is consistent with the normal learning methods of the human animal and hence, may speak with more persuasion and finality than a verbal presentation.

5

Organizing a Personal Injury Case File

How many times have you searched through material in files seeking information you know should be there, that you distinctly recall placing or ordering placed there, yet no matter how intense the search, the results are futile.

Organizing the file is of critical importance in terms of time saved, frustration avoided, and financial economy.

In this day of complex litigation, it is rare indeed that a case can be successfully pursued without multiple files; indeed multiple file drawers, and file cabinets, overflowing with memoranda—legal and factual, pleadings, discovery, and the like.

In every modern office, the development and consistent use of forms is commonplace, indeed mandatory.

Every lawyer should develop a system of organization that works well for his office operation, and careful thought and study must be given to the development of such a system.

5.1 THE TRIAL NOTEBOOK SYSTEM

The trial notebook system is a method of forcing yourself to analyze your trial preparation, to organize the material you have developed for ready retrieval, and to plan for its orderly presentation in the trial. Without this, or some similar system, it is difficult not to appear disorganized or ill prepared if the case is one of more than minimal complexity. Juries or judges seldom reward the appearance of poor preparation or organization.

How does it work?

In the trial notebook system the file is organized, and the pretrial preparation material inserted, in a three-ring notebook having a silent clasp. The notebook may be of the ordinary school variety, but is preferably of a more durable kind. The notebook is then divided into sections, by dividers, containing such information and material as are necessary to the trial lawyer from the beginning of the trial through the end. The notebook commonly includes the following sections:

1. Things to Do
2. Checklist
3. Pleadings
4. Statement of Facts
5. Voir Dire
6. Jurors
7. Plaintiff's Outline of Liability
8. Plaintiff's Outline of Damages
9. The Law
10. List of Witnesses
11. Witnesses
12. Medical and Other Expenses
13. Opening Statement Notes
14. Exhibits
15. Plaintiff's Testimony
16. Defendant's Testimony
17. Argument
18. Requested Instructions
19. Instructions
20. Motions
21. Depositions

Although most of these sections are self-explanatory, some elaboration is in order.

Things to Do

Whatever the system of organization for trial, some place in the file, any place which is readily accessible, there must be a sheet of paper marked "Things to Do." This sheet should contain a reminder of those matters that require attention prior to the attorney's courtroom appearance. All such notations should be made on this sheet by the trial lawyer's secretary, investigator, assistant, or by the lawyer and marked off as soon as the matter has been attended to.

Checklist

The trial lawyer knows that in each case, before entering the courtroom, certain matters must be reviewed. Conferences with doctors and witnesses must be arranged, depositions read and marked, and innumerable other matters attended to prior to trial. The notebook checklist should therefore include the following:

1. A review of pleadings for possible amendment
2. A notation as to whether pleadings have been amended and whether the ad damnum clause has been adjusted so as to place the case in its proper perspective
3. A list of all witnesses
4. A list of all expenses
5. Copies of all bills inserted in the exhibits envelope
6. Information as to whether exhibits have been numbered and listed, subpoenas issued, all doctors notified of the imminency of trial, depositions read and marked, law notes inserted in the notebook, and anticipated requested instructions prepared

The checklist should also contain information with respect to the pretrial conference between the trial lawyer and the medical witnesses and such other expert witnesses as may be required.

A printed or mimeographed checklist inserted in the trial notebook for use in every trial is highly recommended. The checklist should contain all matters to be covered and material to be obtained for use at trial. It is an invaluable aid in trial preparation and organization, permitting the secretary or investigator to follow through on matters that might otherwise be overlooked.

Pleadings

All pleadings in the case should be placed in an easily accessible location after having been carefully reviewed, marked, and checked against the outline of liability and outline of damages, which must be prepared prior to the court appearance. If the outlines of proof have been properly prepared, the trial lawyer should have little occasion to reexamine the pleadings during the actual trial of the case. However, the ready availability of the pleadings, if it becomes desirable or necessary to review them during the trial process, will do much to avoid delay and possible irritation of the jury while the trial lawyer searches his briefcase for the file containing the material.

Statement of Facts

A sheet entitled "Basic Information for Trial" should be inserted in this section of the trial notebook, containing such information as the date of the injury, time of the injury, location of the injury, type of occurrence, (a rear-end collision, a side swipe, or an intersection), the name or names of the defendants, a diagram of the occurrence, the claimed negligent acts of the defendants, the type of injuries sustained, and the name or names of the defense counsel. All of the basic facts necessary to acquaint the lawyer sufficiently with the problems and parties involved should be on a single sheet of paper so that he or she may make such preliminary remarks to the jury, prior to voir dire and in conducting the voir dire, as are appropriate in the jurisdiction.

Voir Dire

In this section of the trial notebook the trial attorney should write key questions to be asked in voir dire, as well as the authority for the asking of such questions. In those jurisdictions where the judge interrogates the juror before accepting the questions from counsel, the questions and authority should be noted on a sheet, and a copy given to the judge in the manner prescribed by the rules.

Most experienced trial lawyers agree that, where counsel is permitted voir dire, he or she starts winning or losing a case with the first question asked of the jury. It is ordinarily the juror's first opportunity to hear the plaintiff's attorney begin presentation of the case. Thus care should be taken to acquaint oneself with the authority for the asking of any special or unusual questions, so that if defense counsel objects, the legal authority for the questions may be readily cited to the court. This section should also contain, as a reminder to trial counsel, a list of all challenges per cause, together with the legal authority for such challenges.

Jurors

There is great divergence of opinion among competent trial counsel as to the most effective method to use in the voir dire and the selection of those who are to serve on the trial panel. There is, however, almost universal agreement that certain basic information must be obtained from the prospective jurors. The trial notebook system devised by Verne Lawyer, one of the co-authors, provides for a system of interrogating six members of the panel, at one-time, as to the background, general experience, and specific court experience of each of them. Listed in columnar fashion under the name of each juror, and printed in such a way that circles can be drawn around the key word, are such items, relevant to the juror's background, as the following: whether the juror has ever lived on a farm, in a town of a population under ten thousand, in a city; whether the juror has ever studied law or medicine, been a nurse, been a teacher; whether the juror has ever worked for a police department; whether he or she has ever worked for, had any interest in, or owned any stock in any automobile casualty insurance company. Space is then provided for other information relevant to the particular case at trial, such as any experience the juror may have had with respect to an automobile collision, personal injuries to any member of the family, experience with lawsuits, either directly or as a witness, and experience driving an automobile.

Every trial counsel must adapt such questions to the technique developed for the selection of juries. The apparent advantage of using the columnar system of key questions is that it lends itself to a rapid interrogation of the jurors and thus avoids unnecessary delay, which irritates the prospective jurors.

Plaintiff's Outline of Liability

Most trial lawyers have developed a system of outlining, prior to trial, the liability aspects of the case. One proven, effective, and simple method is the use of the divided sheet inserted in the trial notebook, listing to the left of the sheet the facts, and to the right, the method by which counsel expects to prove the facts. For example, if it is contended that it is a fact that the defendant was on the wrong side of the road, opposite such statement, under "Proof," counsel should list the names of those witnesses who can prove that fact, together with any key statements that the witnesses have made, or that the trial attorney knows the witnesses will make as a part of their testimony.

Plaintiff's Outline of Damages

The outline of proof of damages is similar in all respects to the outline of liability proof, and the lawyer should follow the same general procedure. For example, if it is a fact to be established that the plaintiff will sustain loss of earning capacity in the future, such a statement of fact is written to the left side of the page, and on the right side of the page, under "Proof," is listed the name of the witness who can be expected to prove this.

It is also suggested that plaintiff's counsel have an outline of the human body, both front and back, with appropriate notations and a diagram of the various areas where injury has been sustained by the plaintiff, so that trial counsel may at a glance understand the injuries and the medical testimony to be adduced.

The Law

The sheet of paper captioned "Law of the Case" should be divided, the left side captioned "Proposition" and the right side captioned "Citation." The trial attorney then notes propositions of law which he or she has reason to believe will be important during the trial of the case. On the right side of the page may be noted the citation supporting the proposition. In this way a written reference is available where questions of law may arise. Any key questions noted on the witness sheet may thus be keyed back to the law section of the notebook by means of numbers. When the question is asked, or the evidence or material is adduced, plaintiff's counsel has in the law section of the notebook a ready reference in support of his or her theory of admission of proof or such other legal propositions as may arise during the trial.

List of Witnesses

A sheet for listing all possible witnessess should be provided primarily as a worksheet to which the practitioner may refer when organizing and listing the names of witnesses who are to appear at the trial.

Most experienced trial lawyers believe that not only must the attorney be well organized prior to entering the courtroom, but also that it should be obvious to the jury that he or she is well prepared and well organized in the presentation of the client's cause. It is suggested, therefore, that all witnesses be listed, and that the undesirable witnesses, or witnesses who may offer merely accumulative testimony, be excluded.

Witnesses

The trial lawyer should prepare a separate sheet for each witness who will appear at the trial. This sheet should contain the name, address, employer, address of employer, and telephone number of each witness, together with data as to whether or not a subpoena has been issued and served, whether the appearance will be by deposition or in person, the date of the appearance, and the time of the appearance. In addition, there should be information on the witness sheet as to whether the witness will testify regarding (1) liability, (2) freedom from negligence, (3) cause, (4) damages, or any other aspect of the case.

The sheet should also contain information as to the type of witness, such as (1) an eye witness, (2) an expert witness, (3) a before-and-after witness, (4) a link-in-the chain witness, (5) a lay witness, (6) a police witness, (7) an at-the-scene witness, or (8) a medical witness.

There should be a short resumé of what the witness can prove and the key questions that should be asked of the witness in order to prove what has already been stated in the plaintiff's outline of liability and damages. Opposite key questions on the witness sheet should be citations referring to the law of the case.

After a study is made of the witnesses who will be produced at trial, each of the witness sheets should be numbered in the order in which the witnesses will appear. It must be recognized that sometimes it is impossible to produce a witness at exactly the most strategic moment, but care should be taken to produce strong witnesses at strategic times. We know from experience that jurors are inclined to remember what they hear first and last, and very little of what they hear in between. If possible, therefore, strong witnesses should be produced at the beginning of the trial or at the beginning and close of each day of the trial. This is a matter of timing and often requires shifting, at the last moment, the time of the appearance of a witness.

Medical and Other Expenses

A list of each of the doctors, together with the amounts of their bills, should be made prior to trial. A list of drug expenses, hospital expenses, property damages, loss of earnings, and other financial losses should also be made prior to the time of trial, and a copy of each bill placed in the exhibit envelope for use at the trial.

Depending upon local practice, it may be advantageous from time to time to prepare, well in advance, the out-of-pocket expense sheet and to make a copy of the sheet available to opposing counsel and the court for reference during the trial. Often this helps to avoid possible future objections as to the reasonableness of the bill in those jurisdictions where reasonableness must be proved. Each bill to be introduced should be assigned an exhibit number and listed on the exhibits sheet.

Opening Statement Notes

Notes should be prepared in advance on matters that the counsel intends to cover in the opening statement. The attorney should also keep sufficient notes of opposing counsel's opening statements for ready reference at the close of the case, when it may appear that opposing counsel has failed to establish by evidence one or more of the matters that he or she indicated would be established.

The modern plaintiff's attorney should avoid such statements as "We expect the evidence will show," or "We expect the evidence to prove," because they lack conviction and force. They are statements of expectation, rather than positive, strong declarations of what the evidence will in fact show. If a trial lawyer does not know what the evidence will prove, and merely states what it is expected to prove, he or she is not a well-prepared trial lawyer.

There are perhaps many phrases which may be used in lieu of "expect to prove," but a few statements that have been found to be effective are (1) "We will offer evidence to prove, and ask you to establish as a fact, as part of your verdict in this case, that..." (2) "We will demonstrate for you by the evidence. . ." and (3) "We will show you by the evidence, and ask you to establish as a fact, as part of your verdict in this case, that. . . ."

All such statements should be positive and confident. They are part of the overall image which the modern trial lawyer must project to the jury, an image of a well-prepared, well-organized, competent attorney.

Exhibits

Counsel should prepare a list of the exhibits, numbered and described, to be used at trial. Opposite the number should be a space for notations to be made when the exhibit is offered and when it is received. Where permissible, the exhibit should be premarked prior to the trial in order to avoid irritating delay in the courtroom. It is a good practice to list all exhibits in advance and to deliver an extra copy of the plaintiff's exhibits list to the judge, reporter, and opposing counsel at the beginning of trial. Some judges require such a list in advance, but even when not required, furnishing a list of the exhibits to the judge fulfills a twofold purpose. First, it assists the judge in keeping track of the exhibits as they are offered and received. Second, it demonstrates to the court that the attorney's case is well prepared, well organized, and well presented. In this section of the trial notebook there should also be an exhibits envelope containing smaller exhibits, such as bills, which may be readily produced as needed.

Plaintiff's Testimony

Most experienced trial lawyers develop prior to trial a checklist of material to be covered in the interrogation of the plaintiff and the plaintiff's witnesses. An example of such a checklist follows:

PLAINTIFF'S TESTIMONY

(Checklist)

IDENTIFICATION AND HISTORY

Name: ____________________

Birthdate: ____________________

Present age: ____________________

Occupation: ____________________

Address: ____________________

Spouse's name and occupation: ____________________

Children: ____________________

Their names and ages: ________________________________

____

1. Where were you born?
2. Where were you raised?
3. Where did you attend high school?
4. What year did you graduate?
5. College or special training?
6. Where?
7. When did you graduate?
8. General state of health during childhood.
9. General state of health during school years.
10. General state of health up to ________________________
    (date of injury)
11. Did you ever have any difficulty with your ________________?
    (here describe area of injury)
12. With your head?
13. With your muscles in your neck?
14. How long did you work at ________________________?
    (place of employment prior to injury)
15. What capacity? What department?
16. Describe duties prior to ________________________
    (date of injury)
17. How much were you earning? Per month? Per Day? After taxes—Per month? Per Day?

DAY OF INJURY

1. Were you involved in an automobile collision on ____________?
   (date of injury)
2. When did you go to work that day?
3. When did you leave work?
4. With whom did you leave?
5. How did you leave?
6. What route did you take?
7. Recall collision?
8. Describe collision.
9. Describe what happened to you.
10. Describe injuries.
11. Describe how you felt.
12. Describe pain.
13. How did you leave scene?
14. Where did you go?
15. What doctor saw you first?
16. What difficulty did you have with your ________________?
    (insert description of area injured)

17. Were you wearing glasses at the time of the accident?
18. Were you hospitalized as a result of this collision?
19. How long were you hospitalized? Where?

EVENTS AFTER INJURY

1. Describe activities the day following the collision.
2. Describe pain and discomfort.
3. What medications did you take?
4. What doctor prescribed them?
5. What medication had you taken prior to ______________________?
   (date of injury)
6. What did you take them for?
7. Who prescribed them?
8. Did they help?
9. When did you first notice pain in ____________________________?
   (area of injury)
10. Describe pain in ____
    (area of injury)
11. Had you ever had such difficulty before? ______________________
12. When did you first notice difficulty with ______________________?
    (area of injury)
13. Describe injury with____
    (other areas of injury)
14. Had you ever had such difficulty before?
15. Describe any other injuries.
16. When did Dr. __________ first see you?
17. When did you have your last general physical checkup prior to your injury?
18. What results?
19. Describe hospitalization____
    (insert date of hospitalization)
20. Where did you go from the hospital?
21. Describe routine at home.
22. How did you feel?
23. When did you return to work?
24. How did you feel?
25. What difficulty were you having with your ____________________?
    (area of injury)
26. How much were you paid? Per month? Per day? After taxes—Per month? Per day?
27. When were you next hospitalized for injuries sustained?________
    (date of injury)
28. What was your difficulty at that time?
29. What doctor ordered you to the hospital?

30. How did you feel?
31. What was your situation with respect to your ________________?
(describe area of injury)
32. Did you receive therapy?
33. Describe your hospital stay in ______________________________
(date of hospitalization)
34. How long were you off work at that time?
35. What date did you return to work?
36. How much was your pay when you returned to work? Per month? Per day? After taxes—Per month? Per day?
37. Describe your condition during the remaining weeks of _______
(state year)
38. Describe the condition of your ______________________________
(area of injury)
during the next year.
39. What difficulty did you have?
40. Were you subsequently hospitalized because of your__________
(injury)
41. When?
42. Describe your condition at that time.
43. Who put you in the hospital?
44. How long were you there?
45. What was your pay the day before entering the hospital this time? Per month? Per day? After taxes—Per month? Per day?
46. How many days were you off work?
47. When did you return?
48. How much did you earn when you returned to work? Per month? Per day? After taxes—Per month? Per day?
49. Have you calculated total lost earnings after taxes?
50. Are you still working?
51. What are your present earnings?
52. What are your present duties?
53. What, if any, difficulty are you having at the present time with your ____?
(insert area of injury)
54. How has it affected your life and your routine at home?
55. At work?
56. Describe your general state of health at the present time.
57. Were you rendered bills for your hospital confinement?
58. Identify them. (Exhibit__________)
59. Were you rendered bills by Dr.__________?
60. By Dr.__________?
61. Identify doctor bills. (Exhibit__________)
62. Were you required to purchase medicine?

63. What was the total cost of the medicine?
64. Identify medical bills (Exhibit__________)
65. What was the cost of the repairs to your glasses?

OFFER ALL EXHIBITS PROPERLY IDENTIFIED AND ADMISSIBLE

Note: This is not intended to be a complete checklist, but a minimum outline of areas to be covered and a reminder of questions to be asked. Where the witness can identify exhibits in the nature of photographs, X-rays, etc. additional reminder questions should be inserted. Refer to witness sheet and proof outline for additional key questions to be inserted.

Comment: Such a checklist is especially important in the interrogation of medical witnesses. It is suggested that counsel, early in his or her trial career, develop a comprehensive checklist of key questions to be asked witnesses in each category.

Defendant's Testimony

This section of the notebook is for notes with respect to the testimony of the defendant and defense witnesses, as well as matters to be covered during cross-examination. A good practice is to draw a line down the center of the page, with testimony on the right-hand side, and on the left-hand side, notes for cross-examination.

There is no question but that a retentive memory is essential to the successful trial practitioner. The fewer the notes that he or she makes, the less chance there will be of failing to hear important bits of testimony produced by the defendant. While no attempt should be made to record all of the testimony, all of the important bits of testimony from any witness should be recorded; namely those portions that bear upon the ultimate fact issues in the case, along with those statements upon which the plaintiff desires to cross-examine the defendant's witness.

Arguments

Since the plaintiff usually has the privilege of opening and closing the argument or summation, notes should be made during the trial in the argument section of the notebook. These may then be used as a reminder of the points upon which counsel intends to base his or her argument. The outlines of proof, liability, and damages, the witness sheets, and the notes made during the trial should afford readily accessible material for use in summing up the case.

Requested Instructions

This section of the notebook contains notes regarding anticipated requested instructions, or requests to charge the jury, which will be presented to the court during the trial or at the close of the case. All requests to charge should be placed in the notebook well before the time for filing so that they may always be quickly available for presentation to the court.

Instructions

This section should contain all of the instructions or charges to the jury actually given so that at the conclusion of the case the trial notebook will have a complete record of the trial.

Motions

Sheets should be provided in the notebook for all notations regarding motions for directed verdict, for nonsuit, or otherwise. The notes are usually made at the time that the motion is made by opposing counsel. All motions made by the plaintiff's attorney should also be placed in this section of the notebook, including motions for new trial or motion for judgment notwithstanding the verdict, and the ruling of the court upon such motions. If the motions are filed in writing, the sheets should be cut with a three-ring punch and placed in this section of the notebook for ready reference and permanent binding.

Depositions

This section of the trial notebook should contain notes and outlines of the discovery depositions that have been taken and that are to be used. Counsel should develop a system of outlining or indexing each deposition, dividing the outline into categories, such as material which may be used for impeachment purposes and material which may be used as substantive proof or as admissions.

6

How and When to Settle

It is amazing that the emphasis in continuing legal education concerns the preparation for and the actual trial of a case, yet very little current literature is helpful to the lawyer in deciding how and when to settle. This is true even though the overwhelming majority of claims and cases are settled without trial. There is apparently an unspoken belief among lawyers that if a case is well prepared for trial, the actual settlement will automatically be a satisfactory one that accurately reflects the full value of the client's injuries.

Nothing could be further from the truth.

It is a sad fact of personal injury practice that a great many settlements represent less than full value recovery for the client's injuries and a few, a very few, represent the full value of the claim. The number of claimants who receive more than the full and fair value of their claim is so small that it is not statistically significant.

Why is this so?

In the first place, only about ten percent of all claimants ever retain a lawyer. The inexperienced claimant is immediately faced with the sophisticated and organized claims industry whose basic function is to protect the assets of the insurance company. It is true that a few companies make an honest attempt to fairly evaluate claims. However, the definition of "fair" and the orientation of the adjuster become critical in the manner in which the system actually functions. Certainly, no one would argue that the adjuster is trained to give away any more of the company's money than necessity demands. The adjuster is trained to recognize the questions of liability, damages, and responsibility that ensue in every case. Not so the claimant.

It comes as a rude shock to many claimants to learn of principles such as "contributory negligence," "cost of litigating," "delay in getting a case to trial if a case is not settled on terms satisfactory to the company." The claimant is often without transportation while awaiting settlement, existing with unpaid medical bills, unable to work, and handicapped in mobility by injury and pain. The insurance carrier, on the other hand, has the premiums already received from insurance purchasers safely invested at handsome interest rates. The sad fact of claims settlement is that time is nearly always on the side of the defendant.

While settlement is delayed, the plaintiff is getting better medically, and proof of initial injuries is seldom accumulated unless the plaintiff has a lawyer. Witnesses disappear or lose their recollection if statements are not taken. (Statements taken by adjusters, of course, are not available to the plaintiff at a later date under most circumstances, since in most jurisdictions, they are classified as "work product.")

Skilled adjusters make every effort to keep the plaintiff from getting a lawyer, pointing out that "the lawyer will take a third or more of what you are entitled to," and in some instances, going so far as to claim that retaining a lawyer will delay settlement of the case. It is seldom pointed out that statistically, a plaintiff usually does not recover a substantial sum without the aid of a lawyer. Most plaintiffs do not even know which items of damage they are entitled to recover, how to preserve evidence, or how to evaluate a claim.

6.1 WHEN TO SETTLE

Usually, a substantial claim should not be settled without filing suit.

Why?

1. Often it is impossible to evaluate the medical injuries of a plaintiff and the degree of certitude of recovery in the first weeks after injury. If the plaintiff waits for "maximum medical recovery" before attempting settlement and cannot settle, suit still must be filed and the weeks and months of delay have been wasted.

2. Many insurance companies do not give substantial settlement authority to their adjusters. (A common limit of authority is $1,500.00 or $2,500.00.) The granting of substantial authority to settle awaits the filing of suit, the attention of supervising claims authorities or defense counsel. All that most adjusters can do is recommend a settlement in excess of their own limited authority. A favorite negotiating technique is for the adjuster to assume the role of supplicant for the injured party, saying that he or she will try to get a specific sum. Then when the

plaintiff's patience and capacity to hold out is nearing exhaustion, the adjuster returns with regret, claiming inability to get the sum represented—but a lesser sum has been approved. Often, the claimant takes it in despair.

3. Many items of evidence can be obtained only with the use of subpoenas and those become available only after suit is filed.

4. Often the adjuster may not appreciate the weakness in his or her case, or the strength of the plaintiff's case, until evidence is developed through discovery procedure. Many adjusters are inclined to underestimate the value of intangible items that sometimes are the greatest items of damage, such as loss of capacity to lead a normal life, emotional distress, etc. Unfortunately, also, the adversary orientation of the adjuster will cause him or her to disbelieve claims of the plaintiff, particularly if inadequately presented by the injured and confused plaintiff. The confusion and poor description of the items of damage is often interpreted as evidence of questionable existence.

There are a few times when a lawyer should not file suit before attempting settlement. When are these?

1. When the injury of the plaintiff is clear, easily recognized and identified, and recovery is complete, certain, and not continuing.

2. When the liability is clear, the amount of insurance is limited, the damages exceed the policy limits, the defendant is without readily reachable assets, and the insurance company is ready to pay its policy limits. (The possibility of exposure on the part of the insurance company above the policy limits under these conditions has begun to serve as a powerful incentive to the insurance company to recognize its responsibility for good faith protection of its assured. Under the circumstances suggested, the company is bound to treat the interests of the assured with at least the same tender care that it would its own, and in this instance offer the policy limits as soon as the facts are ascertained.)

3. Occasionally facts will arise when the negligence of a professional person is clear and the damages are obvious. Under this circumstance, good practice would dictate that the professional be given a limited amount of time to put his or her insurance carrier on notice or otherwise provide for settlement. Unfortunately, few medical doctors appreciate the courtesy and avail themselves of the opportunity to avoid suit.

4. If there are elements of the plaintiff's case that are better not put to test by the rigors of discovery in preparation for trial, early settlement may be advisable. In the best of all possible worlds, all weaknesses would be revealed to all parties and some equation of justice applied. We do not

live in such a world, however. Skillful but concealed capitulation may be the road of wisdom in some circumstances.

6.2 SETTLEMENT DEMAND LETTERS

In order to successfully *evaluate* a client's case, you must have as accurate an idea as possible of the weaknesses and strengths of your client's case—and the defendant's position.

In order to *settle,* you must make sure that the defendant's representative has the same concept of the facts as you do, or at least that he or she does not have a stronger opinion of the case than do you.

If both sides share the same knowledge and opinion of the facts and the conclusions to be drawn from such facts, and if there are sufficient assets available, there is an excellent prospect of settlement. Nobody wants to gamble on a lawsuit if a settlement can be effected that accurately represents the risks of both parties. It costs money and time to litigate.

One effective way to ensure that your client's case is viewed in the same light by the defendant as the plaintiff is to write a demand letter describing the salient and provable facts. If there is a question about a given point that can only be resolved at trial and concerning which there can be an honest difference of opinion, acknowledge this in your letter. If you force defense representatives to state their arguable positions, by the mere process of stating their opinions, they will become more fixed in them.

If you are making a demand that reflects a controverted liability situation or a questionable item of damage, state that your demand reflects the fact that the item or fact is in controversy.

Ask for a little more than you expect to get. The claims industry is set up to bargain. You are not going to change the rules of the game single-handedly. If you simply state a demand with no room for compromise, you increase the chances of having to try the case. Many adjusters want to save a little, and thereby look good to their supervisors, so if your object is settlement, let them save a little off your demand.

All three elements of the settlement triangle must be considered in evaluating and settling a claim. The three elements are: fault, damages, and capacity to respond to judgment. The absence or weakness of any of these elements changes the value of your lawsuit.

An example of a typical demand letter follows. Each demand letter must be tailor-made to the particular circumstances of your case, but the elements that must be considered essentially remain the same. Please note that all demand letters should contain a time limit. Defense counsel and adjusters are very busy people. Your file may remain at the bottom of a stack unless there is a compelling reason to examine it. If there are facts that need documenting because they are not in the possession of the defendant, furnish the proof with the letter if the defendant desires it (such as medical bills, wage loss, etc.). The easier you make it for the defendant to examine and evaluate the file, the more likely he or she is to do so.

Other advantages of demand letters over a verbal demand are that they continue to speak after the phone call is complete. They accurately state your case in one easy-to-review place, and they cannot be forgotten as to what exactly was said.

A TYPICAL DEMAND LETTER

August 10, 19——

John Toughy, Esquire
Clearwater, Florida

A. Scrooge, Esquire
Tampa, Florida

W. Nevermind, Esquire
St. Petersburg, Florida

Re: William Osteen v. Wilkie General Hospital,
Jane P. Baroque, M.D., and N. V. R. Chaste

Gentlemen:

If I may, we would like to address all three parties in this single letter. My partner, J. Good, and I have carefully reviewed our file and we are prepared to submit a settlement proposal to you which will be recommended to our clients.

We, of course, attempt to evaluate every file, as we are sure you do, by taking into consideration liability, damages, and the question of each defendant's responsibility.

Our client's problem began when he was injured in the early evening of November 10, 19--, nearly four years ago. Mr. Osteen had the unfortunate experience of falling on his right shoulder and arm as he tripped over a kitchen bar stool while visiting a friend. Due to the hour of the day and his extreme discomfort, he was taken to the Wilkie General Hospital Emergency Room. At this point, it might be simply stated, his real problems began.

Although he was in great pain, an effort was made to make Mr. Osteen comfortable so that he might return home for the evening. After several unsuccessful attempts to position the arm properly, it became necessary to admit the patient due to unbearable pain. One of the assisting women told Mrs. Osteen that, if they gave him enough medication to sedate him, Mrs. Osteen could not get him into the car. He arrived at the Emergency Room at 10:32 P.M. and at about 1:00 A.M., he was admitted as an inpatient.

The Emergency Room notes disclose a diagnosis of a fracture of the head of the right humerus. The x-rays taken at that time are very clear—this was a fracture dislocation, not a mere fracture. The hospital record also shows that this was a fracture dislocation. The degree of severity of the injury moved from an emergency to an acute emergency.

Dr. Chaste telephoned Dr. Baroque concerning this injury and orders were written for a mere fracture of the proximal humerus. Dr. Baroque did not see the patient until 12:00 noon on November 11, 19--, according to the hospital records. No medical care appropriate to the emergency was given Mr. Osteen for nearly twelve hours after his hospital admission.

Mr. Osteen's physical evaluation at that time revealed that the patient had radial and ulnar nerves intact and sensation intact. This note was dictated on November 10, 19--. Dr. Baroque apparently then reviewed the x-rays and found the dislocation of the humerus at the shoulder joint along with a fractured humeral head. Dr. Baroque attempted a closed reduction with Valium injection on the ward, which was unsuccessful, and the plaintiff had an adverse reaction to the Valium. Laboratory work was ordered and the patient was fasted and prepared for surgery that evening. The patient did not get to the operating room until 6:00 P.M. that evening, approximately twenty hours after being seen in the Emergency Room.

After a number of attempts at closed reduction under general anesthesia were unsuccessful, Dr. Baroque had to do an open reduction on the fractured dislocation. This surgery posed a number of difficulties, but finally, after freeing up the fracture and the biceps tendon, the reduction was accomplished.

Immediately postoperatively, it is noted in the hospital records that the patient had a radial nerve palsy. He was discharged on November 13, 19--, and followed as an outpatient by Dr. Baroque.

His wound healed satisfactorily and he was started on an exercise regimen after adequate time elapsed for the fracture to heal. It was not until the end of January, 19--, that Dr. Baroque noticed that the patient was having difficulty contracting the muscles about his right shoulder. A neurological consultation and EMG were obtained from Dr. Score. This study revealed extensive brachial plexus injury involving C-5 through T-1, with major involvement at T-6, T-7, and T-8.

On February 28, 19--, when Mr. Osteen was an outpatient, Dr. Baroque writes that the brachial plexus injury occurred at the time of the dislocation. Although Dr. Baroque claims she knows this because the axillary nerve sensory area was out prior to attempted reduction, we cannot find any note of this in the hospital record. Dr. Baroque's hospital record indicates no evidence of radial or ulnar nerve damage, and no sensory changes before treatment.

We are prepared to show that, if this fracture dislocation had been diagnosed immediately and appropriate treatment had been ordered, the arm would have resolved successfully. However, the delay in diagnosis made it more likely that permanent nerve damage would result.

We intend to show Dr. Chaste departed from the standard of reasonable medical care by not recognizing an acute emergency and obtaining the appropriate orthopedic management.

The Wilkie General Hospital had as its agent (or ostensible agent), Dr. Chaste, working under the direct supervision and control of the hospital administration and in conformity with the hospital rules and regulations. Moreover, we doubt if a jury would think it reasonable for the hospital to "warehouse" a patient with a medical emergency, and not secure him at least *some* treatment, for approximately twelve hours. We believe a jury would find Dr. Baroque negligent in the delay in examining and treating her patient, and in her operating procedure.

The medical expenses total over $2,600.00, and while this did not break the bank account of our client, it has cost him real dollars.

The wage loss for this successful businessman does not show on paper. We really do not know how much more he would have had today had he not suffered the loss of use of his right arm. He was indeed fortunate that he could keep his business from going under. Likewise, it is heartening to see that he has rehabilitated himself psychologically to his present degree.

Despite Mr. Osteen's efforts to mitigate his misfortune, the net result is an ambitious man who now enters his golden years without the benefit of the use of an extremity. His life is altered from the moment he awakens until he is asleep again. Disability and limitation of the quality of his life are his hourly companions. The tables show his life expectancy is fourteen years and his work expectancy is six years. The benefit of the retirement he expected to enjoy is diminished. Mrs. Osteen will be assisting her husband for as long as she is physically able to do so.

We would recommend $300,000.00 to our clients if a settlement can be promptly reached. If Agreement cannot be reached collectively, we ask $100,000.00 from the Wilkie General Hospital, $200,000.00 from Dr. Chaste, and $100,000.00 from Dr. Baroque. We will hold this offer open for thirty (30) days.

May I hear from you by the 10th of September?

Very truly yours,

Mary Davis

Bcc: To the referring attorney

6.3 SETTLEMENT BROCHURES

Settlement brochures are a dramatic technique for presentation of a major case for consideration.

They should not be used in anything less than the exceptional case. Their promiscuous use in anything less than the "bell-ringer" can destroy the value of the approach and it will not turn the second-rate case into a first-rate one.

What the settlement brochure does in the bell-ringer case is bring the case to the top of the heap for consideration by the claims committee.

Consider the process of settlement from the standpoint of the insurance company. Minor claims are settled, usually by an adjuster within that adjuster's customary settlement authority.

Cases of slightly more significance are settled after consultation with a claims supervisor and frequently defense counsel.

These two decisions are usually made at a local or regional level.

The decision to settle the major case is usually made far away, often at the home office of the insurance company. The decision is made by a claims committee of the senior claims supervisors of the company and several people may contribute their wisdom, experience, and opinion to the settlement decision. Every aspect of the case is likely to be discussed, including the characteristics of plaintiff and defense counsel, the forum, and the judges' habits and prejudices.

In the absence of a settlement brochure, the settlement offer of the insurance company is likely to reflect the average experience around the country with cases of a similar type, modified by whatever unusual information has been provided the claims committee by the local adjuster or defense counsel.

If your case is truly a bell-ringer, there are likely to be personalized, individualized, and subtle but important nuances involved. If you want to settle the bell-ringer, the settlement brochure is a way of presenting

HOW A RISING STAR WAS SNUFFED OUT

Odell W. Vaughn, Jr.
December 9, 1942–June 26, 1972

Death Shoots Down
A Young Man On His Way Up

In one of the last photographs before his death, Odell Vaughn showed the charisma that was "catching on" as a TV newsman.

Odell Vaughn (left) began winning his spurs as a member of the Columbia Broadcasting System (CBS) election coverage team in 1968.

Here Odell Vaughn (center) directs a CBS newsfilm team on location.

TALK ABOUT A FUTURE!

In 1967 Odell Vaughn earned $8,145 as a researcher in the CBS news election unit.

By 1971 his annual income had grown to $30,383 as he "anchored" major network newscasts on radio from New York.

In the year of his death he would have earned more than $48,526. No less an authority than Walter Cronkite viewed him as a "comer."

CBS
Columbia Broadcasting System, Inc.
51 West 52 Street
New York, New York 10019
(212) 765-4321

John A. Schneider, President
CBS/Broadcast Group

Dear Mrs. Vaughn:

Please accept my sincere sympathy on the tragic death of your husband.

Del's career with CBS was one of growth and development that could well serve as a model for others aspiring to the degree of success and professionalism that he had already reached. As an anchorman on the CBS Radio Network, he had many unseen fans -- as well as admiring colleagues -- who will sorely miss him as a person and as a journalist.

A brief note may not go far in easing your grief, Mrs. Vaughn, but I wanted you to know that there are many in CBS who share your bereavement.

Sincerely,

Jack Schneider

Mrs. Odell W. Vaughn Jr.
3065 Octavia Place
Atlanta, Georgia 30340

June 27, 1972

THE FATAL ROLE OF A FAULTY PART

On Monday, June 26, 1972, Odell Vaughn was covering the Harrisburg, Pennsylvania, floods from a Bell helicopter owned by T. H. Cosgrove, Inc.

The helicopter was returning for its landing when it simply "threw a blade." When the blade flew off, the helicopter crashed, killing all aboard.

Subsequent investigation proved that the blade was lost because of a defectively designed and machined retention strap fitting—Bell Part No. 206-010-155-7.

In short, Odell Vaughn was an innocent victim of failure to redesign and replace a part known to be faulty.

A DEVOTED FATHER DISAPPEARS.

Odell and Christine were married in 1963. They had two small sons, Stephen and Matthew.

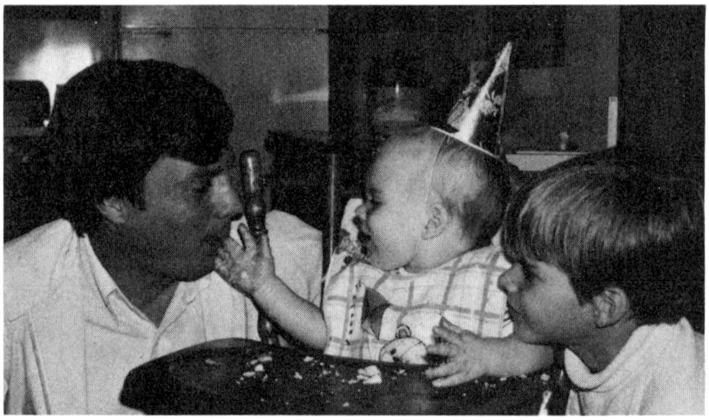

Odell was "Dad," and these pictures show what a fine one he was.

Prepared for settlement purposes only by Verne Lawyer of Lawyer, Lawyer, Dunn and Jackson, plaintiff's attorney, Fourth Floor, Fleming Bldg., Des Moines, Ia., as a courtesy to the defendants and their insurers to assist them in the evaluation of the loss occasioned by the death of Odell Vaughn.

these nuances that might be otherwise overlooked •by the claims committee.

Cost of preparation should not be relevant in the preparation of the brochure. We have purchased machines that permit the preparation of the brochure in bound booklet form. Several copies should be furnished in order that everyone involved in the settlement decision may have a desk copy for consideration.

Needless to state, the brochure is a highly individualized presentation. It should be a work of art and make a statement. Everything in the brochure must be meticulously true. If something is stated as a fact, it must be demonstratively true. Probabilities, opinions, etc., must be labeled as such.

See the sample of one of the shorter brochures here. The form varies and is endless in possibility, limited only by your skill and imagination in presenting the facts of your case.

6.4 STRUCTURED SETTLEMENT—A ROSE OR A THORN?

In recent years, the settlement arrangements sometimes known as structured settlements have come into relatively common use.

No other innovation in settlement is more fraught with possibility for either good or harm to the plaintiff than this technique, depending upon the skill, care, knowledge, and integrity of the plaintiff's counsel.

What is this technique?

A structured settlement calls for the substitution of periodic payments over a certain length of time for the traditional method of settlement by a single lump sum. Usually some of the settlement is in the form of "up-front" cash. The periodic payments may be at a constant rate per month or per annum, or may vary by being increased or decreased by a specified percentage. Increments of additional payments may be agreed upon to be paid at specified times, such as an additional $10,000.00 each five years. The payments may be guaranteed for a set number of years, may terminate on the death of the plaintiff, or may be based upon the joint and several life expectancies of two or more persons, such as the plaintiff and spouse.

Advantages to the plaintiff:

1. Management-free income
2. Tax-free periodic payments for life
3. Financial planning, structured to the individual plaintiff's needs
4. Possible increased net returns because of income tax rulings that currently tax income from annuities, but do not tax proceeds of a properly structured settlement

Advantages to the defendant insurance company:

1. Possible savings in cost

Each of the above will be discussed in turn, together with consideration of the various pitfalls that can beset the plaintiff or the attorney if proper skill and knowledge are not appropriately used.

1. Management-free Income:

Few plaintiffs are equipped by training, experience, or aptitude to handle a large sum of money.

Most plaintiffs' attorneys are neither able nor willing to undertake the continued supervision of the proceeds of a large lump-sum settlement over the lifetime of the plaintiff.

One method of providing the management and the resulting assurance that the proceeds of the settlement will not be squandered is by a structured settlement.

Usually the insurance company is required to purchase an annuity designed to insure payment of the settlement.

Properly done, the structured settlement ensures that mismanagement, improvidence, waste, or fraud are unlikely to affect the plaintiff's long-term security.

Hazard: The plaintiff is not fully protected by the purchase of the annuity, even from a triple A rated company. If the primary obligor, the defending insurance company, goes into bankruptcy, the proceeds of the annuity purchased by the defending insurance company may be treated as a general asset of the bankrupt, and not an obligation of the annuitant to the plaintiff. Further, if the plaintiff retains the right to name the beneficiary of the annuity, it could affect the tax-free status of the payments.

Solution: Look to the security of the primary obligor. If adequate, the hazard is illusory. Some of the major insurance companies are little less likely to become bankrupt than is the United States government (perhaps not as likely).

2. Tax-free Payments for Life:

Present tax rulings indicate that payments made pursuant to a properly structured settlement are not subject to income tax.

See the following IRS Code Sections:

IRS TAX CODE SECTIONS

I. R. C. Section 61 Gross Income Defined

(a) General definition—Except as otherwise provided in this subtitle, gross income means all income from whatever source derived, including (but not limited to) the following items:

(1) Compensation for services, including fees, commissions, and similar items;
(2) Gross income derived from business;
(3) Gains derived from dealings in property;
(4) Interest;
(5) Rents;
(6) Royalties;
(7) Dividends;
(8) Alimony & separate maintenance payments;
(9) Annuities;
(10) Income from life insurance and endowment contracts;
(11) Pensions;
(12) Income from discharge of indebtedness;
(13) Distributive share of partnership gross income;
(14) Income in bequest of a decedent; and
(15) Income from an interest in an estate or trust.

I.R.C. Section 213 Medical, Dental, etc., Expenses

(a) Allowance of deduction.—There shall be allowed as a deduction the expenses paid during the taxable year, not compensated for by insurance or otherwise, for medical care of the taxpayer, his spouse, or a dependant (as defined in section 152)—

I. R. C. Section 104(a)(2)

I. R. C. sec. 104 (1954 Code). (a) IN GENERAL.
Except in the case of amounts attributable to (and not in excess of) deductions allowed under section 213 (relating to medical, etc. expenses) for any prior taxable year, gross income does not include—

(2) the amount of any damages received (whether by suit or agreement) on account of personal injuries or sickness;

REVENUE RULING 65-29

Income realized from the investment of a lump-sum payment representing the discounted present value of a damage award for personal injuries is not excludable from gross income under section 104 of the Internal Revenue Code of 1954.

Advice has been requested whether income realized from the investment of a damage award computed as stated below may be excluded from the taxpayer's gross income under section 104 (a) of the Internal Revenue Code of 1954 for any period of time.

A sued *B* for tortious injury to his spouse. The Court found that due to *B*'s negligence *A*'s spouse was rendered 100 percent and permanently disabled, and that her life expectancy was thereby shortened to 10 years. The reasonable cost of care, medicine, and medical attention was found to be 1*x* dollars per week, totaling 520*x* dollars (1*x* dollars times 52 weeks times 10 years).

The Court awarded *A* 416*x* dollars, which amount represents the present value of 520*x* dollars payable over a 10-year period.

Section 61 (a) of the Code provides that except as otherwise provided in subtitle A, gross income means all income from whatever source derived, expressly including various types of investment income.

Section 104 (a)(2) of the Code provides, in relevant part, that gross income does not include the amount of any damages received by suit or agreement on account of personal injuries or sickness.

As *A* has unfettered control over the lump-sum payment and over the income from the investment of such payment, it is concluded that only the lump-sum payment, 416*x* dollars, is received as damages within the meaning of section 104 (a)(2) of the Code.

Accordingly, it is held that none of the investment income may be excluded from the gross income of *A*, under section 104 of the Code.

PART I. RULINGS AND DECISIONS UNDER THE INTERNAL REVENUE CODE OF 1954

Section 61.—Gross Income Defined

26 CFR 1.61-1: Gross income.

Whether the recipient must include in gross income any part of monthly payments received in settlement of a damage suit. See Rev. Rul. 79-220, below.

Section 104.—Compensation for Injuries or Sickness

26 CFR 1.104-1: Compensation for injuries or sickness.
(Also Sections 61, 451; 1.61-1, 1.451-1.)

Damages; monthly payments; amount excludable. An insurance company purchased and retained exclusive ownership in a single premium annuity contract to fund monthly payments stipulated in settlement of a damage suit. The recipient may exclude the full amount of the payments from gross income under section 104(a)(2) of the Code rather than the discounted present value. Payments made to the estate after the recipient's death are also fully excludable.

Rev. Rul. 79-220

ISSUE

Does the exclusion from gross income provided by section 104(a)

(2) of the Internal Revenue Code of 1954 apply to the full amount of monthly payments received in settlement of a damage suit or only to the discounted present value of such payments?

FACTS

A, an individual, sued *B* for damages for personal injuries. *B* is insured by *M*, an insurance company. Before trial, *A* accepted *M's* offer to settle the suit for a lump-sum payment of $8,000 and *M's* agreement to provide *A* with monthly payments of $250 for *A's* lifetime or 20 years, whichever is longer, the payments to be made to *A's* estate after *A's* death if *A* should die before the end of 20 years. *A* had no right to the discounted present value of the monthly income (the present value of which, at date of settlement, was less than the total monthly payments to be provided) or to control the investment of that amount.

To provide the monthly payments for *A*, *M* purchased a single premium annuity contract from *O*, another insurance company. *M* advised *O* to make payments directly to *A*. However, *M* is the owner of the annuity contract and has all rights of ownership, including the right to change the beneficiary. *A* can rely on only the general credit of *M* for collection of the monthly payments.

LAW AND ANALYSIS

Section 61(a) of the Code and the Income Tax Regulations thereunder provide that, except as otherwise provided by law, gross income means all income from whatever source derived.

Section 104(a)(2) of the Code provides that except in the case of amounts attributable to (and not in excess of) deductions allowed under section 213 (relating to medical and dental expenses) for any prior taxable year, gross income does not include the amount of any damages received (whether by suit or agreement) on account of personal injuries or sickness.

Section 1.104-1(c) of the regulations provides, in part, that the term "damages received (whether by suit or agreement)" means an amount received (other than workmen's compensation) through prosecution of a legal suit or action based upon tort or tort type rights, or through a settlement agreement entered into in lieu of such prosecution.

However, if a lump-sum damage payment is invested for the benefit of a claimant who has actual or constructive receipt or the economic benefit of the lump-sum payment, only the lump-sum payment is received as damages within the meaning of section 104 (a)(2) of the Code, and none of the income from the investment of such payment is excludable under section 104. See Rev. Rul. 65-29, 1965-1 C.B. 59, relating to damages awarded a claimant for tortious injuries in a lump-sum payment of 416*x* dollars over which claimant had unfettered control. The 416*x* dollars represented the discounted value of 520*x* dollars, which was found to be the reasonable cost of care, medicine, and medical attention for the injured person over a 10-year period. Rev. Rul. 65-29 holds that only the lump-sum payment, 416*x* dollars, is received as damages within the meaning of section 104(a)(2). See also Rev. Rul. 76-133, 1976-1 C.B. 34, which reaches a similar conclusion with regard to a court approved settlement awarded a minor and transmitted by the clerk of the court, in the name of the minor, to a savings and loan association for deposit in certificates of deposit.

In the instant case, there is a continuing obligation by *M* to pay $250 per month to *A* for the agreed period. *M's* purchase of a single premium annuity contract from the other insurance company was merely an investment by *M* to provide a source of funds for *M* to satisfy its obligation to *A*. See Rev. Rul. 72-25, 1972-1 C.B. 127, which relates to a similar arrangement made by an employer to provide for payment of deferred compensation to an employee. In Rev. Rul. 72-25, as here, the arrangement was merely a matter of convenience to the obligor and did not give the recipient any right in the annuity itself.

HOLDINGS

The exclusion from gross income provided by section 104(a)(2) of the Code applies to the full amount of the monthly payments received by *A* in settlement of the damage suit because *A* had a right to receive only the monthly payments and did not have the actual or constructive receipt or the economic benefit of the lump-sum amount that was invested to yield that monthly payment. If *A* should die before the end of 20 years, the payments made to *A's* estate under the settlement agreement are also excludable from income under section 104.

REVENUE RULING 79-313

ISSUE

Are payments received by the taxpayer, under the circumstances described below, excludable from the gross income of the taxpayer under section 104(a)(2) of the Internal Revenue Code?

FACTS

In 1977, the taxpayer sustained severe and permanent personal injuries as the result of being struck by an automobile. Thereafter, the taxpayer brought an action against *X*, the owner-operator of the automobile. *X* carried automobile liability insurance with *M*, an insurance company.

In 1979, *M* proposed a settlement of taxpayer's suit against *X*, which the taxpayer accepted. Pursuant to the settlement agreement, *M* agreed to make fifty consecutive annual payments to the taxpayer, the first payment to be made one year after the date of settlement. These payments are for "personal injury, pain and suffering, disability, and loss of bodily function." The amount of each annual payment will be increased by five percent over the amount of the preceding annual payment.

The settlement also provides that the taxpayer does not have the right to accelerate any payment or increase or decrease the amount of the annual payments specified.

Under the agreement, *M* is not required to set aside specific assets to secure any part of its obligation to the taxpayer. The taxpayer's rights against *M* are no greater than those of *M*'s general creditors. *M*'s obligations to the taxpayer result solely from the settlement out of court of the legal action that the taxpayer instituted against *X* who was insured by *M*.

LAW AND ANALYSIS

Section 104(a)(2) of the Code provides that except in the case of amounts attributable to (and not in excess of) deductions allowed under section 213 for any prior taxable year, gross income does not include the amount of any damages received (whether by suit or agreement) on account of personal injuries or sickness.

Section 1.104-1(c) of the Income Tax Regulations provides that the term "damages received (whether by suit or agreement)" means an amount received (other than workmen's compensation) through prosecution of a legal suit or action based upon tort or tort type rights, or through a settlement agreement entered into in lieu of such prosecution.

The annual payments to be received by the taxpayer are amounts received through a settlement agreement entered into in lieu of the prosecution of a legal suit based upon tort or tort rights within the meaning of section 1.104-1(c) of the regulations.

Rev. Rul. 65-29, 1965-1 C.B. 59, holds that, when the taxpayer actually received the present value of an award for personal injury in a lump sum and invested it, any interest earned on the amount invested was taxable. However, in the instant case, even though the settlement agreement provides for increasing payments to be made annually the taxpayer has neither actual nor constructive receipt, nor the economic benefit of the present value of the damages.

HOLDING

All payments received by the taxpayer in this case, pursuant to the settlement agreement, are excludable from the gross income of the taxpayer under section 104(a)(2) of the Code.

TRUST ESTABLISHED BY THE UNITED STATES OF AMERICA

FACTS

An individual sued the United States of America for damages for injuries suffered in the course of a physical examination at a medical facility operated by the United States Government. Pursuant to a court-approved settlement, a trust was established by the United States of America and funded in the amount of $100,000 to pay for the individual's future medical expenses for any physical or mental condition arising from, or related to, or that may have been contributed to by the injury sustained. The settlement agreement also provided that the net income of the trust, and the corpus if necessary, would be distributed in payment of incurred medical expenses, and that net income in excess of incurred medical expenses would be accumulated and added to the corpus. Upon the individual's death, the remaining trust estate (if any) as well as undistributed income (if any) would revert to the United States. If the trust assets are depleted by payment of the individual's medical expenses, the United States is not required to make further contributions to the trust or otherwise pay subsequently arising medical expenses of the individual.

LAW AND ANALYSIS

Section 671 of the Internal Revenue Code of 1954 provides the general rule that in cases where the grantor or another person is regarded as the owner of any portion of a trust, there shall be included in computing the taxable income and credits of the grantor or person who is regarded as the owner those items of income, deductions, and credits against the tax of the trust that are attributable to that portion of the trust to the extent that such items would be taken into account in computing the taxable income or credits against the tax of an individual. The circumstances under which the grantor is regarded as the owner of a portion of the trust are set forth in section 673 (reversionary interests), section 674 (power to control beneficial enjoyment), section 675 (administrative powers), section 676 (power to revoke), and section 677 (income for benefit of grantor).

Section 677(a)(2) of the Code provides that the grantor shall, in general, be treated as the owner of any portion of a trust, whether or not treated as such owner under section 674, whose income, without the approval or consent of any adverse party is, or in the discretion of the grantor or a nonadverse party, or both, may be held or accumulated for future distribution to the grantor or the grantor's spouse.

In this case, the trust agreement provides that any trust assets remaining, including any net income in excess of the incurred medical expenses that had been accumulated and added to the trust corpus, will revert to the United States upon the individual's death. Accordingly, the United States of America is considered the owner of the entire trust pursuant to section 677(a)(2) of the Code.

However, because the owner of the trust, the United States of America, is not subject to Federal income tax, any income earned by the trust will not be subject to income tax, whether the income is distributed to the individual, retained by the trust, or distributed on termination of the trust.

In addition, benefits received by the individual through distributions made from the income or corpus of the instant trust in payment of the individual's medical expenses are amounts received through a settlement agreement entered into in lieu of prosecution of a legal suit based upon tort or tort type rights and are, therefore, excludable from the individual's gross income under section 104(a)(2) of the Code.

HOLDING

To the extent medical expenses arising from or related to the injury are compensated for by the United States and not by the individual, the individual is not entitled to a medical expense deduction for such expenses under section 213 of the Code.

No one can guarantee that this will always be the ruling of the Internal Revenue Service. Its rulings are not set in concrete, nor has consistency been the primary criterion in its holding. However, it would require a change in a long series of rulings. The resulting political resistance would furnish a substantial obstacle to change.

If the plaintiff takes a lump sum and invests it, the interest income is subject to taxation. This can make an enormous difference in the net benefits received by the plaintiff over a period of years.

3. Factors to Be Considered in Planning for the Individual Plaintiff's Needs:

Financial management usually requires specialized skill and facilities for long-term supervision of assets.

Financial planning, while still enormously important, can usually be accomplished in a few days. It requires foresight, common sense, empathy, and a high degree of ethical responsibility. However, it is a task that is well within the scope of the experienced legal practitioner. If the lawyer feels uncertain of his competency in this area, obviously he should seek the advice of others.

It is imperative that in planning you consider the present and future needs of the entire present and prospective family.

The fact that a spouse may have rights that are represented in the settlement must not be forgotten. The possibility of divorce and the consequent divergence of economic interests of the members of the family must be considered.

The joint life expectancy of the members of the family should be considered.

Often the plaintiff may have a shortened life expectancy. This must be considered in the settlement. The insurance company should not be permitted to obtain unconsidered windfall savings by the early death of the plaintiff. Payments guaranteed for a minimum period of time or enhanced payments based on the shortened life expectancy should be considered.

The effect of inflation can be devastating and must be considered.

An example analysis of one plaintiff's position and the factors considered with the resulting solutions is as follows:

Young John Sage was the illegitimate five-year-old son of a young woman who was killed in an auto accident, leaving no estate. He was accepted into the family of his aunt, a school teacher, but not adopted. The foster family had limited income. The foster mother was pregnant at the time the trial approached. John was reasonably bright in school and it appeared possible that he might have the ability to attend college, although the income was not available other than from the lawsuit. He was entitled to approximately $330 per month in social security benefits that would not be affected by the settlement.

The following settlement was worked out. It cost the defendant $850,894, but would have a guaranteed value to John Sage of $3,177,262 and a projected payout of $7,995,929 if John Sage lives out his life expectancy.

The settlement involved the following:

1. $400,000 in cash "up-front"
2. $2,500 per month for life, increasing at five percent per annum compounded, guaranteed for thirty years
3. An additional $150,000 at age 25, and each five-year interval thereafter, for a total of nine payments of $1,350,000, guaranteed

It was contemplated that the $400,000 would take care of the attorney's fees and advanced costs, and would produce a moderate amount of cash for the estate which, in turn, could reimburse the grandmother and aunt in part for funeral expenses and medical expenses paid on behalf of the deceased mother, and produce a small amount of cash for home improvements where the surviving child, John Sage, lived.

The $25,000 per month would take care of the living expenses of John and the increase of 5 percent compounded annually would take care of inflationary factors.

It was believed that excess of income over living needs from the time of the settlement until age eighteen would provide for college needs.

The $150,000 at five-year intervals beginning at age twenty-five was intended to give John Sage successive career opportunities, and assumed that his first business or professional venture might not be successful and, in fact, might be a learning process.

The fact that part of the payouts were guaranteed was intended to provide reward, either to the faithful aunt and grandmother, should John Sage die prematurely, or if he subsequently married and had children, to enable him to exercise his option to provide for them.

A lump-sum settlement of the same cost to the insurance company would have provided only a fraction of the benefits, would have left ill-prepared guardians to manage money in a complex and difficult financial circumstance, and would have left all income made on investments subject to income tax.

4. Possible Increased Net Returns Because of Income Tax Rulings:

As discussed above, the differences in net revenue to a plaintiff can be enormous over a period of years because of the fact that income earned on investment is taxable to the plaintiff, whereas payments under a structured settlement are currently not taxable. Postulate a settlement that nets a million dollars to a plaintiff after attorney fees and costs. Assume a fifteen percent return on investment. Income taxes could consume perhaps $75,000.00 the first year. Translate that into costs compounded over twenty or thirty years and the failure to earn interest on the money lost to taxes. Consider the fact that the costs of administering the million-dollar investment are continuous, recurring every year.

The difference in yield or result to the plaintiff can amount to a full provision for the plaintiff's needs or an inadequate and incomplete settlement.

Advantages to the insurance company: Contrary to the commonly held belief of many plaintiff attorneys, the insurance company does not have any magic capacity to purchase the annuity at a cheaper price than anyone else. Even the companies that have interlocking relationships are prevented by financial and accounting realities from buying "discounted annuities" to meet their obligations.

The advantage to the insurance company can be cost and negotiating flexibility.

If the difference in the tax treatment can produce larger net possible benefits to the plantiff through a structured settlement, the insurance company can legitimately expect to share in these advantages. After all, they are making available the resources of money management and are assuming the additional administrative costs required to make periodic payments over a number of years.

Attorney's fees in structured settlements: Ordinarily, the settlement should provide a certain amount of "up-front cash." Usually in substantial settlements, the up-front cash can and should be structured to take care of attorney's fees, costs, and the immediate needs of the plaintiff. Worker compensation liens or other liens should be provided for. (Please note that Worker Compensation liens may not be enforceable on the settlement until the date that the money becomes available to the plaintiff, often over a period of years. This creates a situation that would favor negotiation between the compensation carrier and the plaintiff on terms that might be unfavorable to the plaintiff. Also, if the plaintiff negotiates a settlement with the Worker's Compensation carrier, this settlement must be provided for in the "up-front cash" in the settlement with the defendant in the third-party lawsuit.)

Some attorneys have been willing to take their fees in payments that are made over a period of years. This can create a substantial risk to the attorney and this risk should be considered in making such a decision to accept fees in the form of periodic payments. If the Internal Revenue Service rules that the whole fee is taxable in the year earned, and the actual fee is not received for a period of years, the attorney might find himself in the unlovely position of facing substantial tax obligations, without the income concomitant therewith. This risk can be substantially diminished if the defendant pays the entire periodic payment to the plaintiff, who then pays the attorney. If the attorney continues to render some service over the period of the payment of the fees, the risk of being taxed on income the attorney has not yet received becomes much less.

Some attorneys have suggested that in those states in which contingent fees are limited by schedules resulting from court order, larger fees can be received by the attorney by accepting deferred payments. We believe this to be both dangerous, unworthy, and probably unethical.

One problem that the plaintiff's attorney must face is in determining the basis on which the fee is calculated in a contingent-fee case. The one basis that seems appropriate is the present money value of the settlement received. This is often closely related or identical to the "cost of the settlement" to the insurance company, including the up-front cash and the cost of the annuity. Some insurance companies will try to avoid telling you the cost of the annuity, and will allege that to do so may endanger the tax-free aspects of the structured settlement. This is not so, and this claim is merely negotiating technique by the insurance carrier. However, the plaintiff's attorney should avoid placing the offer to settle in terms of "we will take either a lump-sum of X dollars or a specific structured settlement," as there are indications that this mistake could affect the tax-free characteristics of the settlement. In any event, this problem is one for the plaintiff to be concerned about and not the insurance company. We believe in every case, the plaintiff should demand to know the cost of the settlement.

How to determine the cost of a particular annuity: The plaintiff's attorney should retain a competent insurance specialist whose duty runs to the plaintiff, who can obtain firm bids from class triple-A rated insurance companies on the particular annuity involved. This specialist must be paid a fair consulting fee regardless of success in negotiating the structured settlement. The specialist can get firm bids from suitable insurance companies. These bids will all be subject to time limitations, as conditions in the money markets constantly change. The defendant insurance companies will also be obtaining bids on the annuity. There will nearly always be a fairly substantial fee payable to the insurance specialist placing the annuity for the insurance company. This fee is often of surprising size. Contrary to the belief of most insurance companies and plaintiff's lawyers, the representative of the defendant insurance company cannot and often does not get the lowest and best bid. In the dozen or so structured settlements negotiated by one of us in the past year, only in one instance did the defending insurance company succeed in getting a bid lower than the one obtained by the representative of the plaintiff from comparable companies. In one instance, the bid obtained by the plaintiff's representative on the annuity involved was $400,000.00 less than the amount actually paid by a major insurance group.

The costing information obtained by the plaintiff's insurance specialist is essential in determining the actual value of the settlement being negotiated, and is also critical in determining the basis for the contingency fee.

In every case, the plaintiff's attorney should seek a private letter ruling from the Internal Revenue Service or from a tax specialist on the tax aspects of the settlement in self-protection and in protection of the client.

A careful inquiry as to the solvency of the settling insurance company is essential since, for reasons described, the ultimate security of the plaintiff is related to that fact and not to the solvency of the company from which the annuity is purchased.

How to explain a structured settlement to your client: It is essential that all aspects of the settlement be explained in full to the plaintiff as often and in as many ways as necessary, to make certain the client fully understands. If there is any doubt of the plaintiff's understanding, even though he or she is enthusiastically acquiescing, good practice would be to explain the settlement to the plaintiff in the presence of the judge with a court reporter present. In the case of minors or incompetents, this would be required. If the judge is unwilling to assist in this regard when the plaintiff is not incompetent (usually the judge is glad to assist), the plaintiff's attorney may wish to have another outstanding lawyer retained at the attorney's own expense to review the settlement and advise the plaintiff of his or her opinion. In the minimum, the settlement needs to be thoroughly explained, in writing and orally, to the plaintiff and spouse.

EXPLANATORY LETTER—STRUCTURED SETTLEMENT

August 26, 19--

Mr. and Mrs. Robert Edline
Sebring,
Florida

Re: Edline v. Shaw Manufacturing Company

Dear Bob and Linda:

The purpose of this letter is to summarize numerous things which we have told you orally. As you know, we have settled your case against Shaw Manufacturing Company (the machine manufacturer) and your pending workmen's compensation claim, with your knowledge and approval. We are still negotiating with the insurance carrier for Rooter, the engineer.

We have an appointment set for 4:00 P.M. on September 1, 1981, with John Robot, the attorney for Shaw Manufacturing Company, to close that file. We already have in our possession papers that are the first draft of the proposed settlement with Shaw Manufacturing Company. We are in the process of working out the necessary closing papers and obtaining the court's approval in the workmen's compensation claim.

To summarize what we have told you as to what we have tried to do and what we think we have accomplished, we would like to set forth the following. Our goals have been to obtain sufficient money up front to take care of your immediate needs, such as a better house, and to provide an income for you both for life. We have also attempted to provide some income to each of your three children about the time they would either be finishing high school or beginning college. We have accomplished this through the use of what is called a "structured settlement." A structured settlement has a number of advantages over the receipt of a large amount of money in a lump sum.

1. In the first place, very few people are equipped to handle and invest a large amount of money. One mistake in judgment can cost them the remainder of their security for a lifetime.
2. There are distinct tax advantages in a structured settlement, if it is worked out correctly. If we receive a lump-sum settlement and invest it, or you invest it, the interest income on the lump-sum settlement is taxable, frequently at very high rates. A structured settlement can be arranged so that the income is not taxable.
3. The value of the benefits that we are able to obtain through a structured settlement is often much larger than we can obtain in a lump-sum settlement. For example, our experts have indicated that the actual cost to the insurance company for Shaw Manufacturing Company will be in the neighborhood of $1,936,000. However, if each of you lives out your life expectancy as listed in the standard ordinary mortality tables, the payments that you would jointly receive would, according to our best estimates, total $6,550,999 or over six (6) million dollars. If after execution of the settlement papers with Shaw Manufacturing Company both of you were simultaneously killed, we believe that nevertheless the value of the guaranteed payments and upfront cash would be over three (3) million dollars.

You will both recall that you were offered two separate annuity options—one of them called for a separate annuity to Linda in the amount of $1,600.00 a month and a separate annuity to Bob of $6,733.33 a month. You were also offered a joint annuity based on a life expectancy of both of you and combining the annuity interest of each of you separately in the combined monthly amount of $8,333.33 or $100,000 per year guaranteed for sixteen (16) years and payable over the lives of either or both of you. Both of you have indicated that you prefer the joint annuity, since that amount will be payable for both your lives even if one of you dies first.

Linda's portion of the joint annuity amounts to about 19.2 percent of the annuity, based on the fact that a separate annuity to her would have been $1,600.00 per month.

You should also recognize that the $8,000.00 payment every four years for 44 years was intended to cover the cost of additional prostheses for Bob and that Linda has no financial interest in this, although the payments are joint payments and therefore payable to Linda if Bob dies first. The cash payment that will be made to you as part of the settlement was also intended to be apportioned between you two with 19.2 percent of it being attributed to Linda's interest and the remaining portion to Bob's. Of course, the $75,000 workmen's compensation payment is for Bob's claim only, since a spouse has no claim under the workmen's compensation law.

It was not our intention in structuring this settlement that the payments to be made to your children would in any way represent anything other than a monetary interest running to them.

Please feel free to ask any questions that you care to ask. For our own protection, if you understand and agree with the terms of this settlement, please sign below at the indicated place and we will move forward with completing the settlement as rapidly as we can.

We admire and respect both of you and hope that you are pleased with this result of our efforts.

Yours very truly,

JOHN DAVIS

We understand and agree with the terms of the settlement as outlined above.

____

____

Date: ________________________

7

Eleventh-Hour Trial Preparation

The culmination of months of preparation occurs shortly before trial. Witnesses have long since been located and deposed, evidence secured and safeguarded, legal positions taken and solidified. No matter how complete the early preparation, however, in the last days and hours before trial, the pace inevitably quickens. All of the accumulated effort of months must be brought together and organized. Decisions as to tactics, often deferred in the early stages of the case, must be made. Midnight approaches—and final preparation must be completed.

7.1 WHY CONTACT WITNESSES EARLY?

All of the witnesses should be contacted as soon as the trial date is scheduled, and notified that they will probably be needed at the trial. This procedure is particularly important with respect to doctors, since it often eliminates the necessity of their rescheduling operations. Subpoenas should be issued at about the same time as the witnesses are contacted. All witnesses should be subpoenaed, including friendly ones. The court will usually declare a mistrial or grant a continuance if a witness who has been subpoenaed fails to appear, but will rarely do so if the witness has not been subpoenaed.

7.2 SELECTING THE WITNESSES TO BE SUBPOENAED

Subpoenas should be issued to expert witnesses, witnesses who have knowledge of the liability factors in the case, and witnesses who have knowledge of the effect of the accident on various aspects of the plaintiff's life. Some of these last would include witnesses who have observed evidence of physical pain and suffering on the part of the plaintiff, e.g. neighbors, relatives, and friends who have observed the altered life of the plaintiff; fellow employees or superiors on the job who can testify as to the plaintiff's diminished capacity to properly carry out work assignments; nurses who may have attended the plaintiff in the hospital; and members of the family or others who can testify as to the effect of the accident upon the plaintiff's personality.

7.3 PICKING YOUR ASSOCIATE'S BRAIN

Sometime prior to trial, after the attorney has freshly reviewed the case and has every detail and aspect of it in mind, he or she should sit down, preferably with someone else whose judgment is respected, and consider every aspect of the trial and the manner in which the case will be presented. If the case is one that will hinge on the acceptance or rejection of a given witness's testimony, attention must be carefully focused on this witness's testimony and how it should be approached on cross-examination or direct examination. Has the witness said anything in any depositions or statements that could be misinterpreted and shake the value of the testimony? Are there any inconsistencies between the witness's testimony and that of other witnesses as to the physical circumstances surrounding the accident? Does the witness have any interest in the case which might affect his or her willingness or ability to tell the truth?

7.4 ALWAYS DEVELOP A CASE THEME

One of the important factors to be decided in the pretrial planning is what the theme of the particular case should be. Assume, for the sake of an example, that a small boy has fallen into a pit in the back of a house, in a construction area partially filled with terrazzo mud and slake lime, and has suffered severe damage to his eyes. Assume that the attorney knows that the testimony of the defendant's witnesses will be that this is the customary procedure in the construction industry for disposing of terrazzo mud and slake lime. Certainly one of the themes that should be developed in the course of the trial is that the entire industry is negligent, and that by the rendering of its verdict the jury will give emphasis to the need for additional safety devices and safety planning on the part of this industry. Assume, in the same case, that the child's father is a man of limited education and limited intelligence. Will the jury be reluctant to render a substantial verdict if they feel that the father will be incapable of handling the money? Under these circumstances it should be demonstrated to the jury that the court or other competent individuals will place any funds received for the child in trust, to be dealt with in a way appropriate to the needs of the child.

7.5 FACE THE UNFAVORABLE ISSUE SQUARELY

Assume that the plaintiff is an individual of extremely unsavory character, perhaps drunk at the time of the accident, for whom the jury is likely to feel little empathy. Would not the attorney be wise to face this issue squarely, and from the beginning of the case openly admit the questionable morals of the client, but at the same time also stress the fact that, notwithstanding this, in the particular instance the client was blameless and received genuine injuries for which he deserves compensation?

Is the client someone who has the tendency to complain more than is warranted by the injury, and are his complaints consistent with those which would be expected from this kind of injury? Can the client's complaints be legitimately explained by a theory of traumatic neurosis? If so, can this explanation be persuasively presented to the jury in such a way that the client will not be penalized for the excessive complaints?

7.6 IMPORTANCE OF TIMING

In the course of planning the trial, preliminary consideration should be given to the timing of the witnesses' appearance on the stand. A basic psychological principle is involved in the selection of the first and last witness. Two of the rules of learning, as established by scientific experiment, are the rules of "primacy" and "recency." These principles state that the first material and the last material presented in a sequence are more likely to be remembered and to influence the minds of the listener than the material in between.

In the courtroom situation, this, of course, does not necessarily mean that the first witness presented need be the strongest witness, since most courts permit an opening statement and ordinarily the attorney will have an opportunity to state his or her case as forcefully as possible. On the other hand, the first witness should in all probability be a witness who can create interest and can start to tell, to some extent, the central theme of the case and the "whole story."

The last witness, of course, should be as strong a witness as possible and one who can restate the theme of the case. Frequently the plaintiff, in a plaintiff case, makes a good last witness, since he or she has a chance to restate the theme of the case. Moreover, the plaintiff is sufficiently accustomed to the conduct of the courtroom so that he or she is no longer nervous.

7.7 SHOULD YOU CALL THE ADVERSE PARTY EARLY?

On occasion the plaintiff may wish to call an adverse party under the rule, and interrogate him or her as one of the first witnesses, provided that the deposition of this party has been taken and the plaintiff is certain that the story to be told is either incredible or one of such a nature that it should be placed in the record in order to have it contradicted or impeached by the testimony of subsequent witnesses.

7.8 THE PRETRIAL GROUP WITNESS CONFERENCE—AN IMPORTANT TOOL

7.8.1 How to Do It—What to Say

An immediate pretrial witness conference should be scheduled with all witnesses except expert witnesses, who must be interviewed individually and separately. This conference is essential to adequate preparation for the trial. Often more is accomplished in a few minutes during such a conference than is accomplished in many hours of prior preparation.

Contacting the Witnesses

Once the subpoenas have been issued, each witness should be contacted and told something along the following lines:

"Ms. Jones, as you know, a court order called a 'subpoena' has been served on you by the sheriff, requiring that you appear to testify as a witness on behalf of our client, Mary Smith, on January 19th. There are, of course, a number of other witnesses who have been subpoenaed, and obviously not all of them can testify at the same time. In order to schedule the appearance of witnesses and to save you time, we are scheduling a witness conference on Sunday night at 7:00 o'clock in our office. At that time, also, we will discuss with you any out-of-pocket expenses that you may incur while attending the trial, and methods of reimbursement for these expenses. We will also tell you what questions we expect the other side to ask of you in cross-examination, and will discuss with you any questions that you feel we should ask you. It has been our experience that such a witness conference saves the witnesses many hours and enables them to do a much more creditable job in presenting their testimony."

Approached in this manner, very few witnesses will refuse to attend. In the first place, it is greatly to their advantage to be present because by spending half an hour or so at such a witness conference they can save themselves, under some circumstances, days of time. In addition, many witnesses are appearing for the first time in court and are concerned about how to act and what will happen during the course of the trial. The only persons who should be exempted from attending such a witness conference are those who are professional witnesses, such as doctors, engineers, law enforcement officers, etc. Even hostile witnesses should be invited to be present.

7.8.2 Setting the Stage

Basic Orientation of Witnesses

The group conference should be held in some suitable place, preferably in the library or conference room, around a conference table. Coffee or tea may be offered prior to the beginning of the conference. When all of the witnesses have arrived, the attorney responsible for conducting the conference should begin as follows:

"Ladies and gentlemen, let me first thank you for coming to this witness conference tonight, since I realize that it involved some sacrifice on your part. In the long run, however, we believe that attendance at the conference will save you many hours, and in all probability a great deal of inconvenience. Before we adjourn the meeting we will wish to have the telephone number of each of you, and a method of contacting you. We will wish to know approximately how long it will take to reach the courthouse after you are telephoned, in order that we may contact you in ample time for you to be present to give your testimony. This will eliminate the necessity for all of you sitting around from the time the trial begins, on Monday morning at 9:00 o'clock, until you are called as witnesses, perhaps two or three days later. We will also wish to know from you the approximate time that is the least inconvenient for you to appear, in order that we may cooperate with you by attempting to schedule you at that time. Before we obtain this information, however, we would like to discuss with you some of the aspects of testifying in general, since we believe that many of you are appearing for the first time as witnesses. Many times witnesses have the wrong concept of what it is like to appear at a trial. They have perhaps seen "Perry Mason" on TV, and believe that a trial is something like this, when in fact it bears very little similarity to that portrayed on TV.

"The court will ordinarily set several cases for trial on Monday morning and expects the lawyers and witnesses to be ready to start at 9:00

if necessary. In this particular instance, however, we are the second case set for trial, and although we must be ready to go on trial Monday, it is entirely possible that we will not actually begin our case until a previous case is finished. We have talked to both of the lawyers involved in the case ahead of us and believe that the case they are trying will take them approximately two days. Thus, although your subpoena reads Monday morning, it is very probable that we will not actually begin our case until Wednesday morning. Assuming that we do begin the case on Wednesday morning at 9:00, the first thirty minutes to two or three hours will in all probability be taken up with the selection of the jury. After the jury is selected, each of the lawyers for their respective clients is permitted to make a brief opening statement. By this time it is usually somewhere between 10:30 and noon. Thus, ordinarily we do not really start to put any witnesses on the stand until the afternoon. You can expect that the other side will ask the court to 'invoke the rule,' which means that the witnesses, except for the parties who are actually involved in the case, will not be permitted to sit in the courtroom and listen to the other witnesses testify. We will call each of you in sequence, as needed, and after you have testified we will ask the court to excuse you. Under most circumstances the court will grant this motion and will permit you to return to your jobs or homes, as the case may be, in order to minimize the inconvenience to you."

Instructions Re Testifying: Telling the Truth

"I would like to talk about the general process of testifying. The first and most important thing for you to remember in the trial of a lawsuit is to tell the truth about everything. If you tell the truth about everything it eliminates many of the hazards of cross-examination. Even if you should make some minor mistake in testifying, if you are attempting to tell the truth, and your testimony basically reflects that fact, jurors in general recognize this. None of us have absolutely perfect memories, and it would be very unusual for a person to be completely accurate in his or her estimates as to time and distances, or in recollection of the exact sequence of events. We will discuss some of these factors with you a little later, but you should not be concerned about the fact that a year or more has passed since the accident and that there may be some phases of the accident that are no longer crystal clear to you, as though the accident were now happening in front of your eyes.

"This matter of telling the truth about everything involves, of course, basic things such as whom you have talked to about the case. One of the oldest tricks of lawyers is to ask witnesses if they have talked to anybody about the case. Because witnesses will sometimes feel that something is wrong about having talked to an attorney or an investigator about it, they will say no, they have not talked to anyone about the case. This is, of course, a mistake, since it deviates from the basic principle of telling the truth about everything. It is also a rather foolish position to be caught in, since any attorney who is worth anything at all is not going to put a witness on the stand until he has some idea of what that witness's testimony will be. Consequently, if you are asked this question you should in this, as in everything, tell the truth and name any persons whom you have talked to about the case. If you have talked to your wife, or husband, or neighbors, or friends, or to our investigators, or to me, of course you should state this. If you are asked what we told you to say after we talked to you, you can tell them that we told you to tell the truth about everything which is virtually the first thing we have told you in this witness conference tonight."

Compensating the Witness for Expenses

"The same applies to any questions that may be asked of you as to whether you are being compensated for your lost time or for your out-of-pocket expenses in coming to the trial. The law states that we are legally entitled to reimburse you for your out-of-pocket expenses, and some lawyers even believe that they have a duty to do so. Consequently, it is not only not improper, but indeed quite proper for us to reimburse you, for your out-of-pocket expenses, out of any recovery that we expect for our client, Ms. Smith. Some of you may not wish to accept this compensation, since it is coming out of the recovery of Ms. Smith, but that is of course a decision for your to make." (Note that it is perhaps of some value to let the prospective witnesses know that this money is coming out of their friend's pocket rather than out of the attorney's. Neighbors and friends of the client are frequently unwilling to accept reimbursement under these circumstances, and thus some money is saved the client.)

Inconsistent Versions

"Each of you, in telling the truth, should not be concerned about the fact that your testimony may be different from that of the other witnesses who are here tonight. I am sure that all of you have heard the old story that if there are ten witnesses on a corner, each of whom has observed an accident, each of them will have a slightly different version of what happened. In some instances the versions will differ so greatly that it is difficult to tell whether the witnesses are actually describing the same accident. Merely because your story may be different from that of the other witnesses here, you should not change it, but should give a truthful account of what you saw, and testify to those things of which you are sure. Of course if you did not observe anything, or merely have an impression about something, but are not actually certain, you should state this."

The Group Conference and the Hostile Witness

At this point the attorney has fulfilled most of the intended purpose of the conference as far as the hostile witnesses are concerned. There are sound psychological reasons, however, for having them present.

A few years ago an article in *Scientific American* recounted the results of an experiment which had been performed by certain clinical psychologists. The initial purpose of the experiment was to determine whether one racial group, or certain racial groups, might have a greater tendency to social conformity than other racial groups. The experiment was performed as follows:

Three booths were set up; they looked like telephone booths except that the front doors to the booths were opaque. In two of the booths were tape recorders on which prerecorded statements were contained and controlled in such a way that by pushing the switch the experimenter could cause each of the booths in turn to play the next material on the tape. The person to be tested would be brought into booth number three. Some coats would be hanging in the booth, and the testee would be informed that there were two others persons being tested with him and that they were already in the booth. After being instructed to enter the booth and close the door, he would then be told that three musical notes were to be sounded, one of which was lower than the other two, and one of which was higher. He was told to indicate which of the three notes was the highest, which was the lowest, and which was in the middle. After sounding the notes, the tape recorder in booth number one would erroneously state which of the three notes was higher. Then the tape recorder in booth number two would state which of the three notes was the highest, and the same error would be made. The person being tested in booth number three would then be asked to determine which of the three notes was the highest, and in an astonishingly high percentage of cases the opinion conformed to the opinion previously stated on the two tape recorders. Even with those individuals who stated opinions different from the first two, conformity could be elicited if one of the tape recorders was made to say something like "Well, what's wrong with his ears?" or "Who does he think he is?" On retesting after such a statement, a significant percentage of testees tended to alter their opinions to conform with that of the group.

If this psychological tendency to conform to a group is considered with reference to the pretrial witness conference, it is apparent that the hostile witness who is present with perhaps fifteen or twenty other persons will be somewhat curious as to exactly how his testimony differs from theirs. (As a matter of fact, all of the witnesses present may be testifying as to the effects of the accident on the plaintiff rather than as to how the accident occurred, but this, of course, is not known to the hostile witness.)

Excusing the Hostile Witness

At this point in the conference the attorney conducting the case should call the hostile witness to one side, and say, "Mr. Jones, I know, of course, from what my investigator told us, (or "from our previous conversations") that it was somewhat inconvenient for you to come tonight, and we are therefore going to let you go at this time. We appreciate your coming, and if you will give me your telephone number and address, should it be necessary for you to testify, we will call you in adequate time to have you present." The hostile witness is then permitted to leave. (Since hostile witnesses are nearly always the only persons who object to coming to such a witness conference, that they have experienced some difficulty in being present is almost invariably true.)

This witness has been told to tell the truth and not to deviate from his testimony even though it may differ from that of other witnesses, but at the same time he has left a roomful of ten to twenty persons whose testimony, insofar as he knows, differs from his to some extent. While the witness will still tell the truth under virtually all circumstances, at the same time he approaches the whole problem of testifying with much less self-assurance and is more vulnerable to effective cross-examination than if he had simply been placed directly on the stand. Under some circumstances, when the witness is not completely hostile and some portions of his testimony are useful to the attorney, after the hostile witness is taken aside it may be advisable to discuss parts of his statement with him, pointing out that these are the portions of the testimony which the attorney is anxious to use, and asking him if his story still conforms to the facts described in these particular parts of his statement or deposition. This, of course, serves the function of making certain that he has not deviated from previously given statements or from the deposition. These same statements can be elicited in cross-examination, if necessary. After the hostile witnesses have been excused, the attorney should continue as follows:

7.8.3 Enhancing the Witness's Credibility

"I would like, first, to discuss with you the general theory of our case and what we expect to prove. Not all of you know everything about all of the phases of the case, and naturally we wish you to talk only about that phase of the case about which you have personal knowledge. Before we talk about this, however, let's talk about some general principles of testifying. In addition to telling the truth about everything, it is important that you tell the truth in a way that is acceptable to a court jury. The impression that we would like to get across to the jury is that of dignified sincerity. If a question is asked of you, do not attempt to be evasive about it, but answer it as well as you can. However, you should testify only to facts, and should avoid expressions of any opinions, or the repetition of any hearsay testimony. For example, assume that you are asked whether you observed the plaintiff after the accident. If you were to state, 'Yes, I observed the plaintiff after the accident,' you would be testifying only to a fact. Assume the next question to be 'Would you tell us what you observed about her?' and that your reply is 'I observed her when she was in the hospital, and every time she started to move she would have an expression or grimace of pain on her face. It was necessary for me or for others of her friends to assist her in moving about in the bed. I also noticed that the nurse came in several times to give her pain pills while I was visiting with her, and I myself assisted her on several occasions in taking such pills.' Such testimony, of course, is not hearsay, but provides the basis of your observation, which led you to draw the conclusion that the plaintiff was in pain. You may state the basis of your observation, for the jury to draw their conclusions, but you may not state your conclusion. The same is true of statements such as 'I saw the plaintiff at work, but she just was not able to do what she did before the accident.' This, too, constitutes an opinion as to what she could or could not do. You may, however, state, if true, 'Before the accident I noticed that she was able to stoop and bend and was one of the most active persons in the shop. Following the accident, if she had to pick up anything, it was necessary for her to receive assistance. I myself helped her move a chair about. I noticed, too, that she took long periods of rest, whereas before the accident she was virtually tireless and worked as hard as anybody in the shop. I noticed changes in her personality also. Whereas before the accident she was happy-go-lucky, gay hearted, and concerned about people around her, after the accident she was quiet, withdrawn, and had no desire to participate in any of the fun that went on around the shop.' This testimony, of course, permits the jury to draw a conclusion from the same facts on which you based your opinion that she was in pain or discomfort, or was limited in her activities."

Listening Carefully to Questions

"In addition to the kind of impression that you would like to make while testifying, you should be aware of one or two other things. You should listen carefully to the questions put to you, and under no circumstances answer a question you have not completely heard or do not fully understand. If you have not heard a question or do not understand it, all that is necessary is to ask the lawyer to repeat it, or to tell the court that you do not understand the question. If you do understand a question, however, you should answer it fully and completely, but answer only the questions that you are asked, without volunteering information irrelevant to the questions that have been put to you."

Keeping Your Temper

"You should be very careful that you do not lose your temper in the course of the trial, and you should be courteous to opposing counsel and certainly to the judge. You may rest assured that opposing counsel is a good lawyer, and a good lawyer will virtually never lose his or her temper in a courtroom. If a lawyer does on occasion pretend to lose his or her temper in order to evoke anger on your part, you may be assured that it is a deliberate policy and that your testimony has been harmful. A good lawyer knows that you catch more flies with sugar than you do with vinegar, and in all probability will be extremely kind to you. If the lawyer does pretend to be angry, recognize that this is a deliberate effort and that he or she is aware that a person cannot be angry and think at the same time."

Courtesy to Court Officers

"Thus I would urge you to kill the lawyer with kindness regardless of how you are treated, and to say 'Yes, sir,' 'Yes, ma'am' and 'No, sir,' 'No, ma'am' according to the question. Even though you may not feel that a lawyer personally merits this address, nevertheless in the courtroom he or she stands as an officer of the court. Just as in saluting army personnel who we might feel do not merit the salute, we are in fact saluting the uniform, so should we similarly respect the position held by an officer of the court. This is part of the courtroom protocol which should be followed by you. In the event that the judge addresses any remarks to you and you have occasion to reply you should refer to the judge as 'Your Honor,' saying 'Yes, Your Honor' and 'No, Your Honor.'"

Speaking Up

"Try not to act nervous as you testify. One of the important things to remember is that you must talk loudly enough for the jury to hear you. Many of the courtrooms in which we try cases have good acoustics, but others have air conditioning noises or other background noises which prevent the jury from hearing everything that is said. During the course of the examination I will in all probability stand by the juror farthest away. If you will talk loudly enough for me to be able to hear your answers, in all probability the jurors will be able to hear them. It may be necessary, however, to ask you to talk more loudly."

Looking at the Jury

"Please look at the jurors as you testify, since they are really the only people in the courtroom who matter very much in the course of the trial. The judge is there, of course, to see to it that the rules of procedure are followed, but except for instructing the jury and making certain that the lawyers follow the ordinary rules of practice, the judge's function in the actual decision making is really very little. Thus it is important to look at the jurors, since this helps to keep their attention and is an effective part of the process of persuasion. Talk to the jurors in a normal, relaxed way, as though you were talking to any of your neighbors or friends. Most of them are really the kind of people that you would ordinarily associate with anyway in your daily lives had you had the opportunity to meet them."

Personal Appearance

"I think it probably unnecessary to tell you that you should not chew gum and that you should, of course, wear fairly good clothes. You should wear the same kind of clothes that you would wear if you were going to church, since this is a somewhat formal occasion. There is an exception to this, of course, and that is if any of you are working at the time and, for example, wearing a uniform or other clothing appropriate to your job. In this case, you would simply come as you are, since jurors are basically practical people and will understand that you did not have the time to go home and change from your uniform into the clothes that you would normally wear to come to court."

The witnesses' manner of dress should be carefully noted at this time, in an attempt to determine the probable effect of their appearance on the jury. If a witness is dressed in a manner that would offend the jurors, or arouse their anger rather than their confidence, take that person aside after the witness conference is over and thoroughly explain the need for correcting his or her appearance.

7.8.4 Explaining Theory of Case

Once the witnesses have been thoroughly instructed as to the general procedure of testifying, the case should then be discussed in order to give the witnesses a general idea of the theory of the case. For example, the attorney might state, "Now this is of course a case in which our client, Ray Smith, had stopped at a stoplight for several seconds, when the defendant's automobile approached from the rear and banged into the back of the plaintiff's automobile. This caused the plaintiff's neck to be jerked to the rear and flung forward. We will offer medical testimony which will show that this caused a stretching and tearing of the ligaments and nerves and muscles in his neck, resulting in a tremendous amount of pain and discomfort. This is probably the most common type of automobile accident which occurs today, and we know from experience that when a person has been through as much as Smith has been through, in this case, there is usually scar tissue left in the neck to replace the soft tissue originally injured. This scar tissue will sometimes press on nerve roots and other portions of the nervous system and under some circumstances will cause permanent discomfort. Some of the things we expect to prove are how the accident originally happened and the immediate effects of the accident on the plaintiff, such as the fact that he was unconscious for a few minutes before he was removed to the hospital and was in severe pain and discomfort in the hospital. We hope to prove through some of you that he was able to move his neck only in a guarded fashion, that he was confined to bed, where he was put into traction by various doctors, and that for a considerable period of time it was necessary for him to take medication to alleviate the pain he was suffering from as a result of his injuries. We expect to show that after he returned home he remained confined to his bed for approximately three weeks and that he gradually began to get around the house and increase his activities. We will show that even after he returned to work, although he pushed himself as far as he could in an effort to carry out his normal activities, he simply was not able to perform his job the same as he did before the accident. We expect to prove through his job supervisor that he lost a promotion because of the fact that he was unable to carry out his work. We will show through his wife and neighbors and friends that because of the physical pain and discomfort he has had he has been increasingly irritable, harder to get along with, and has evidenced what amounts almost to a change of personality. We expect to show that he has dropped out of his regular golf foursome, dropped out of bowling, and as a matter of fact has done very little except attempt to work and to drive his car to and from work. We will show that before the accident he took pride in his yard and used to do most of his yard work, but that now his wife mows the lawn, and the general appearance of his house indicates that it has fallen into a state of considerable disrepair."

7.9 HOW TO DETERMINE WHICH WITNESSES TO CALL

At this time it is usually wise to begin questioning the witnesses as to name, address, telephone number, and the amount of time it will take them to get to the courthouse. It is then advisable to go into particular aspects of their testimony, once again making certain that statements of opinion, hearsay testimony, etc., are eliminated. This also affords an opportunity to listen to the witnesses talk, and to decide which of them are likely to make satisfactory witnesses. In the beginning, when the witness conference is set up, it is a good idea to have more witnesses present than the attorney actually intends to use, since some of them will undoubtedly prove to be unsatisfactory. In this manner witnesses may be selected who are best able to express their opinions articulately to a jury.

7.10 SCHEDULING THE ARRIVAL OF WITNESSES

Any special problems of the witnesses relative to scheduling or absence from work can be considered and dealt with at this time. If the witness is in need of transportation, this, of course, can be arranged at the time of the conference. Often it is wise to arrange a tentative time for the witness to appear, but it should be determined how long it will take the witness to come after being telephoned. Then, with the assistance of an investigator or an associate at the trial, while one witness is on the stand, one or two witnesses may be kept waiting, and others on the way. In this manner the total loss of time to the participants of the trial is kept to an absolute minimum. It is generally wise to arrange for the plaintiff and perhaps one or two other witnesses to be present at the outset of the trial. At all times two or three witnesses should be present in order that the attorney may avoid the embarrassing dilemma of being asked by the court to put his or her next witness on the stand and not having one present.

Learning from the Witness

After each witness has been interrogated, and necessary information secured, the witnesses should be given a chance to ask any questions and to contribute any additional ideas they may have. These conferences in general help the witnesses to understand what they are doing, and help to remove some of the awesome mysteries associated with going to court.

7.11 PREPARATION OF PRETRIAL WITNESS STATEMENTS

The courts of many states, and many of the Federal Courts, require pretrial conferences. Although many lawyers who specialize in trial practice have come to doubt the complete utility of pretrial conferences, feeling that the original hopes of the pretrial conferences have not been realized, nevertheless these conferences should be expected and prepared for in most jurisdictions. The local rules of court in most areas do not require a written pretrial statement; however many trial specialists think that this is a useful adjunct in a case in that it (1) assists the court in rapidly grasping the issues which are involved in the case, and (2) compels the attorney to organize material for presentation at the pretrial conference in such a way as to minimize the possibility of forgetting some essential item of preparation. A sample pretrial statement utilized by many law firms is set out. Once the use of such a form has become customary, an experienced secretary can perform most of the work in preparing such a pretrial statement, requiring only correction and supervision by the attorney.

A SAMPLE PRETRIAL STATEMENT

IN THE CIRCUIT COURT OF THE FIFTEENTH JUDICIAL CIRCUIT OF FLORIDA, IN AND FOR PALM BEACH COUNTY. AT LAW.
CASE NO.

MARY JOHNSON and EMANUEL JOHNSON, her husband,
Plaintiffs,
vs. PRETRIAL STATEMENT
WE HAUL THEM RAILWAY COMPANY, a Florida corporation,
Defendant.

1. Designation of Pleadings on Which Case Goes to Trial:

Complaint: **Count I:** For personal injuries sustained by the Plaintiff, Mary Johnson, who was riding as a passenger in an automobile owned and operated by John Jones, when the said vehicle was struck by the defendant's train that was backing across State Road 72, approximately .2 of a mile south of Air Harbor, Florida.

Count II: Emanuel Johnson, husband of the Plaintiff, claims damages for medical treatment of his wife's injuries and loss of consortium.

Answer: Defendant admits that he owns and operates the We Haul Them Railway Company, but denies all other allegations of the Complaint, and alleges that Plaintiffs were guilty of contributory negligence.

2. ISSUES TO BE TRIED:

(a) Negligence of the Defendant

(b) Contributory negligence of Plaintiffs
(c) Plaintiff's damages

3. EXHIBITS AND DOCUMENTS:

(a) Engineering drawing of railroad right of way
(b) Two aerial photographs of the scene of accident
(c) 26 black and white 8″ × 10″ photos of scene and vehicles
(d) 4—3″ × 4″ black and white photos of Plaintiffs
(e) Medical bills:

Palm Beach Limb & Brace, Inc.	$ 6.00
Palm Beach Limb & Brace, Inc.	$ 7.00
Palm Beach Limb & Brace, Inc.	$ 10.00
St. Mary's Hospital	$245.00
Dr. James F. Young	$ 90.00
Air Harbor Memorial Hospital	$379.00
Jones Pharmacy	$400.00

4. WITNESSES

Mary Johnson
512 S. Tree Road
Air Harbor, Florida

Mary Jones
729 Main Street
Air Harbor, Florida

Emanuel Johnson
512 S. Tree Road
Air Harbor, Florida

L. A. Read
Kissimmee Road
Norfolk, Virginia

5. RESERVATIONS OF RIGHTS:

(a) Mortality tables
(b) Blackboard and charts
(c) Skeletal devices
(d) Current medical bills
(e) Hospital records
(f) X-rays
(g) Names of additional witnesses

SMITH, JOHNS & HARRY
512 Public Street
Air Harbor, Florida

____

____

Attorneys for Plaintiffs

Preparation of Jury Instructions

In many states the court expects counsel to prepare suggested jury instructions. Instructions should be inclusive, covering every possible desirable charge. It should be understood that these instructions may be eliminated or not even requested by the party at the time of the conference on jury instructions. It is convenient to include a place, at the bottom of each suggested instruction, where it may be quickly recorded whether the charge was given, denied, given and modified, or otherwise ruled upon by the judge. Most courts will require copies to be furnished to opposing counsel as well as to the court; hence the instructions should be prepared in sufficient quantity to comply with this requirement.

7.12 MOTIONS IN LIMINE—WHY AND HOW TO USE THEM

One of the most effective weapons in the defendant's arsenal is prejudice. You can look in any volume of the *Defense Law Journal,* under "Trial Tactics," where defense attorneys will tell you how they win their cases, and you will find that a majority of these cases are won on prejudice; that is, the defendant's attorney catches the plaintiff not telling the truth on some minor matter, or introduces evidence not material to the issues but so prejudicial to the plaintiff as to affect the jury's verdict.

The Double Standard. We may not like it, but there is a double standard in most of the courtrooms today. When a plaintiff and his lawyer come into court, they are suspect. Whether this is the result of the continual propaganda campaign which is being conducted by the insurance companies, or because the burden of proving the case is upon the plaintiff, or both, is academic. Regardless of the reason, the double standard is there, and the plaintiff's attorney must face it and cope with it.

Importance of Eliminating Prejudicial Evidence. Because the plaintiff carries the burden of proof, prejudicial evidence brought in against the plaintiff will be far more harmful that any brought in against the defendant. Hence, it behooves the plaintiff's attorney to keep the case as free from prejudicial evidence as possible.

The Motion

Purpose of Motion in Limine. One of the best ways to accomplish this is through a motion *in limine* [lim-ih-nee; i.e., at the very beginning; preliminarily.] For those who are not familiar with this, it is a motion heard in advance of jury selection which asks the court to instruct the defendant, his counsel, and witnesses not to mention certain facts *unless and until permission of the court is first obtained outside the presence and hearing of the jury.* An example of such a motion follows.

SAMPLE MOTION IN LIMINE

COMES NOW, plaintiff in the above entitled and numbered cause, and before trial and the selection of the jury, moves the Court in limine to instruct the defendant and all his counsel as set forth below on the following grounds:

1. Since it is immaterial to this suit whether or not:
   (a) Plaintiff had a driver's license on the occasion in question;
   (b) Plaintiff was issued a ticket as a result of the collision in question;
   (c) Plaintiff has ever been convicted of the offense of driving while intoxicated;
   (d) Defendant was not issued a ticket as a result of the collision in question;

   the defendant is precluded from using any pleading, testimony, remarks, questions, or arguments which might inform the jury of such facts.

2. Were any of the above facts made known to the jury, it would be highly improper and prejudicial to plaintiff, even though the Court were to sustain an objection and instruct the jury not to consider such facts for any purpose. This motion should also be granted because there is no other way the problem can be properly handled at the trial of this cause, and in all probability any such attempt would result in a mistrial.

   WHEREFORE, plaintiff respectfully requests the Court to instruct the defendant and all counsel not to mention, refer to, interrogate concerning, or attempt to convey to the jury in any manner, either directly or indirectly, any of the above-mentioned facts, without first obtaining permission of the Court outside the presence and hearing of the jury; and to further instruct the defendant and all counsel not to make any reference to the fact that this motion has been filed and granted; and to warn and caution each and every one of their witnesses to strictly follow these same instructions.

Need for Motions in Limine

Recognized by Courts. "An examination of the case digests shows that in the last twenty years there has been a decided increase in the percentage of jury cases wherein complaint has been made of prejudice suffered by reason of the misconduct of counsel in the examination of witnesses. Much of this misconduct has consisted of knowingly asking improper questions. In many cases the attorney complained of has persistently pursued a wholly unjustified and prejudicial course of interrogation, notwithstanding objections made and sustained, clearly calling to his attention, if such a thing could be deemed necessary, that the questions asked were without any plausible legal foundation . . ." 109 ALR at 1089.

This was written in 1937. Since then the need for motions *in limine* has steadily increased.

Condra Funeral Home v. Rollin (1958) 158 Tex 478,314 SW2d 277.

Besides the clear-cut situations referred to in the above quote, many times there is a legitmate difference of opinion between "logical relevancy" and "legal relevancy," which cannot be resolved without the court's ruling.

If prejudicial matters are brought before the jury, no amount of objection or instruction can remove the harmful effect, and the plaintiff is powerless unless he or she wants to forego the chance of a trial and ask for a mistrial. Once the questions are asked, the harm is done. Under the harmless error rule, many of these matters would probably not be reversible error even though they have a subtle and devastating effect upon the plaintiff's case. Perhaps the greatest single advantage of a motion *in limine* is the avoidance of objecting in the jury's presence to evidence which is "logically relevant." Jurors cannot be expected to understand why they should not be allowed to consider *all* evidence which is related to the case, and will usually resent the fact that an objection kept them from hearing it.

Another advantage of these motions is that they allow the trial judge an opportunity to study the question and the authorities involved. If a brief of these is presented in advance of trial, so that the court has time to study it, the court will be more inclined to grant the motion.

Arguments for Use of Motion in Limine. One of the best arguments for use of a motion *in limine* is that the granting of the motion as worded above cannot be reversible error.

Hartford Accident & Indemnity Co. v. McCardell, (Tex 1963) 369 SW2d 331, 6 Sup Ct, J 549; *Aetna Casualty and Surety Company v. Finney* (Tex Civ App, n.r.e., 1961) 346 SW2d 917; *Alamo Express, Inc. v. Wafer* (Tex Civ App, 1960) 333 SW2d 651.

It is only when the evidence is offered out of the presence of the jury, and then excluded, that possible reversible error occurs. The appeal is taken on the basis of the rejection of the evidence tendered, not the granting of the motion. This rule is no different from the rule concerning other evidence questions; that is, in order for a complaint to be made upon appeal, the excluded evidence must be in the record so that the appellate court will know what it was and will be in a position to determine the effect of its exclusion.

Power of Trial Court. The power of the trial court to grant such a motion is inherent in its right to admit or exclude evidence and will probably not be specifically mentioned in the procedural rules. The *in limine* practice is rapidly growing in Texas [and across the nation].

Bridges v. City of Richardson (1962) 163 Tex 292, 354 SW2d 366; Kronzer, "Advantages to Be Gained by Trial Motions for the Plaintiff", 6 *So Tex L J* 179 (1962).

The practice has been at least suggested elsewhere.

Crawford v. Hite (1940) 176 Va 69, 10 SE2d 561.

7.12.1 Examples of Use

Collateral Source Rule Enforcement

The type of evidence that can be excluded by a motion *in limine* is determined by the particular facts of each case and by counsel's ingenuity. Some of the more common and obvious types of evidence fall within the "collateral source rule."

"The Collateral Source Rule and Full Special Damages," *Trial and Tort Trends* (1957) Central Book Company, Inc., New York, 1958, Page 642; 22 *NACCA LAW J* 159; 46 Minn L R 669; 95 ALR 575; 18 ALR2d 659 (food and lodging); Matthew Bender, *Personal Injury Newsletter,* Vol. 3, Page 218.

Such types of evidence are the following:

1. Medical Care:

—Paid by insurance—*Chapman v. Evans* (Tex Civ App, w.o.m., 1945) 186 SW2d 827; *Graves v. Poe* (Tex Civ App, dismissed, 1938) 118 SW2d 969; *American Cooperage Co. v. Clemons* (Tex Civ App 1963) 364 SW2d 705; 13 ALR2d 355.

—Furnished without charge:

(a) VA Hospital—*City of Ft. Worth v. Barlow* (Tex Civ App, n.r.e., 1958); 313 SW2d 906; 22 *NACCA Law J* 159.

(b) Servicemen—68 ALR2d 876; 20 *NACCA Law J* 193; *Bell v. Primeau* (1962) 104 NH 227, 183 A2d 729; Matthew Bender, *Personal Injury Newsletter,* Vol. 3, Page 225.

2. Sick Leave and Vacation Time:

—Paid by insurance—*Texas Cent. Ry. Co. v. Cameron* (Tex Civ App, refused, 1912) 149 SW 709.

—Paid by employer

(a) Voluntarily—*Missouri Pacific Ry. Co. v. Jarrard* (1886) 65 Tex 560; *Houston Belt & Terminal Ry. Co. v. Johansen* (1915) 107 Tex 336, 179 SW 853; *McCullough Box & Crate v. Liles* (Tex Civ App. w.o.m., 1942) 162 SW2d 1055; 21 *NACCA Law J* 125;

Beaty v. Buckeye Fabric Finishing Co. (ED Ark WD 1959) 179 F Supp 688.

(b) Credited against sick leave or vacation—*Mikell v. LaBeth* (Tex Civ App, n.r.e., 1961) 344 SW2d 702; *Louisville & N. P. Co. v. Utz* (1945); 299 Ky. 765, 187 SW2d 439; *Calci v. Brown* (RI 1962) 186 A2d 234; 52 ALR2d 1451.

(c) Serviceman—*Bell v. Primeau* (1962) 104 NH 227, 183 A2d 729.
—Paid by partnership—*Dumas Milner Chevrolet Co. v. Morphis* (Tex Civ App, n.r.e., 1960) 337 SW2d 185.

3. Social Security and Pensions:

—During diability period only—*Texas Cities Gas Co. v. Dickens* (Tex Civ App 1941) 156 SW2d 1010, affirmed 140 Tex 433, 168 SW2d 208 (1943).

—After employment ceases

(a) Railroad retirement fund—*Mosley v. Texas & Pac. Ry. Co.* (Tex Civ App 1955) 191 SW2d 55; *Missouri Pacific v. Wellingham* (Tex Civ App 1961) 348 SW2d 764; *New York, New Haven & Hartford Ry. Co. v. Leary* (1st Cir 1953) 204 F2d 461.

(b) Social Security, pensions and government payments—*A. H. Bull Steamship Co. v. Ligon* (5th Cir 1960) 285 F2d 936; *Price v. United States* (ED Va 1959) 179 F Suppl 309; *Healy v. Pennert* (1961) 9 NY2d 202, 173 NE2d 777; *Labick v. Vicker* (Pa 1962) 186 A2d 874; *City of Pueblo v. Ratliff* (Colo 1958) 327 P2d 270; 75 ALR2d 885.

4. Withholding from Salary:

MKT P. R. Co. v. McFerrin (1956) 156 Tex 90, 291 SW2d 931; *Texas & N. O. Ry. Co. v. Pool* (Tex Civ App 1954) 263 Sw2d 582; *Buckner & Sons v. Allen* (Tex Civ App 1956) 289 SW2d 387; 63 ALR2d 1393.

By excluding mention of these matters, you not only add to the amount of damages which the jury will award, but you also avoid getting in the prejudicial position of asking the jury to award damages that you have not actually lost.

Slight materiality to other issues should not make any of the above matters admissible, since the prejudicial effect far outweighs any legal relevancy which the evidence might have.

On length of disability—*Dumas Milner Chevrolet Co. v. Morphis,* supra; *A.H. Bull Steamship Co. v. Ligon,* supra; *Louisville & N. Ry. Co. v. Utz,* supra; *Dilbert v. Ross Pattern & Foundry Development Co.* (Ohio App 1957) 152 NE2d 369; *Calci v. Brown,* supra (sick leave); *Clark v. Piccillo* (1962) 75 NJ Super 123, 182 A2d 381. On manner in which injury occurred—*Green v. Texas & P. Ry. Co.* (1935) 125 Tex 168, 81 SW2d 669.

Nor should such evidence be introduced for impeachment purposes, since it concerns a collateral matter.

Can't impeach on a collateral matter—*3 Wigmore on Evidence*, Sec. 1001-1003; *Texas Employers' Ins. Assn. v. Yother* (Tex Civ App, n.r.e., 1957) 306 SW2d 730; *Texas Employers' Ins. Assn. v. Garza* (Tex Civ App, n.r.e., 1957) 308 SW2d 521.

Use in Death Actions

In death actions a motion should request the exclusion of such matters as the remarriage or engagement of the surviving spouse.

Gulf C. & S. F. Ry. Co. v. Younger (1897) 90 Tex 387, 38 SW 1121 (husband); *Texas Elec. Ry. v. Stewart* (Tex Civ App, refused, 1920) 217 SW 1081 (wife); *The City of Rome in re Ocean S.S. Co. of Savannah* (SD NY 1930) 48 F2d 333; 24 *NACCA Law J* 229 (1959); 30 ALR 121 (1924).

Other matters for exclusion, which would fall under the "collateral source rule," are the surviving spouse's income from employment, life insurance, Social Security, pensions, and Veterans Administration pensions.

Texas & N. O. Ry. Co. v. Tiner (Tex Civ App, n.r.e., 1953) 262 SW2d 769; *Welch v. Ada Oil Co.* (Tex Civ App, n.r.e., 1957) 302 SW2d 175; *Lipscomb v. Houston & T. C. Ry. Co.* (1901) 95 Tex 5, 64 SW 923; *Lehr v. City of New York* (1961) 219 NYS2d 308; 25 *NACCA Law J* 345 (1960); 84 ALR 2d 764.

The exclusion of a fact such as the remarriage or the engagement of the surviving spouse should also prohibit the defendant's counsel from arguing to the jury, in summation, that "this nice looking little girl certainly isn't going to have any trouble finding someone to take care of her."

Excluding Criminal Convictions

Only certain criminal convictions are admissible, usually those involving moral turpitude.

Texas Employers' Ins. Assn. v. Yother (Tex Civ App, n.r.e., 1957) 306 SW2d 730; *Texas Employers' Ins. Assn. v. Garza* (Tex Civ App, n.r.e., 1957) 308 SW2d 521; 20 ALR2d 1421.

However, a check of the cases in your jurisdiction will disclose that there are many crimes that have been held not to involve moral turpitude. Of course indictments and charges are never admissible, nor is the fact that your client received a traffic ticket in connection with the collision, or that the opposite party did not receive a traffic ticket.

Condra Funeral Home v. Rollin (1958) 158 Tex 478, 314 SW2d 277; *Allen v. Ellis* (Kan 1963) 380 P2d 408; Matthew Bender, *Personal Injury Newsletter,* Vol. 3, No. 15, Oct. 10, 1960, Page 141, and Vol. 6, No. 6, June 3, 1963, Page 44; 28 *Fordham L R* 369; 25 *Ins Counsel J* 480 (Oct. 1948); 38 *Tex L R* 336.

Evidence of Prior Suits

Prior claims, prior suits, and prior settlements are likewise inadmissible.

St. Paul Fire & Marine Ins. Co. v. Murphree (Tex 1962) 357 SW2d 744; *Burger v. Van Severen* (Ill App 1963) 188 NE2d 373; 18 NCCA 3rd 129.

While the plaintiff, in pleading aggravation of a prior injury, may go into the details of the extent of the injury, the manner in which the injury occurred, whether by automobile accident or falling off the front steps of the home, would be immaterial, as would the fact that a lawsuit was filed, or a claim or settlement made. None of these matters have any relationship to the extent of the injury, but they can be very prejudicial to the plaintiff.

Opinion of Investigating Officers

The opinions of investigating officers are not always admissible.

Patron v. Department of Public Safety (Tex Civ App 1962) 358 SW2d 726; *Flores v. Barlow* (Tex Civ App, n.r.e., 1962) 354 SW2d 178; *Chronister v. City of San Antonio* (Tex Civ App, n.r.e., 1960) 337 SW2d 233; *Figueroa v. Treece* (Tex Civ App, n.r.e., 1960) 337 SW2d 400; *Flores v. Missouri-Kansas-Texas R. Co.* (Tex Civ App, n.r.e., 1963) 365 SW2d 379; *Morlan v. Smith* (Kan 1963) 380 P2d 312; 38 ALR2d 13; 66 ALR2d 1048; 69 ALR2d 1148, 14 NCCA3rd 382.

Most investigating officers are firm in their opinions, which carry a great deal of weight, and their opinions can have a decisive influence upon a jury. A check of the cases in your jurisdiction will determine what opinions are not admissible. For instance, it has been held in Texas that a police office may not give an opinion, concerning the speed of a vehicle, which is based upon the damage done to the vehicles. *Flores v. Barlow* (Tex Civ App, n.r.e., 1962) 354 SW2d 173.

Many police departments have a space in their official report form for the officer to estimate the damage to the vehicles. Often this is a very low, conservative estimate, since it is usually for statistical purposes only. If this estimate is stated by the defendant, it can be very prejudicial when you are asking for three or four times as much. Nearly all police officers, if asked, will admit that they are not qualified to give an opinion as to the value of the damage. However, unless the defendant is instructed in advance not to ask this question or state this information, it may be introduced, and its effect cannot be removed.

Circumstances of Attorney's Retainer Inadmissible

When, where and how the plaintiff engaged his attorney is also inadmissible and can be prejudicial. The fact that he went straight from the accident to an attorney is not material to any issue which the jury will decide. Its only purpose would be to show the plaintiff's litigiousness, which in most jurisdictions is not a legitimate item of proof.

Houston & T. C. Ry. Co. v. Johnson (1919) 103 Tex 320, 127 SW 539; *Martinez v. Williams* (Tex Civ App 1958) 312 SW2d 742; *Southern Truck Leasing Corp. v. Manieri* (Tex Civ App, n.r.e., 1959) 325 SW2d 912.

However, unless ruled out, these prejudicial matters will usually be brought in by the defendant.

Fact of "Family Corporation" Inadmissible

It would also be to the plaintiff's advantage to prohibit the defendant's attorney from proving that the corporate defendant is a "one-man" or "family" corporation or even a local corporation. Since the plaintiff cannot prove the wealth of the defendant, likewise, the defendant cannot prove his "poverty."

Wilmoth v. Limestone Products Co. (Tex Civ App, n.r.e., 1953) 255 SW2d 532; 122 ALR 1408.

The effect of this prejudicial proof is obvious, and the defendant should be instructed in advance not to tender such proof.

Compensation from Other Sources Inadmissible

In third party negligence cases it is not proper to show that the plaintiff was covered by or received workmen's compensation benefits.

Myers v. Thomas (1945) 143 Tex 502, 186 SW2d 811; 77 ALR2d 1153.

Likewise, in a Jones Act case, evidence that the plaintiff accepted payments under the Longshoreman's Act is inadmisible. *Tipton v. Socony Mobil Oil Co. Inc.* (5th Cir 1963) 315 F2d 660.

7.13 MOTIONS TO SEVER

Another way in which motions in advance of trial are useful is in the situation where "good old Joe," who has a wife, thirteen children, and a dependent, sick, widowed mother, injures your plaintiff while in the course of his employment for "Big Dog" Corporation. Often your suit will be against "Big Dog" Corporation alone and will not include "good Old Joe" as a defendant. Under these circumstances the insurance company is very likely to bring in "good old Joe" as a third party defendant, so that the jury will believe that any judgment they enter will be against "good old Joe" and that he will be the one who will ultimately have to pay it. Under these circumstances a motion to sever should be made upon the grounds that the joinder is prejudicial to the plaintiff.

Goodhart v. U. S. Lines Co. (SD NY 1960) 26 FRD 163; *Hanley v. Standard Oil Co. of Texas* (HD Tex 1948) 8 FRD 354; *Bridges v. Evandotte Worsted Co.* (1961) 239 SC 37, 121 SE2d 300.

Hence a third party defendant should not be brought in unless the defendant has a cause of good action against him. Now, in our hypothetical case, since "good old Joe" was driving during the course of his employment, he was obviously driving with permission, and is also insured under the standard omnibus clause of the same policy that is protecting "Big Dog" Corporation. Since "Big Dog" Corporation is insured, it will not have to pay the judgment and can consequently sustain no loss; therefore it has no cause of action against "good old Joe". Of course the insurance company that is defending has no cause of action against "good old Joe," since he is its own insured. *Buckholz v. Michigan Motor Freight Lines* (ED Mich 1956) 19 FRD 407.

This motion to sever also has an additional advantage in that it makes "Big Dog" Corporation's liability policy material and, therefore, discoverable in that this information is necessary to establish the fact that "Big Dog" Corporation has no cause of action against "good old Joe."

Even in those circumstances where you want "good old Joe" as a defendant, the cross action by the employer should be "motioned out." The liability of the employee to the employer is a legal question and is a matter with which the jury is not legitimately concerned. Therefore, it is immaterial to the jury whether or not the employer has cross acted over against the employee. The only effect is to prejudice the plaintiff's case, and a motion should be granted instructing the employer not to read to the jury his pleading on the cross action, or to allow the jury to know that the employer is seeking a judgment over against the employee.

Another common situation in which similar motions can be very useful is in a suit for injuries to a minor. In such a suit the manner in which the minor rode or drove his vehicle prior to the collision would not be material. *Mrs. Baird's Bakeries, Inc. v. Roberts* (Tex Civ App, n.r.e., 1962) 360 SW2d 850; 18 NCCA 3rd 129. Nor would the fact that he was unlicensed be material. (29 ALR2d 963). However, the defendant will often claim as a defense that the parents were negligent in allowing the minor to ride a bicycle or motor scooter, or drive an automobile, because they knew or should have known that he was a careless, unlicensed, reckless driver. Even though the court would instruct the jury that such evidence was not to be considered insofar as the minor's case was concerned, the prejudicial effect could not be removed.

Since such an allegation is immaterial to the final determination of the lawsuit, it should be motioned out. Even assuming that the parents were negligent in allowing the minor to ride or drive a vehicle, nevertheless, as a matter of law, their negligence is not a proximate cause of the collision unless the minor was negligent in some specific manner at the time of the collision. This law has been established as a result of the negligent entrustment cases where recovery has been attempted against the employer or owner of the car for entrusting it to an unlicensed, careless, or reckless driver. In those situations, the courts have usually held that the negligent entrustment cannot be a proximate cause, as a matter of law, unless the driver was negligent at the time of the collision.

Mundy v. Pirie-Slaughter Motor Co. (1947) 146 Tex 314, 206 SW2d 587; *Spratline v. Butler* (1951) 150 Tex 369, 240 SW2d 1016; *McIntire v. Sellers* (Tex Civ App, n.r.e., 1958); 311 SW2d 886; *Carter v. Montgomery* (1956) 226 Ark 989, 296 SW2d 442; 69 ALR2d 978.

In cases of this type the employer has stipulated that since, if the employee was negligent, the employer was liable anyway, the employer's negligent entrustment was not material to the case. Hence such allegations and proof were excluded. This same reasoning can be used in the parent-child case to exclude all evidence concerning the prior driving habits of the child.

Conclusion

There are many other uses of motions *in limine* and similar motions in advance of trial. Each case will be different. It is hoped that these random examples have stimulated your thinking and given you some idea of the advantages that can be gained from the use of such motions, and that from now on if you lose your cases it will not be for the wrong reasons, but for the right reasons.

8

Selecting and Motivating a Jury

8.1 IMPORTANCE OF VOIR DIRE

The voir dire, at least in many of the state courts, is the only time in the trial of a lawsuit when the trial attorney may speak to prospective jurors without time limitations or judicial restrictions.

In those states where voir dire is restricted, the litigant is far less assured of an impartial jury.

8.2 FOUR FUNCTIONS OF VOIR DIRE

There are four functions of the voir dire. The first is to root out members of the panel who might be unperceptive, unintelligent, or unresponsive to your client's cause, and to retain, if possible, the more intelligent members of the panel, as well as those who by reason of temperament or experience might tend to favor your client's version of the controversy.

The second function is to ascertain the background of specific jurors in order to determine which lines of reasoning or argument a given juror would be most receptive to.

The third function is to predispose the jurors to certain ideas and positions. The last function is to impart information.

Emotional Susceptibility and Prejudices

Much of the knowledge that is helpful to the advocate during voir dire cannot be gained from law books, but rather from books dealing with psychology and sociology. Jurors do not come to the box with minds like blank pages, on which the advocate may imprint arguments, like mathematical formulae, that his client should win. Rather, the prospective juror comes to the box with prejudices and emotional susceptibilities arising out of his experiences and temperament. It is the function of the advocate to discover those prejudices and susceptibilities and to use them in order to reach a desired verdict.

Most decisions are not made on a coldly logical basis. As a matter of fact, emotion precedes thought in almost all decisions. Therefore, the advocate must appeal to emotion as well as to logic. If the emotional drive can be evoked, and a rationale suggested by which the satisfaction of the drive may be justified, the desired verdict is more likely to be attained. Even if such a rationale is not provided, if the jury can be psychologically motivated to desire the same ends as your client, more often than not they will find a way to produce the verdict which satisfies the emotional drive. The significant question is, *Which* emotional drive?

Selecting Favorable Jurors

In selecting jurors who favor his or her client, if possible, or at least those who do not disfavor him or her, the trial lawyer should employ certain criteria:

1. Absence of personal bias potentially damaging to the client's interests.
2. Predictability of response.
3. Psychological tendency to favor the client's side of the case.

Eliminating Biased Jurors. Specific personal biases, potentially harmful to the client's interests, may often be revealed by the following measures:

(a) Securing full information about the juror, including marital status, business or profession, former businesses or professions, whether juror has children, and if so, their ages.
(b) Determining those jurors who may have had contact with the parties involved in the litigation, with witnesses, or with counsel.
(c) Exploring the possibility of the juror's experiences with other litigation, whether as a party, witness, or juror.
(d) Exploring the possibility of the juror's family experiences with respect to the above-mentioned.
(e) Determining whether the juror knows any of the other jurors, and if so, the extent of acquaintanceship with them.
(f) Determining the attitude of the juror toward specific aspects of the case, and persons involved in it.

Eliminating the Unpredictable Juror. It is advisable to eliminate the "abnormally unpredictable" juror. By this is meant the social misfit, the iconoclast, the professional reformer, the professional rebel-against-society, the problem drinker, etc. The reason for this should be clear. The trial attorney must persuade a given number of persons to agree. A hung jury is a victory for no one. The perpetual rebel or reformer, for example, may be difficult to persuade to agree with fellow jurors. Moreover, since time in the closing argument is always limited, counsel's arguments must be such that they are persuasive to all normal people. An argument is a good gamble only if the result of the argument is reasonably predictable. The "odd ball" juror, therefore, should be eliminated.

Selecting a Jury that Favors Your Case. The selection of jurors with a psychological tendency to favor your side of the case is implicit in the second function of voir dire: ascertaining the background of specific jurors in order to determine which lines of reasoning or argument a given juror would be most receptive to. Trial lawyers have differed greatly as to the principles involved in the selection of jurors and still have been successful. Some lawyers, at times, advise favoring or disfavoring jurors because of national background, religious background, economic status, the type of job held by the juror, sex, and educational level. It is not suggested that these factors be ignored, but rather, that an attempt be made to determine the attitudes which might be influenced by them. It is also suggested that a given juror may be a "plaintiff's juror" or a "defendant's juror," depending on the arguments or evidence used in order to elicit a particular emotional response. In order for arguments or appeals to have a maximum effect on jurors, they should be aimed at specific prejudices and attitudes. This requires analysis, to the extent possible, of the character traits of each juror.

Persuading a Jury—Personality Types in Modern Society

The "Inner-Directed" Juror. In his book *The Lonely Crowd,* David Riesman discusses some dominant personality types observable in modern society. One such type is the "inner-directed" personality, where a conscious or subconscious image exists of what the individual would like to be. Examples may be seen in the puritan, the self-made businessman or businesswoman, the business tycoon, and the religious zealot. This type of person may make little attempt to conform to society, but rather an attempt to be like the inner image, regardless of the opinion of society. If a juror appears to represent this type, obviously the first task is to ascertain, to the extent possible, *his* concept of the ideal inner image, and then appeal to *her* sense of duty, *his* sense of pride, or *her* prejudices. Arguments which the juror already subconsciously accepts are more persuasive than arguments that are strange or new.

The "Other-Directed" Juror. Another common personality type is the "other-directed" type, where the individual seeks less to conform to an inner image than to the group of which he is a part and the accepted standard of conduct for that group. It is important to note that the peer group for a given individual may radically differ from the peer group of another individual. The youth who is a member of a slum gang will be concerned about conforming to a pattern of conduct different from that of a Palm Beach dowager. The important question, from a trial lawyer's standpoint, is whether or not appeal should be made to group conformity, and if so, which group. The decision is usually delicate, and the time for consideration short, but the trial lawyer *does* make a decision with each argument.

Combine Appeals to Both Types. Because personality types overlap, and because of the danger of error in judging them, it is often well to include appeals to both group conformity and specific images. Perhaps some examples will help clarify the above discussion. It is not suggested that these examples be used, but merely that they are representative of a *type* of argument.

An example of an appeal to group conformity:

"Ladies and gentlemen of the jury, as you know, we are suing for a substantial sum in this case because we have substantial injuries. I am glad that we no longer live in an age when jurors or judges could condone miserly awards of $10,000 or $20,000 for the loss of the breadwinner of a family, or when hours of agony could be squared, with a good conscience, by awards of $5,000 and $10,000."

An example of an appeal to a specific image, assuming that there is a preacher's son on the jury, and a Negro plaintiff:

"Gentlemen of the jury, this is an age when increased emphasis upon Christian doctrines has sharpened the conscience of, and enlightened mankind. The courts of justice, too, have benefited from this enlightenment, for they now say that an award should be full and complete for any injury, regardless of race, or creed, or color."

Appealing to deep-seated prejudices must be done with great delicacy. If a juror ever suspects that you are attempting to appeal to his or her prejudices, resentment can be disastrous. The violin should be gently stroked, not pounded.

Eliminating the Juror's Bias

The third important function of the voir dire is to predispose the jury to certain ideas and positions. This function is familiar to all experienced trial lawyers, and will not be discussed except for one or two examples.

Assume that you wish a jury to consider each item of damage separately:

"Ladies and gentlemen of the jury, Her Honor, the Judge, will charge you, we believe, that if the plaintiff proves that she is entitled to recover there are certain items of damage which she is entitled to have considered if we prove that these items exist. If the Judge does so charge you, and you find for the plaintiff, will you consider individually each of the items on which we present proof?"

Assume the factor of drinking on the part of the plaintiff:

"Ladies and gentlemen of the jury, the evidence will show that the plaintiff had two cocktails in the late afternoon before dinner, and one drink after dinner. The accident occurred between 1:00 a.m. and 2:00 a.m. If Her Honor, the Judge, charges you that the fact that the plaintiff had three drinks early in the evening must not be a factor in your judgment, unless you find that it contributed to the cause of the accident, will you follow Her Honor's instructions?"

Transmitting Information to Jurors

Although voir dire may be safely used, in certain situations, for the purpose of imparting information, its use here is limited. Since there is the possibility of being stopped or reprimanded by the court, or of committing reversible error, attempting to use voir dire extensively for this purpose is inadvisable. There are, however, circumstances where, if opportunities are seized, information or ideas may legitimately be imparted during the voir dire examination. Two examples are offered:

The juror has indicated that he has a brother who is a claims adjustor. If he is removed instantly, in such a way as to make it obvious that the relationship is the reason for removal, unless the jury is unbelievably dense, it will immediately see the connection.

A long trial is anticipated and you are afraid that the jury may become impatient. Tell them, "Ladies and gentlemen of the jury, this is a case, as in all cases, where the burden of proof is on the plaintiff. We do not intend to ask you to accept our case on faith, but will present proof on each issue. This will take time. We believe, and opposing counsel has stated that she shares our view, that this case will take three to four days, even if both sides and the Judge do everything possible to expedite the trial. Do you have time to listen to us, remain patient until we have given you the evidence that you need to render a verdict, and then carefully consider your verdict?"

8.3 PRETRIAL JURY INVESTIGATION

The writers believe that investigation of members of the jury panel before trial, to the extent possible, is an absolute must. In some areas of the state of Florida, a jury investigation service is available. This service, if properly handled, can unearth information that cannot be obtained through voir dire. A few examples follow:

In one instance, one of the writers represented a minor plaintiff in a case involving an attractive nuisance theory. A potential juror and his wife hated children so much that they had strung barbed wire all through the hedge surrounding their yard, and burst into violent rage whenever a child trespassed on their property. This potential juror, during the course of voir dire, smilingly stated that he and his wife loved children and fondly wished they had some (to eat, perhaps?). He did not serve.

In another case, a thrice-divorced woman, badly burned, was the plaintiff. A potential juror, twice divorced, was paying alimony to two ex-wives. He did not serve.

Although these illustrations would alone more than justify the use of a jury investigation service, they are obvious and specific. The real yeoman duty is performed by the jury investigation service in revealing broad information about general personality traits. For example: "He and his wife entertain often and have many friends. He is always ready to help others." Or, "He and his wife are little known to their neighbors. In their quiet, secluded lives, they make few friends."

Whether the empathetic individual, who forms warm, personal ties, or the recluse, who has little affection for others, would make the best plaintiff's juror or defendant's juror depends, of course, upon the particular case and the specific, emotionally charged issues involved. In any event, a good jury investigation service is of invaluable assistance in rendering reliable information as to the personality characteristics and possible prejudices of a juror which might influence his verdict.

8.4 USE OF PSYCHOLOGIST IN JURY SELECTION

For many years, it was a closely guarded secret that lawyers, the truly successful ones, frequently used the services of body-language experts and psychologists in the jury selection process. The secret is out. Today, in any significant case, you should explore the wisdom of employing such assistance. The reasons are obvious. A truly good body-language expert can pick up juror responses that are often missed by the attorney busy with interrogation. Such emotions as hostility, acceptance, disbelief, and the like concerning you and your client, defense counsel, and defendant, are important, indeed vital, information. Have the expert present in the courtroom during all the voir dire, opening statements, and plaintiff's testimony. A good one can tell you who on the jury needs to be convinced.

Summary

When the voir dire examination is complete and properly done, the ideal result is to have a jury without personal experience causing them to be inherently hostile to your side of the case, and, if possible, a jury with a psychological tendency to favor your cause. Seeds may be planted, in the minds of jurors, which may be cultivated by evidence and argument.

If, at the time of voir dire, the jurors have promised a full and fair award, remind them in your argument. If they have promised to consider intangibles, such as pain and suffering, after giving such evidence, remind them of their promise in the closing argument.

The trial lawyer, for maximum efficiency, must weld the techniques of psychology and law and utilize them in voir dire, demonstrative evidence, and closing argument.

8.5 OPENING STATEMENT

8.5.1 The Opening Statement Can Be Dynamite

An opening statement is permitted in practically every state in the Union and in all Federal Courts. The usual provision is that the plaintiff may briefly state her claim and the evidence by which she intends to prove it, and that the defense attorney may briefly state the defense and the evidence by which he intends to prove the defense. In most instances the opening statement immediately follows the impaneling of the jury. The party having the burden of proof, usually the plaintiff, has the right to make the first opening statement.

Trial specialists consider the opening statement one of the most important phases of the case. Its importance would seem to be borne out by a recent study at the University of Chicago, where a number of mock trials were taped for jury study. A poll of the jury after the entire case had been submitted to them indicated that only 20 percent of the jurors ever changed their minds with respect to liability after the opening statement. The other 80 percent appeared to have made a decision at the close of opening statements, a decision which never changed at any time during the trial in spite of evidence introduced by the defense.

8.5.2 Purpose of Opening Statement

The basic purpose of the opening statement should be to disclose the evidence which will be produced in support of the plaintiff's claim. In order to be persuasive, the opening statement must be accurate, sincere, and should capture the interest of the jury. It should be presented in such a way that the jury may understand, and, you hope, favor such evidence. Like the cover of a magazine, it should be designed to attract attention, creating a theme which should be maintained throughout the trial, and which will keep the interest of the jury sustained.

The lawyer should never make an opening statement without having carefully prepared it in advance. It is imperative that the lawyer interview in advance all witnesses whom he intends to use, and that he know all of the important evidence which will be introduced at the trial.

In order to determine whether the opening statement is effective or not, the attorney should ask himself, "If the jury were to retire immediately after the opening statement, would they feel compelled to return a verdict for the plaintiff?" Hence the opening statement should be such as will convince the jurors that the plaintiff's position is a correct one, and that only by their finding for the plaintiff can justice be genuinely served in the case.

Should You Make an Opening Statement?

The party having the burden of proof should without exception make the first opening statement. The plaintiff's attorney should outline accurately and emphatically the evidence intended to be offered in support of the claim. The evidence should be broken down into two parts: liability and damages. The defendant's conduct giving rise to liability, and the damages, with all of the aspects that can be shown, should be thoroughly reviewed for the jury.

Sometimes the defense waives the opening statement. Counsel for the plaintiff should advise the jury, at the close of her remarks, that the defendant has the right to make such a statement and that they should listen with interest to the proposed defense. This has the effect, if properly done, of making the plaintiff's counsel seem fair and gracious. Such a tactic at the same time requires the defense counsel either to make a statement or to have the jury wonder why he did not.

8.5.3 Essential Characteristics of an Opening Statement

Introducing the Parties

Although the parties to the suit are usually introduced by the court or the attorneys during the voir dire examination, a reintroduction of the parties during opening statement is ordinarily a good practice. The parties should be asked to stand and should be identified for all the jury to see. At the same time some "vital statistics" about the plaintiff should be furnished to the jury so that at the outset the plaintiff becomes a real person to the jurors.

Setting Forth the Issue

After the introduction of the parties, counsel should state briefly and concisely the real fighting issues in the case. Thus if the problem boils down to the question of whether the defendant was speeding, counsel can advise the jury that this is the real issue in the case, and, if the evidence established that he was speeding, the amount of compensation which should be paid by the defendant to the plaintiff for his injuries.

Good trial lawyers follow the practice of narrowing the issues as much as possible, and of pointing, in opening statement, to the real controversy between the opposing sides. All the experts agree that simplicity should be the goal of the lawyer in every case. Most jurors lose interest if the task before them appears to be a complicated one. Making it clear to the jury, in the opening statement, that the issues and problems before them are really very simple, after all, will do much to encourage a receptive attitude.

Describing the Occurrence

After stating the issues, counsel should describe in vivid detail the scene of the occurrence, using such aids as the trial court will permit in order to fully advise the jury as to the terrain, the surrounding structures, etc. A vivid and accurate description of the actual occurrence—collision, fall, or other instrument of injury—and the manner in which it caused the injury, should also be given at this time.

Careful thought and deliberation are required at this phase of the opening statement. Counsel should try to paint a word picture which portrays the scene accurately and graphically. She should use simple words, such as "before" instead of "prior," "after" instead of "subsequent." Counsel should remember that she must make herself clearly understood to the least educated juror in the box. Jurors, like all people, resent a lawyer who talks over their heads, and the lawyer who does so violates an important principle of persuasion.

Description of Damages

The University of Chicago studies concerning jury deliberation present an interesting conclusion. A case involving several items of damage was submitted to numerous juries in two different ways. On the one hand, a separate verdict was rendered by the jury on each item of damage, while on the other hand, a lump-sum verdict was rendered.

Where separate verdicts were returned on each of the items of damage, they totaled a higher amount than where a lump-sum verdict was returned. This would indicate that it is the duty of the attorney, in states where the use of per diem formulas is allowed, to use them in cases where separate items of damage exist.

With regard to opening statements, certainly great attention must be paid to separating the different items of damage. It should be stressed to the jury, from the outset, that the only way that they can accomplish justice is to calculate a separate award for each of the separate items and then add them up to arrive at a fair total award. Accordingly, counsel should detail every item of damage which it is expected that the court will submit to the jury, and state briefly in his opening statement some of the evidence which will be produced to prove each item.

In describing injuries it is important that the lawyer do so in simple, readily understandable, layman's terms. He should not try to impress the jury with his vast store of medical knowledge, but should call a fracture a broken bone, a disc in the back a "disc," and not a "herniation of the nucleus pulposis."

Arousing the Jury's Interest

Another important function of the opening statement is creating interest in the litigation on the part of the jury. Use of the newspaper technique, that is, identifying the case by type, such as a "Rear-End Case," "Dog-Bites-Man Case," and the like, can be effective. "Headlining" those aspects of the case that are attention getters can be very advantageous in getting the case off the ground and on to a flying start.

In her opening statement the lawyer must keep in mind that communication with the jury is effective only if the jury fully grasps the information she is attempting to impart. Charts, photographs, and other exhibits which will be introduced at the trial and which are permitted by the court, on occasion, to be shown to the jury in opening statement enhance such communication and should be used for this purpose.

Being Informative

Above all, counsel should be informative. The information should be given in an interesting, conversational manner. Some lawyers visit with the jury. Some make it a chatty affair. No successful trial lawyer ever harangues the jury.

Most important, the attorney should be himself, with his own style of delivery. He may use the ideas and suggestions of others, but should never attempt to imitate. An attempt to copy another lawyer's style will result in an appearance of insincerity.

Developing the Theme

In each case a theme should be developed in the opening statement. If the case is a dog-bite case, use the "dog bite" as the theme. If the case is a rear-end case, refer to it as a "rear-end case" and use the rear-end collision as the theme. If the case involves speed on the part of the defendant, and if it is logical to develop the theme of the case around speed, call it a "speeding case." If it is a right-of-way case, call it a "right-of-way case."

The theme of the case should be determined in advance of opening statement. The reasons are obvious. The theme helps set the tone of the evidence to come. It helps pinpoint the problem. It makes the problem seem less complicated and directs the jury's attention to what plaintiff's counsel contends is the real issue in the case. Repeat the theme several times during the beginning and at the close of the opening statement. Do not permit the defendant to develop a theme first. Permitting him to do so will allow him to gain advantages that should be yours.

Photographs and Models

Many Federal Courts and some state trial judges permit in opening statement the use of photographs, models, and other aids which will enable the jury to have a better understanding of the evidence that will later be produced. One of the advantages of a pretrial is that such exhibits may be marked and identification waived. This procedure lays the foundation for a later request to use the exhibits during opening statement.

The trial is a search for the truth. The term "verdict" literally means "to speak the truth." If the trial court will agree that all possible means should be used to assist the jury in discovering the truth, there should be little valid argument against the use of photographs, models, and other such obvious jury aids in opening statement. Therefore, in every trial, counsel should request that they be permitted during opening statement. Permission or denial is largely discretionary with the court, and most modern judges will respond favorably when properly alerted to the obvious value of such exhibits.

If the request for use of exhibits during the opening statement is denied, individual ingenuity must be used. Some attorneys, for the purposes of demonstration, use the counsel table, the jury rail, or other objects which the jury can see. Some use books or anything else which will help to represent cars, people, etc. If distance is a factor, it is suggested that the courtroom be measured before trial. Counsel can tell the jury that he will prove the length of the room, that it is so many feet. He can describe the distance in terms of courtroom lengths, counsel table lengths, jury rail lengths, or anything else within the courtroom which the jury can see. The jury must be made to picture, understand, and grasp the evidence to come. They are a captive audience. Many of them don't really want to be there. Hence the attorney must make the case interesting to them and present the evidence in such a way that it is easy for them to follow.

Oral Testimony—Witnesses

Oral testimony, which gives life to every case, requires a special approach. Should the lawyer identify each witness and what he or she will say? If the witness's testimony is detailed, counsel risks the possibility that the witness will not hold up on direct examination, and consequent criticism by the jury for having misled them. However if the lawyer does not describe the witness and her testimony, some vividness may be lost.

The best rule seems to be this: If the witness is "solid," describe not only his testimony, but the witness as well. For example, if he is a tall, redheaded man, tell the jury about him. Describe him as a tall, redheaded man. Tell them where he was at the time of the accident. If the court permits the use of photographs in the opening statement, pinpoint, on the photograph, his location with respect to the accident scene. Hence, when the witness makes his appearance in court, the jurors can say to themselves, "Oh yes, this is the man she told us was standing on the northeast corner of the intersection." By describing the witnesses, the lawyer makes her case come to life.

It is usually a good practice to ask that the witnesses remain outside the courtroom during opening statement as well as during testimony. Thus, when the witnesses take the stand, their testimony will seem more spontaneous and credible. If, however, they are present in the courtroom when the lawyer tells the jury, as she invariably should, that she has talked to the witnesses before trial, she should say it loudly enough for the witnesses to hear. This way the witnesses may prepare themselves for future cross-examination and the age-old question "Have you talked with the lawyer about your testimony here?"

The Client

Introduce the client to the jury, as vividly as possible. Have him stand up. Tell the jury who he is, where he lives and works, and the sort of person he is. Tell them about his background, his childhood, his education, his life. Tell them about his work, his wife and children. Make the jury know him.

Tell them about his injury, how it occurred and what has happened to him since the injury. Use descriptive terms. Help the jury understand his medical problems by describing them in lay terms. If bones are fractured, tell the jury about the bone and its fracture. If the femur is involved, tell the jury about it, that it is the longest bone in the body, that it is a weight-bearing bone, that it is important to walking, lifting, running, squatting, and so forth. Describe the healing process, the reason for pain. Describe the soft tissues in the areas of the fracture, the tendons, muscles, blood supply, and nerves. If rib fractures are present, describe the function of the ribs, the expansion and contraction while breathing, why it hurts when the client breathes. Add up the number of breaths taken during the day and tell the jury. Even in states where the per diem argument is not permitted, most courts will permit such testimony, and reference to it should be made in opening statement in order to help the jury accept and understand it.

Refer to the client by his name, and never as "the plaintiff." The word "plaintiff" is too impersonal, and sometimes is confusing to the unsophisticated juror. If the plaintiff is a young person or a child, refer to him by his first name. If he is an older person, call him or her "Mr. or Mrs. . . . ." Where the given name and the surname are particularly pleasing to the ear, use them together. Make your client a real person with a name and personality to which the jury can respond.

Evidence

The jury should be told in the early phase of the opening statement just what evidence is, and what is the nature of the evidence that will be used to prove the claim. They should be told what articles, models, or other exhibits will be used to illustrate the evidence so that they may better understand it as it is offered. This should include a description of photos, models, charts, medical drawings, x-rays, skeletal models, and the like. The jury should be advised that many such articles will not be introduced, but used merely to illustrate the testimony.

Where depositions are to be used, an explanation of the deposition process and the purpose and use of the deposition should be given. Where portions of the defendant's deposition are to be used to prove admissions and in support of the plaintiff's case, the jury should be told in opening statement that the defendant has previously testified under oath about these matters. The portions of the depositions to be utilized should be selected. If there is doubt as to their admissibility, approval of the court should be sought in advance, either at pretrial hearing or by a motion in limine.

Where the defendant is to be called to the witness stand and examined under the adverse witness rule, the jury should be advised in advance unless the element of surprise might be so effective as to be an overriding factor.

Brevity

Though the rules usually provide that the plaintiff may briefly state his claim and the evidence by which he intends to prove it, the term, "brief" is relative. Obviously every case requires careful individual consideration in this regard. While the attorney should be brief, he should, more important, be thorough. Do not, for the sake of brevity, fail to touch upon all important aspects of the case. Discuss the highlights of the testimony and the important bits of evidence which will, when pieced together by the jury, establish the claim of the plaintiff.

Avoiding Argument

Some attorneys make an opening statement as if it were a final argument. Most alert judges and opposing counsel recognize argument when they see it, and any effort to argue the case in the opening statement may be met with successful objection. Furthermore, jurors tend to respond unfavorably to any attempt to argue the merits of the case in opening statement, and many lawyers have lost the jury's sympathy, understanding, and even their attention in opening statement by attempting to inject argument into it.

Avoiding Levity

The representation of an injured person is serious business, and usually jurors regard their task as a serious one. The injection of levity, the telling of jokes, the effort to be funny on the part of the plaintiff's counsel can do much to alienate the jury from the plaintiff and his attorney. Few attorneys are adept at joke telling. Almost none are capable of "joking" a jury into a verdict. The telling of jokes gives an appearance of insincerity and certainly detracts from the gravity of the plaintiff's situation. The attorney should try to create an impression of sincerity and a tone of seriousness.

Avoiding Exaggeration

Exaggeration has in all probability ruined more good lawsuits than any other single act on the part of the plaintiff's counsel. One single statement, one single representation, of evidence to come, that is an exaggeration of the truth, can destroy an otherwise valid claim. New York lawyer Moe Levine suggests that the best course is to understate the case, and to overstate the defects in the case. He suggests that the lawyer, after doing so, say to the jury, "Please stand by and wait for all the evidence. Don't form your judgment. We would not be here if we did not have things to tell you. Wait until we have told you all."

The advice is sound, for the jury usually trusts a candid lawyer. Such a technique also prepares the jury to be tolerant. If counsel tells them the defects in the case, they will surely believe him or her; but they will also believe that there must be justification for the case despite the defects, and they will wait for the evidence. When the defects appear, less serious than counsel said they were, the jury is likely to be extremely pleased with him or her for not having lied to them.

The Positive Approach

One of the basic principles of persuasion, as set forth by Professor Minnick*, is projecting sincerity and conveying the impression that what you are saying you genuinely believe. A positive approach serves to further belief in your cause. Any display of doubt can be fatal. If you display doubt you cannot expect to convince others. Be positive in what you say, but not to excess, so that you are guilty of exaggeration. Make it clear to the jury that you are merely stating what the evidence will be and the facts you expect to unfold from it.

The Principles of Primacy and Recency

The trial lawyer must understand the principles of primacy and recency and give full application to the principles throughout the trial, including during the opening statement. The principle of primacy is that in the human mind the first belief about a subject is most deeply believed. The first belief also resists change most firmly. Recency is the principle that you will remember most easily that which you last heard.

There is considerable difference between the two. One involves the intensity of belief and the other involves the ease of recollection. Since the attorney wishes to promote intense belief in her cause, early in the case she must take full advantage of the principle of primacy and make her best point first. The plaintiff's lawyer usually speaks first during opening statement. If she fails to make a strong opening statement, she may be certain that the defense will; and plaintiff will lose the advantage of the principle.

The principle of recency is commonly applied at the summation of the case, but should be borne in mind by counsel when, at the close of the opening statement, she reiterates the important evidence with which she will prove his case.

---

*Minnick, *The Art of Persuasion* (Houghton Mifflin, 1957).

8.5.4 When to Object to an Opening Statement

Counsel should always advise the jury that the opening statement is not an argument, that any attempt to argue the case at this stage would be improper and a violation of courtroom protocol, and that the jury should properly take offense at any counsel who attempts to argue the facts before any evidence has been presented. This procedure lays a foundation for future objection should counsel for the defense attempt to argue during the opening statement.

Never object unless you have good reason to believe that the court will sustain the objection, and then only if it appears that the jury will not be critical of the objection.

Always object if counsel attempts, during opening statement, to inject statements of evidence that have been barred by the court's ruling on a motion *in limine* filed at the beginning of the trial. If counsel persists in violating the court's order, do not hesitate to "make a record" and move for a mistrial if such motion appears in order.

8.5.5 Can an Admission in an Opening Statement Be Binding?

Where definite, unqualified admissions are inadvertently made in the opening statement, they can be binding and classified as admitted facts. For example, where counsel for the defendant has admitted in the opening statement that his client was operating the vehicle involved in the occurrence, and the plaintiff has failed to make proof of such fact, the defendant may not, on appeal, assert want of proof of the defendant's involvement. *Peterson v. General Rug & Carpet Cleaners, Inc.* (1947) 33 Ill App 47, 77 NE2d 58.

Remember, the power of the court to act upon facts conceded by counsel is as plain as its power to act upon the evidence produced. *Ascanyan v. Arms Co.* (1880) 103 US 261, 263.

It is good practice to insist that the opening statement of both the plaintiff's counsel and defense counsel be reported in full. Such a procedure eliminates the possibility of later dispute as to what was admitted by counsel in his statement, and in the event of an appeal, a more complete record is available for both the trial court and the appellate court.

8.5.6 Ending the Opening Statement

The close of the opening statement should recapitulate the highlights of the testimony and the evidence to come. It should briefly restate the theme of the case, and the evidence that will show the defendant's wrongful act. It should review the injury and the damage factors; and in some cases, where permitted, should state the amount, as shown by the evidence, that should be assessed, or the obligation or debt owed by the defendant.

Some counsel refrain from mentioning amounts during the opening statement. Some states prohibit mention of this. Hence care should be taken to abide by the local rules. In cases where it is permissible, counsel should state the amount only after careful deliberation.

The close of the opening statement should always urge the jury to listen carefully to the evidence. Usually it is good to request the jury to hold you to your version of the facts as they will be revealed by the evidence, and to hold defense counsel to his version as well.

SAMPLE OPENING STATEMENT ON LIABILITY

Members of the jury, you have been selected to settle the dispute between John Brown, who is known in the law as the plaintiff in this case, and the defendant, Roberta Jones. This is an automobile collision case. It is an intersection case. It involves the failure on the part of the defendant to yield the right-of-way by ignoring a stop sign requiring her to stop before entering into the through street upon which the plaintiff was operating his vehicle.

This is an opening statement. It is not an argument. It would be improper for me or counsel for the defense to attempt to argue the case at this time. No evidence has been yet presented and you should, with justification, take offense if anyone should argue the merits of the claim or defense until the proper time at the close of the case. Under the law of this state, John Brown has the right and duty to outline to you at this time the evidence which will be produced to prove his claim and to generally advise you of the matters in dispute.

The evidence will show that this is a case of indebtedness on the part of the defendant. The defendant created the debt by her failure to follow the rules of the road in the operation of her vehicle; namely, in failing to yield the right-of-way to the plaintiff at the scene of the collision. The evidence will show that the defendant, while operating her vehicle in an easterly direction upon School Street in the City of Des Moines, approached the intersection of School and West 34th Street, ignored the red stop sign then in place requiring her to bring her vehicle to a halt and to ascertain before entering the intersection that she could do so with safety, and did in fact drive her vehicle through the stop sign into the path of the vehicle approaching from the north, being driven by John Brown at that time. As a result of the defendant's failure to conform to the rules prescribed by law; namely, yielding the right-of-way, a collision occurred between the two vehicles and John Brown sustained the injuries as a result of the defendant's wrong driving, which injuries I will describe in more detail shortly.

Let me describe the scene: 34th Street in the City of Des Moines runs in a generally north-south direction. It is a well-traveled street and is one of the main thoroughfares in the city. School Street, which runs in a generally east-west direction, intersects 34th Street approximately a block and a half east of the street known as Beaverdale Drive. School Street abuts into Beaverdale Drive approximately a block and a half to the west of the scene of the collision. The evidence will show that the defendant turned off Beaverdale Drive onto School and proceeded eastbound up to the intersection of 34th and School and without stopping her vehicle for the stop sign or ascertaining whether she could drive into the main thoroughfare known as 34th Street, drove into the intersection directly into the path of the vehicle driven by John Brown. The collision occurred at approximately the center of the intersection and evidence will show that just prior to the time of the collision John Brown turned his vehicle violently to the left in an effort to avoid colliding with the defendant. The evidence will show that Mr. Brown had practically no warning of the misconduct of the defendant and of her violation of the rules of the road. The evidence will show that at the time of the collision Mr. Brown was thrown from his car onto the pavement, and that he suffered injuries which he will have the rest of his life. Mr. Brown's claim against the defendant, giving rise to the debt which you will settle in your determination of this case is as follows:

1. That the defendant failed to stop at the stop sign when she was under legal compulsion to do so.
2. That the defendant failed to yield the right-of-way by driving into the intersection at a time when she had failed or refused to ascertain that the same could be done with safety.
3. That the defendant failed to maintain a proper lookout for Mr. Brown who was then and there lawfully using the thoroughfare upon which he was operating his car.

These are the charges and these are the wrongs committed by the defendant, which the evidence will prove and from which evidence we will ask you to determine the amount of the debt of the defendant to Mr. Brown.

9

Trial Tactics, Demonstrable Evidence, and Appeals

Trial lawyers are always faced with the problem of whether a given item of information can be considered by the court or the jury—in short, is the evidence "admissible?" To know something is true is not the same as being able to prove it in court. Solid grounding in the rules of evidence and their artful application is necessary to the proficient trial lawyer.

9.1 EVIDENCE

9.1.1 What Makes Evidence Admissible?

Evidence is not admitted because it is competent, but because it is not shown to be incompetent. *Plumb v. Curtis* (1895) 66 Vt 154, 33 A 998; *Sallec v. Routson* (1956) 247 Iowa 1220, 78 NW2d 516. All evidence relevant to the ultimate substantive issue is admissible, unless excluded by some rule of evidence. It is assumed that all lawyers are familiar with the rules of evidence and the basic reasons for them, and that in preparing their lawsuits they are completely aware of the evidentiary problems confronting them. However, the technique of applying these rules is often neglected. A timely and proper objection may serve to keep out of the record evidence which might prejudice a cause, while an objection improper in form, or untimely, may fail to do so. If the offered evidence is objectionable and should be excluded, but is admitted by reason of failure to make proper and timely objection, there is no relief on appeal.

Chief Justice Thompson of the Iowa Supreme Court once made this observation: "It may be that in the courtroom scenes popularly, and generally inaccurately, portrayed on television and radio, a mere 'I object' or 'objection' is sufficent; but it is the good fortune of the trial courts in Iowa that something specific and definite is required and that reversible error may not be predicated upon an objection which does not tell the court the ground upon which it is based."

Our discussion here will be presented in two parts: first, the technique of applying the rules of exclusion from the standpoint of good trial tactics; and second, the technique of applying the rules of exclusion for the purpose of properly preserving the record.

Trial Tactics

In General. Good trial tactics require not only that the lawyer recognize evidence which is inadmissible, but also that he or she know when to object. Some lawyers, it would seem, acquire most of their trial technique from watching the "Perry Mason" show, and proceed on the theory that the mark of a good trial attorney is to object as often as possible.

9.1.2 Avoid Incessant Objections

Experienced trial lawyers agree that incessant objections are bad trial tactics. This is true even of good objections, such as objections to leading questions on immaterial matters, or objections to opinion, and is equally true of constant motions to strike after objections have been made and overruled. It has been said that the damage of overobjection is clearly apparent when the other attorney is abusing the privilege, but not so apparent to the one engaged in the process.

Guard Against Harmful Evidence

An advocate's duty is to maintain a constant and determined guard against the introduction of harmful, incompetent evidence. If the evidence is inadmissible and considered harmful, prompt and vigorous objection should be made. Knowing when to object and when not to is never easy. It is not subject to any fixed rule. Trial practice is not a science, but an art, and one that no lawyer completely masters.

Plan Ahead

The lawyer who expects to object to evidence successfully must plan ahead. A thoroughly prepared lawsuit should reveal the problems of proof on both sides. The lawyer must know what he has to prove and what evidentiary questions will confront him in the proof. By proper use of discovery, he may determine very clearly what his adversary must prove and the problems of evidence which he will have as well. It is possible, in fact almost essential, for the attorney to plan in advance what substantive evidence he will want to admit and exclude. The attorney should have tried his case at least several times in his mind before going to trial, making a few imaginary objections, planning their timing, and mentally playing them back to himself. Like the best ad-libs, good objections are planned in advance.

If Testimony Isn't Harmful, Don't Object

If the attorney has no reason to believe that the testimony will hurt his cause, he should not object, even if the question is objectionable. For example, a question asking the witness whether it is not true that she is a certain age should not be objected to as a leading question. If a question is objectionable *only* because it is leading, it should be left alone. As a rule, the answers given to leading questions are more harmful to the examiner than to his adversary.

Only when the examiner uses leading questions to steady a faltering or confused witness should the attorney rise in indignation and make his objection, prefaced, of course, with the comment that he has been extremely patient throughout the trial in the face of repeated leading questions, but that this time the examiner has gone too far.

Often, too, there is overobjection to opinion. For example, if the witness could actually testify as to the facts, but the question calls for his opinion, obviously the latter testimony is less effective than the former.

Object Without Argument

All objections should be made distinctly and without argument. The making of an objection coupled with a lengthy argument in support of it is certain to brand the attorney as inexperienced. More than that, it is not proper trial conduct, and a good trial court will not permit it. If it is desirable to argue the law applicable to an objection, permission to do so should be requested of the court, and in all cases it should be done in the absence of the jury.

Avoid Repeating the Same Objection

Unless required in the particular jurisdiction, repetition of the objection should be avoided. If the proper objection has been made and overruled, ordinarily it is not necessary to make the same objection to questions pertaining to the same matter. Failure to object to evidence of the same character is not ordinarily a waiver of an objection previously made. In most jurisdictions, repeated objections to questions similar to those held proper by the court are useless. It should be noted, however, that this applies only to objections that have been overruled. If an objection to inadmissible evidence is sustained, most courts require repeated objections to offers of similar proof.

9.1.3 How and When to Object

If an objection appears to be in order, good trial tactics require that it be made early. Although there is no unanimity of agreement among the states, it is generally unsafe not to object to testimony in one instance, and then, later in the trial, to object to the same type of testimony produced by another witness.

Have a Purpose in Objecting. All objections and motions should be made for a definite purpose, based upon authority and logic, rather than simply for the sake of making them. For example, in most jurisdictions if an objection is made to a question, and the objection is overruled, it is unnecessary to follow with a motion to strike for "all the reasons and upon all the grounds as stated in the foregoing objection." Most courts hold that the record has already been made by the objection and ruling, and that the motion to strike adds nothing but length to the court reporter's notes.

Proper Objections to Preserve the Record

In General. There are only a few rules pertaining to this subject. The failure to understand them and invoke them properly at the right time may, however, not only prevent a desirable ruling by the trial court, but may also effectively deprive the lawyer and client of a review on appeal.

Purpose of Timely Objection. In those states requiring the attorney to make proper and timely objection, the purpose is to alert both opposing counsel and the judge to the improper nature of the question, so that opposing counsel may correct the error by reframing the question, and the court may properly and intelligently make its ruling. Often the appellate courts will not predicate reversible error upon an objection that does not tell the court the ground upon which it is based.

Stating the Objection and Reason. Good trial tactics require the attorney to state the objection and the reason for her objection at the time that it is made. The attorney should not expect, nor can she expect, the trial court to try her case for her or make the record which she as counsel should make. A trial is a process in which the attorney's efforts and skills are measured by more than her willingness to attend a pretrial conference.

Where only part of the evidence called for is objectionable, an objection to all of it is ordinarily too broad. Effective trial tactics require the attorney to extract the objectionable portion and make the objection to it alone.

Rules Governing General Objections. The following are general rules which must be considered by the trial attorney, who should determine whether they are applicable in his jurisdiction:

1. Ordinarily a general objection *justifies* the exclusion of the evidence on any possible grounds. See *Gettre v. Healy* (1953) 245 Iowa 294; 60 NW2d 541.

2. Usually a general objection, if overruled, is insufficient for review, and reversible error may not be predicated upon it. *Ferris v. Riley* (1960) 251 Iowa 400, 101 NW2d 176; 3 *Am. Jur.*, Appeal and Error, Section 263, Page 41, 4 *C.J.S.*, Apeal and Error, Section 290 (b), Page 879.

The general objection may be "I object," or "objection," or even "hey, wait a minute," and is usually intended to denote "incompetent, irrelevant, and immaterial." Strictly speaking, each of these terms refers to something different, but they are so interrelated that there is little purpose in attempting to separate their meanings. Dean Mason Ladd (22 *Iowa L Rev* 626), Wigmore (1 Wigmore, *Evidence,* Second Edition, 1923, paragraph 18), and Jones (6 Jones, *Evidence,* Second Edition, 1926, paragraphs 2518, 2519, and 2524) all express some different thoughts as to what each of the words "incompetent," "irrelevant," and "immaterial" means, but all of them agree that they are implicit in the general objection.

It should be clearly understood that ordinarily where the general objection is made, and the evidence is properly excludable on any grounds, the trial court is not in error in sustaining it. Likewise the trial attorney must understand that the general rule is that some ground for the objection be stated. Usually if evidence is excludable on some ground, but only the general objection is made and the ground for it not specifically stated, the trial court is not in error in overruling the objection. One appellate justice stated the principle as follows: "A sweeping objection in general and indefinite terms is not to be made use of as a mere dragnet or screen for a specific objection held in mental reservation by counsel, to be brought to light only when the case has become the subject of appellate jurisdiction."

Value of General Objections. Is a general objection of any value? Yes. While it is often overlooked, it can and does perform a valuable function. As previously pointed out, while a general objection may be ineffective for preserving error when the objection is overruled, it does protect the record when the objection is sustained.

There are, moreover, times when improper evidence is called for so unexpectedly as to afford little opportunity for deliberation on the part of the trial attorney. The attorney often senses the impropriety of the question before actually being able to analyze what it is, much less have time to specifically and succinctly advise the trial court. While the advocate can't "strike between wind and water" during the trial, and then go home to the books to study objections and urge them, it is not too much to ask that on some occasions he be permitted to interpose an objection just to give himself time to think and determine what is really wrong with the question asked. Often the general objection is used for this purpose, to be followed by the proper specific objection.

The general objection may also be used at times as a device to break the continuity of the testimony. It is especially useful where it appears that the witness is telling a well-rehearsed story and must preserve his train of thought in order to tell it as rehearsed. This technique sometimes has the effect of disrupting opposing counsel's train of thought as well.

Separating the General and Specific Objections. A word of caution. The general objection should be separate and distinct from the specific objection. Some courts have held that a general objection followed by a specific objection can lead the trial court into believing that the general objection is urged only for the reasons stated in the specific objection. The specific objection alone is considered. Good tactics require that the specific objection and the general objection be considered and weighed separately.

When to Make the Objection. Ordinarily an objection must be made at the time that the question is asked. If cause for objection to testimony is apparent at the time that the question is asked, generally it is too late to make a motion and objection after the answer is given.

Motions to Strike Testimony

There are occasions when counsel does not have the opportunity to interpose an objection. When this occurs, a motion to strike the testimony may be made on two principal grounds: first, if the answer was given before counsel had time to object; and second, if the answer was so nonresponsive as to take counsel by surprise.

In many jurisdictions these grounds, even if true, are not in and of themselves sufficient to cause the motion to be sustained. They are regarded only as excuses for failure to object. Under such circumstances, in order for the motion to strike to be sustained, counsel must also urge the same grounds for exclusion which should have been urged in an objection to the question.

If the question is improper, but an admissible answer is given, or if the question is proper and the answer is admissible, but not in response to the question, the motion to strike the testimony will ordinarily not be sustained. While there may be a reason justifying the failure to object, there is no independent ground upon which the answer can be excluded.

The best trial technique is to move to strike the testimony by first stating the grounds for failure to object, and then specifically stating why the answer is incompetent or otherwise inadmissible. Some trial lawyers vary the practice by receiving permission to have the objection precede the answer, but even if it is then sustained, ordinarily a motion should be made to strike the answer.

In many jurisdictions, the mere sustaining of an objection to an answer already given does not effectively remove the answer from the record, and the motion to strike must be made and sustained. Care should be taken by the trial attorney to examine the law of his state in this regard.

A nonresponsive answer may be challenged as such by the examiner only, not by his adversary. Usually the latter may successfully move to strike it only when it is both nonresponsive and otherwise objectionable.

Where evidence has been admitted, which appeared at the time of admission to be admissible, and it later appears that such testimony was in fact inadmissible, a motion to strike should be promptly made.

9.1.4 Offering Evidence for Limited Purposes

In general, evidence is frequently admissible for certain limited purposes, but inadmissible for other purposes.

General Offer Before the Specific

Where testimony is offered that is admissible for a limited purpose only, its exclusion by the court is usually not reversible error unless the limited purpose for which it is offered is pointed out. If, however, the evidence is offered without any limitation, and no proper objection is made to it, it is then generally admitted for all purposes. 133 ALR 1454, 1455.

A trial tactic used by many successful practitioners is to offer the evidence at first as a general offer. If no objection is made, the evidence is in the record for all purposes. If an objection is made, counsel then informs the judge, opposing counsel, and jury of the limited purpose for which the evidence is tendered.

The Requested Instruction

The failure of the court to instruct the jury that such evidence is to be considered by them solely for the limited purpose for which it is received is probably not reversible error unless a requested instruction to that effect has been made. *Dagget v. Atchison, Topeka, & Sante Fe R. Co.* (1957) 46 Cal 2d 655, 313 P2d 557, 64 ALR2d 1283.

Examples

Medical Testimony. An attending physician may testify as to the statements made to her by the patient in connection with the accident, to the extent that the statements have bearing upon the injuries sustained by the patient. The history given by the patient to the doctor is ordinarily admissible for the purpose of allowing the doctor to give the basis for her medical opinion. It is not admissible for the purpose of proving the truth of facts, detailed to her by the patient, having no bearing upon the diagnosis.

For example, a statement made by the patient to his doctor that the car in which he was sitting was hit violently from the rear, throwing him first backwards, and then forward into the windshield, could be of some importance to a doctor in diagnosing an injury to the neck and lacerations of the face. However, skid marks made by the other car, or the fact that the other driver was drinking, would be irrelevant to the doctor in her diagnosis, and therefore could not ordinarily be properly admitted as a part of the history given to her by the patient.

Evidence of Repairs. Repairs made after an accident are generally held to be inadmissible for the purpose of showing negligence on the part of the defendant. However, such repairs may be admissible for the purpose of showing control over the premises by the defendant (64 ALR2d 1296, 1311) and to aid in identification (64 ALR2d 1296, 1309). It has been held that such evidence is also admissible for the purpose of showing the existence of a defect when that is an issue. *Millman v. United States Mortgage and Title Guaranty Co.* (1938) 121 NJL 28, 1 A2d 265.

Evidence of Drinking. Evidence of drinking on the part of a driver does not, in and of itself, ordinarily constitute negligence, but such testimony is admissible in many jurisdictions as bearing upon the ability of the party to accurately relate the facts, and it may also have a bearing upon whether the party was careful and reasonably prudent under the circumstances. It has been held that evidence of drinking on the part of the deceased at the time of the accident and at other times tends to show his drinking habits and how they may have affected his earning power and the amount of loss sustained by his estate.

Speed Prior to Accident. Speed at a time just prior to the accident often is held admissible, not as proof of the speed at the place of the accident, but only to corroborate the testimony as to the speed at the place of the accident. 46 ALR2d 60.

Evidence of Prior Accidents. Evidence of prior accidents at the same place or with the same instrumentality, under substantially similar circumstances, is ordinarily admissible, not for the purpose of showing independent acts of negligence, but as tending to show a dangerous and unsafe condition and knowledge thereof by the offending party. It has been held, however, as a corollary, that proof of no such accidents having occurred at the same place or with the same instrumentality, under substantially similar circumstances, is admissible as tending to show absence of danger and lack of knowledge thereof by a party claimed to be at fault.

Admissions Against Interest. Admissions ordinarily constitute substantive proof. However, inconsistent statements of a witness who is not a party to the litigation may not be admissible as substantive proof of the matters described in the statement. Such inconsistent statements are usually admissible only for the limited purpose of impeachment of the witness. 133 ALR 1454, 1455.

Photographs. A photograph containing structures and other matters obviously inadmissible may nevertheless be admissible for a limited purpose. For example, photographs made long after the occurrence, even if the scene has been substantially changed, may be admissible as showing that part of the scene which remains unchanged. Counsel should state promptly, clearly, and concisely the specific purpose for which the photograph is offered.

Multiple Defendants. Often multiple defendants appear as parties. Damaging admissions may be made by one of them, and such testimony is properly admitted as against the interest of the party making such statements. However such statements are not admissible as against the interest of the other defendants except under certain circumstances where the relationship of the parties is that of employer and servant, business partners, or some similar relationship. Good trial tactics require that the counsel representing the defendant or defendants does not make an objection to these admissions, and if he does not, the evidence is generally admitted without qualification, and its admission ordinarily will not, on appeal, be deemed an error. 106 ALR 647.

Conclusion

The trial attorney should tender the testimony or evidence admissible for limited purposes after careful thought. Where such evidence is offered by his adversary, it is imperative that proper objections be stated, and where such testimony is admitted, the court should be requested to advise the jury of the limited purpose for which the testimony is received.

9.1.5 How and When to Make an Offer of Proof

An offer of proof in practice is nothing more nor less than the words imply. It means, simply, offering to prove that which the trial court has ruled inadmissible as evidence.

An offer of proof may be used, and indeed is necessary, in many trial situations; for example, where the evidence a party seeks to introduce is seemingly neither relevant nor competent. An offer of proof is frequently made on cross-examination to show the pertinence, not otherwise apparent, of a question to which an objection has been raised by the opposing party.

Purpose of Offer of Proof

The purpose of the offer of proof is to inform the court of the evidence tendered so that the court may rule intelligently upon the objections to questions that have been asked. An offer of proof also completes the record, thus permitting the appellate court to determine whether reversible error was committed in excluding the evidence sought to be introduced.

Making the Offer of Proof in Proper Form

Although the courts vary in strictness, as a general rule the offer of proof must be in proper form. It should clearly and fully state the facts that counsel desires to prove, and the means and evidence by which he proposes to prove them. Ordinarily it is not an error for the trial court to reject an offer of proof that is vague and unspecific, that fails to disclose sufficient facts and states mere conclusions, that fails to state the purposes for which the evidence is offered, or that fails to disclose that the evidence is admissible; that is, competent and relevant.

Effect of Failure to Make Offer

Where no offer of proof is made, the trial court must determine the admissibility of evidence without being sufficiently informed of that which the examiner intends to prove by the question. Obviously counsel must clearly show to the court the purpose of the question and the answer the witness would give if the question were permitted an answer. When the court is required to rule without the benefit of an offer of proof, the record is such that the appellate court ordinarily cannot and will not consider questions of error in the exclusion of the evidence.

Methods of Making Offer

There are two basic methods of making an offer of proof. The first and simplest method, and the one most often used, is counsel's asking leave of the court to make an offer of proof in the absence of the jury. Generally the request is made after objection to a question has been sustained; however some jurisdictions require it to be made before ruling by the court. The court will ordinarily grant the request, excuse the jury from the courtroom so that the offer can be made in the courtroom, or retire to chambers and permit the offer to be made there. In either event, the request should be recorded by the court reporter. The offer may be stated in the following narrative form:

"If the witness, John Doe, being present in court, were permitted to testify, he would testify substantially as follows:" (Here counsel states the testimony of the witness.)

This method is particularly dangerous because it might well be considered an "offer in bulk," and some courts have held that if any part of the offer in bulk is objectionable the entire offer in bulk may be properly excluded.

Another narrative form that may be used is the following:

"If the witness, John Doe, being present in court, were asked the following question (here state question), he would give the following answer:" (Here state answer.)

Where this narrative form is used, counsel should make a separate offer of each question and a separate offer of the answer to each question, so that each question and respective answer can be ruled upon by the trial court and reviewed by the appellate court. If each question and respective answer is not separately offered, the same danger exists that the group of questions and answers may be considered an offer in bulk and that the entire offer may properly be rejected if any part of the same should be excluded.

Though the narrative methods demonstrated above appear to be the most commonly used, such methods are not recommended since it would appear that the trial courts and the appellate court view them with some disfavor.

The most effective method, and one that appears to be favored by the courts, is the offer of proof by direct and specific questions put to the witness under oath on the witness stand, where the witness is permitted to give direct answers to the questions. Each question and respective answer should be separately offered to eliminate the same possibility of their being considered an "offer in bulk."

Tactics that Determine Value of Offer

The substance of the offer and the tactics of the trial attorney determine the value of the offer of proof. The offer must be made in such a manner as best serves the case, stating the purpose for which the offer is made and satisfying the jurisdictional requirements. Questions and answers must be germane, competent, and material. Questions and answers must be such that the appellate court has sufficient evidence to properly review the offered testimony.

Offer for Limited Purpose

In some jurisdictions an offer of proof may be made for a specific limited purpose only. For example, the testimony may not be generally admissible, but if it is admissible for some specific purpose, and the purpose is stated, then the offer may be allowed even though the jury may consider the evidence for an improper purpose as well. However, it is a common practice for the court, upon request, to instruct the jury that such evidence is admitted for a specific purpose, and to state the purpose.

Conclusion

In summary, the following rules pertaining to offers of proof should be kept in mind:

1. The offer must be made in proper form, in keeping with the rules of local practice.
2. The recommended procedure is direct questioning of the witness, offering each question and answer separately.
3. Questions and answers shoud be framed in such a way as to make it abundantly clear to the trial court what is intended to be proved by the testimony, thereby assisting the court in properly ruling upon the proposed testimony.
4. The offer must be an offer of fact, and not of conclusion.
5. The offer must be specific.
6. If the witness is not in court at the time, the witness must be named, and it must be shown that he is available to testify and will testify in accordance with the offer.

9.1.6 Evidence of Experiments

As a general rule experiments, or evidence of experiments, are admissible if the conditions under which the experiment is or was conducted are substantially similar to the conditions existing at the time of the occurrence. 20 *Am. Jur.*, Evidence, Section 755-762, pp. 627-633; 8 ALR 18; 78 ALR 152; 85 ALR 480; 76 ALR 2d 346; *Ackman v. Beckwith* (1954) 245 Iowa 791, 64 NW 2d 275; *Knalowski v. Grand Trunk Ry. Co.* (1887) 64 Mich 279, 31 NW275.

In the past the courts refused to permit experiments or to admit evidence of experiments because it was felt that (1) to allow experiments would be to permit parties to manufacture evidence, and (2) to allow experiments would raise too many collateral issues, because experiments on behalf of the opposing party would have to be allowed. 15 ALR 221; 85 ALR 479. The trend, however, in recent years has been toward a liberalization of the use of experiments and the admission of experiment evidence. 85 ALR 479.

Judicial Discretion

Whether the experiment was conducted under substantially similar conditions is a matter within the sound discretion of the trial court. Ordinarily such discretion will not be interfered with unless it has clearly been abused. 20 *Am. Jur.*, Evidence, Section 755, p. 628.

Under the general rule, evidence both of experiments conducted in the presence of the jury, and experiments conducted outside the courtroom is admissible. There does not appear to be any distinction between the two types of experiments as long as the court has found that the experiment was or is being conducted under circumstances substantially similar to those prevailing at the time of the occurrence. 20 *Am. Jur.*, Evidence, 757-758, p. 630. However, most courts do not permit the making of tests or experiments by the jury itself. 20 *Am. Jur.*, Evidence, 755, p. 628. Testimony regarding experiments is usually admissible despite the fact that the opposing party was not present when the experiment was conducted.

Proper Foundation for Offering Evidence of Experiments

It is essential that proper foundation be laid for the introduction of testimony regarding both experiments conducted outside the courtroom and those conducted in the presence of the jury. When experiment evidence is sought to be admitted, the court determines whether there is such similarity of circumstances as to render the evidence competent. The attorney must therefore meet the requirement of similar conditions before offering the experiment or the experiment testimony. 8 ALR 18; 85 ALR 480.

Experiments in the Courtroom

Because of the general reluctance of courts to permit the jury to receive evidence outside the courtroom, it is recommended that experiments be conducted in the courtroom, in the presence of the jury, if at all possible. 60 ALR 574, and *Tarr v. Carroll Lumber and Constr. Co.* (1928) 106 W Va 109, 144 SE 881.

Experiments Outside the Courtroom

However, if necessary, some courts will permit the jury to be taken to the place where the experiment is to be conducted. *Stockwell v. C. C. and D. R. Co.* (1876) 43 Iowa 470.

Experiments in Rebuttal

The courts appear to allow greater latitude, so far as the requirement of similarity of conditions is concerned, in cases where experiment evidence is offered in rebuttal of experiment evidence that has already been received. 20 *Am. Jur.*, Evidence, Section 277, p. 293; 8 ALR 23; 85 ALR 479; 78 ALR2d 160, 164, 176.

Court's Attitude Toward Experiment Evidence

Some courts strongly favor experiment evidence. It has been pointed out that there are numerous advantages of experiment evidence over some other kinds of evidence; however trial lawyers frequently overlook its possibilities for use.

Examples of Experiment Evidence

Experiment evidence has been admitted in cases involving tests or experiments with respect to motors, locomotives, automobiles, fire, explosions, electricity, gases, smoke, furnaces, firearms, knives, ladders, identification marks, footprints, noises, stains, alcohol, blood, skin, teeth, paint, glass, wax, foods, drugs, cosmetics, insecticides, seed, livestock, cement, plaster, water, wood, weather, cloth, fur, cleaning compounds, intersections, light, visibility, time, and distance.

Experiments by Nonexpert

Experiment evidence does not always require the use of expert witnesses. Moreover, a review of the many cases involving experiment testimony reveals that in many of them the witness who conducted the experiment was a lay witness and not an expert. Frequently the witness is one of the parties.

Appellate Review

As a general rule, if a trial court permits the introduction of experimental evidence, the appellate courts affirm the use of such evidence unless it is clearly shown that there has been an abuse of discretion.

Pretrial Discussion of Experiment Evidence

Good trial tactics require the attorney who intends to use experimental evidence at the trial to discuss the matter with the court and opposing counsel prior to the commencement of the trial. The pretrial conference is an excellent time to mention to the court and opposing counsel that experimental evidence will be tendered. The court is then in a better position to rule upon the admissibility of such evidence after the foundation for it has been laid at trial. The attorney should advise the court as to the conditions under which the experiment was conducted, or the conditions under which she proposes to conduct such an experiment in the presence of the jury. A brief should be submitted to the court in advance of the trial, indicating that the current trend is to permit such evidence.

Effectiveness of Courtroom Experiments

Experiments or tests conducted in the presence of the jury are more effective than those conducted away from the jury and described by a witness. It is doubtful that there is any more effective evidence than tests or experiments conducted in the presence of the jury. However, the trial attorney should be wary of conducting experiments in the presence of the jury when he is uncertain of the results.

Variations in Conditions

In laying the foundation for the introduction of experimental evidence, the examiner should have the witness explain any differences between conditions as they existed at the time of the occurrence and at the time of the experiment. If variations or departures are minor, and counsel has in good faith demonstrated to the court that he has attempted during the experiment, insofar as possible, to simulate conditions existing at the time of the occurrence, he is more likely to persuade the court as to the competency of the evidence.

9.1.7 Posed Photographs and Models

The value of photographic evidence, though not as great as that of experimental evidence, is well known to the trial lawyer. Posed photographs and models ordinarily are not real evidence, but are used as visual aid or "demonstrative evidence" for the purpose of explaining and demonstrating a witness's oral testimony. The majority of the courts have held that posed photographs, based on recollection of the position of persons or movable objects, are admissible as illustrative of the testimony of witnesses. Where these are offered, preliminary testimony must show that the photographs are fair representations of the scene at the time of the actual occurrence. 19 ALR2d 877.

9.1.8 The Witness

Introduction

To the trial lawyer facts are the weapons of her client's cause; words are the missiles that carry the message, and win or lose the case.

Most evidence produced in court is oral in nature. The witness speaks from the stand under oath. He talks, and when he talks, what he relates is often not so important as the manner and words he uses in saying it.

To be persuasive, the witness must use persuasive words that carry an impact. They must be words of conviction. They must sell not only the witness's version of what he observed or heard, but they must be properly interpreted by the jury.

The Value of the Descriptive Phrase

There are many ways to describe an observation made. In describing movement, which is one of the most common observations a witness is called upon to make, one may state simply that "the car passed by," or, "I saw him moving." These phrases describe movement; but they are not descriptive of the manner in which the movement was made. Let us go one step further. Suppose the witness says, "I saw the car pass. It was going fast." The term "fast" describes speed, but speed is relative. To a witness driving 10 miles per hour, an auto passing at 30 miles per hour might appear to be going fast. Yet this word does not necessarily engender in the minds of the jury a vision or sensation of speed. What if the witness should say, however, that the car went "like a streak" past him. Here we have a stark description of extreme speed.

A defense lawyer was once heard to complain that the plaintiff had won his case because of the use of just two words—"white streak." He perhaps didn't know it, but he was paying homage to the power of words. The devastating power of words. What do we mean? It seemed that the defendant had driven a white vehicle. A witness, when asked to describe the movement of the defendant's vehicle, had answered that it appeared as a "white streak." He gave no testimony as to speed. He gave no estimate in terms of miles per hour, or estimate or guess as to how far the vehicle had traveled in a given time. His testimony as to his observations simply was that the vehicle appeared as a "white streak."

Why did the defendant's counsel complain that the case had been lost because of the words? Let us analyze them. What did the witness say? First, he used a potent word of action—of power—the word, "streak." Now, what "streaks?" Comets streak across the sky; jet planes streak to their destination. The word is a word describing extreme speed. How many times have you heard the statement, "he went by like a blue streak"? The witness, wittingly or unwittingly, by the use of the term called to the minds of the jury a picture of very rapid motion. How much more effective this was, rather than to describe the vehicle as "going very fast" or "moving rapidly." A "white streak." The word "white" happened to describe the color of the defendant's vehicle. Yet even white" lights up the word "streak" and gives more sense of motion to the mind.

The Lawyer's Duty

What technique is employed by the trial lawyer to encourage the witness to use descriptive terms? How far can the trial lawyer go in encouraging witnesses and clients to use words of impact, power words? Often it isn't what is said that leaves the lasting impression. The trial lawyer must encourage client and witnesses to use words of impact and power.

Lawyers owe a duty to their clients, to the court, to the jury, and to their profession to be as effective as their ability will permit. Just as they must orient clients and witnesses to the courtroom scene, so should they impress upon them the value of words. The value of descriptive terms, the power of words. Lawyers have every right to suggest effective methods of telling the *truth*—not what to say, but how to say it.

Example of Indirect Emphasis

Some years ago I chanced into a courtroom wherein an accused was on trial for statutory rape. The young prosecuting attorney, who incidentally is now one of the most effective plaintiff's personal injury lawyers in the midwest, had done his homework well. Picture this scene. On the stand, a young, obviously under-age prosecutrix (you could tell by her dress and pigtails), giving testimony of the events just prior to the attack.

Q: What happened then?

A: I heard footsteps on the stairs.

Q: Whose footsteps were they?

A: I didn't know at the time.

Q: Go ahead.

A: I heard them reach the top of the stairs. The door to our apartment opened and the defendant walked in.

Q: What happened then?

A: He hurt me!

The words "he hurt me" produced visible reaction among the jury members. I watched in fascination as the young attorney with vision and imagination led his witness through the ordeal of explaining what she meant when she said, "He hurt me." It no doubt was the truth. How much more effective than to have the witness describe, step by step, the action of the defendant. And, keep in mind, the witness told nothing but the truth. The defendant did hurt her. The use of the terms; the impact words, accomplished much. It resulted in a prompt conviction of the accused. In terms of technique, it described an occurrence, the unlawful intercourse; it demonstrated a reluctance on the part of the modest young girl to volunteer the details of a sordid act; and it moved the jury to action.

Importance of Words

What is so important about the use of words—how they are said—rather than what is said? Witnesses and clients are people. Jurors are people, and react to their past and their environment. Some words generate sympathy. Some words generate animosity. Some produce a feeling of uneasiness; others, a reaction of kindliness and affection for the person speaking. The witness should be alerted to the importance of using descriptive words. Words that persuade, that tell the story of what the witness saw and heard.

9.1.9 The Lawyer

Introduction

Every trial lawyer talks; he or she uses words. Without them, there could be no trial, no advocacy, no rapid communication of thoughts, ideas, or principles. We sometimes take our language, the words we use, for granted. Many lawyers, including those committed to trial practice, function at minimum rather than maximum efficiency. No effort is made to improve the effectiveness or efficiency of the spoken word. Yet, just as the winner at golf must practice his game, sharpen his eye and improve his stroke technique, so must the trial lawyer constantly practice at the use of his language—his use of words—to win.

The Study of Semantics

The study of semantics—the meaning of words—is a fascinating study. What have the people of the ages said about words? Consider these:

"We rule men with words."—Napoleon

"Words are the voice of the heart."—Confucius

"Words are the instruments that make thought possible."—Emerson

"With words we govern men."—Disraeli

"Words are the pegs to hang ideas on."—Beecher

We might add, as trial lawyers, our own quote—"With words we influence people," or, to be more down-to-earth, "With words we win cases."

Perhaps the most important and the least studied aspect of our professional life is our understanding of, and ability to use, the right words, the right phrase, at the right time. When was the last time you consciously sought to improve your vocabulary? The last time you deliberately used a word designed to shock, to move or motivate someone? Your answer, "Every day!" and it's true. But these are the unconscious efforts, the habitual words engraved in your speech routine. How about the last time you debated with yourself as to the choice of words—asked the question, which one will be the most effective?

Dr. Wilfred Funk, the noted author and publisher of dictionaries and encyclopedias, says that though it is hard to believe, just nine words carry one-fourth of the burden of our letter writing and conversation. Do you know what they are? Here is the list: "and, the, be, to, have, will, it you, of."

Surprising? Yes, but even more so when one realizes that by adding just 34 more words, we have one-half the words actually used in everyday American speech.

Dr. Funk's great little book entitled, *Six Weeks to Words of Power,* which should be "must" reading for all lawyers, lists verbs by category, such as those dealing with human traits, denial, general value, action, and violence. He discusses verbs of exceptional power, of deep emotion about fellow men, of energy, and violent criticism. He analyzes nouns of unusual power, of personal characteristics, of emotion, human traits, pleasant meaning, and insult. He describes adjectives suggesting unpleasant ideas, adjectives describing size, those of disagreeable meaning, those that describe friends and enemies, and those that suggest strength.

Improve Your Vocabulary

It has been said that clarity is most important in the use of words. Oliver Wendell Holmes once remarked that language is the blood of the soul! Emerson said, "each word was at first a stroke of genius." Since words are indeed the instruments that make thoughts possible, the trial lawyer should constantly seek to improve his vocabulary of descriptive, power-packed terms. Consider the description, the impact of words used by a witness describing the speed of an automobile by testifying that it "zoomed," that it "streaked," that it "roared," that it "careened," that it "zipped," or that it "rocketed" past the scene.

Everyday Courtroom Words

What about the words that we use every day in the courtroom? The oath administered to the witness contains the word "truth." In describing the testimony of a witness and in analyzing it for the jury in an effort to demonstrate the truthfulness of the witness, consider the use of the words: frankness, sincerity, candor, openness, honesty, straightforwardness and veracity. Good trial lawyers rarely suggest that a witness has lied on the stand unless the circumstances suggest such intemperate language. Rather, the witness was "inaccurate," "mistaken," "misled or misleading," or perhaps even "uninformed." Why does the word "malinger," bandied by the defense, often produce jury reaction? Because it is a word of power. It describes a human trait. What are some other power words that the trial lawyer should incorporate into his language?

Verbs of Action and Energy

Consider the verbs of action: to devastate; to enjoin; to instigate; to expedite; to coerce; to commandeer. Some verbs suggest violence, such as: to lacerate; to ravage; to subvert; to sabotage; to jeopardize. Other verbs express deep emotion, such as: to harangue; to be obsessed; or to enthrall. What about the verbs: to desecrate; or to emasculate; or to mulct? Are they not terms of power that the trial lawyer may use with effectiveness? Some verbs describe energy. The verb, to catapult, for example. He was "catapulted" from the car. How much more effective is this than "he was thrown from the car." These examples, and many others, are described and analyzed by Dr. Funk in his book.

Words that Move

The trial lawyer should be constantly on the alert for words that move men to action. Some of the great trial lawyers spend part of each day studying words and effective composition. If we analyze the effective jury summations and the witness testimony technique of the truly effective trial lawyer, we find that he or she truly generates "thoughts that breathe and words that burn."

Words and Phrases to Avoid

Some lawyers are trapped by their own habit into using words and phrases that are ineffective and often meaningless. Sometimes phrases handed down to us through legal history cause us to use weak and ineffective terminology. Consider, for example, the phrase, "pain and suffering."

One of the authors has removed from his courtroom vocabulary the word "suffering" for this reason: the word "pain" is a power word and a descriptive term capable of only one interpretation. It means one thing. It means, "It hurts." When we speak of pain, we describe a sensation, physical or mental, that all jurors can understand. But what about the word "suffering"? "Suffering" is a word weak in nature and capable of many interpretations. It detracts from the impact of the word "pain." A juror was once heard to say that all the plaintiff's lawyer talked about was pain and suffering, pain and suffering, pain and suffering. The juror reached the point where the word "suffering" grated noticeably upon his nerves. He was reacting much as others react to a word producing an unfavorable response. We suffer for many reasons. We suffer if our child is hurt. We suffer if our parent is ill. We suffer if things do not go well—none of which suffering is produced, necessarily, by a traumatic experience.

Lawyers Judged by How It Is Said

Lawyers are judged not only by what they say, but by how they say it. We use voir dire examination, not only to elicit information, but to condition the jury (see Chapter 8). Never say, "Are you going to give a full award to this man in your verdict?" but rather, "Are you going to give him full justice?" The implication is obvious. You have come there to seek justice, not to seek an award.

Don't speak of your plaintiff as "the plaintiff," rather, say as "the victim," or "the widow," or "the little boy." When you use such terms, they mean something to the jury. The word "plaintiff" means very little.

Talk about the debt the defendant owes to the victim. Don't talk about awards. Talk about justice instead of a verdict. In a death case, talk about death, not awards. Talk about balancing the scales of justice.

You will find that not all words have meaning. Choose words that fly, words that hit the point, words that strike the bull's eye.

"We are not here to demand anything—we are here asking for your help to attain justice."

9.1.10 Visual Aids in the Courtroom

Some years ago, the Socony Vacuum Oil Company conducted tests to determine whether visual aids were actually helpful in the teaching process. The studies demonstrated that indeed they were. For example, it was learned that when a person merely hears oral statements, such as testimony, the average person remembers only about 10 percent of what he or she heard after the lapse of three days. When the same people were shown something, such as a picture or model, they remembered roughly 20 percent of what they had seen. Interestingly, however, the tests proved that when the person is both told something orally and at the same time shown something that supports or demonstrates the validity of the oral statement, the listener and viewer remembers about 65 percent of what he or she has been told and shown.

The courtroom is, in a sense, a classroom. The lawyers, the witnesses, and the other evidence are the teachers; the jurors are the students. Every lawyer strives to get the point across—to win the case. No modern trial lawyer can afford to overlook the importance of visual aids in the courtroom.

Medical Charts and Drawings

Since the trial of a personal injury case today primarily involves educating the jury with respect to the medical problems involved, most trial lawyers make liberal use of medical charts and drawings. The Froshe charts, used in every medical school and hospital in the country, are standard. They serve to assist the doctor in explaining anatomy, nerve distribution, location of muscles, and such other matters as may be important in a case. The Medical Atlas for Attorneys, published by the Berkley Press of San Francisco, California, is an excellent set of medical charts, drawings, transparencies, and overlays, which may be used alternately on the opaque projector or the overhead transparency projector. Many attorneys use medical illustrators for medical drawings of the injury in the particular case.

The attorney should be careful to make use of such material only when it will better educate the jury as to the medical problem involved. Jurors are quick to sense when a lawyer is attempting to put on a show and will react unfavorably to the lawyer who does this.

Blackboard or Whiteboard

Although trial by blackboard is thought to be of recent origin, blackboards have been used for many years in the trial of both civil and criminal cases. Here again, we are simply using an additional aid in the education of the jury, and the blackboard has certain obvious disadvantages. One of the old defense lawyer's tricks is to erase the blackboard as soon as possible after it has been used, under the pretense of needing it for his own use.

One of the most effective methods of combating this technique is to use what is sometimes referred to as the "whiteboard." This consists of large sheets of paper, which may be obtained from any stationery store, and which are often used by artists. The felt pen, in such colors as red, blue, green, black, or brown may be effectively used to demonstrate and emphasize certain aspects of the case. An additional advantage of the so-called whiteboard is that the charts and notations made on the sheets of paper may be preserved for use in an appeal, if necessary, whereas those depicted on the blackboard, if some later claim is made that it was improper, usually will have been erased before there has been a chance to photograph or preserve it.

In determining whether to use the blackboard or the whiteboard, the attorney should consider just what he or she is attempting to do, and whether there is any question about the propriety of the material.

Skeletons and Models

Some trial attorneys make extensive use of skeletons and models. Most architects and engineers are capable of producing models in almost any area. Some of the larger law firms have a model-making department which prepares models for use in most of the cases to be tried. Models take many forms. A model may be a mock-up or model of a railroad crossing, showing all of the various adjacent structures, or a model car, or the model of a cockpit of an aircraft, depending upon the particular features of the case and the imagination of the attorney.

Models of the human anatomy, such as joints and bones, full skeletons, and the like, are in common use throughout the country, and in most states are admitted upon the basis of the doctor's assertion that they will make it easier for her to explain, and the jury to understand, her testimony. Models are seldom actually introduced into evidence, but are identified as exhibits and used for illustration purposes only. Here again, the trial attorney must be careful not to overuse models to the point where the jury concludes that he is merely trying to put on a show. The judicious use of models, however, can be, and usually is, beneficial, since the party producing them has the advantage of permitting the witness not only to tell in words what he or she knows about the case, but also to illustrate visually for the jury the problems involved in the case.

Experiments

Experiments conducted both outside and inside the courtroom can be very effective as instruments of persuasion. Experiments made outside the courtroom often are photographed either with a motion picture camera or a still camera, and the photographs produced in court for the purpose of demonstrating to the jury the experiment results. Although they are risky, experiments conducted in the presence of the jury can be shockingly effective. Such experiments can be the most illustrative testimony obtainable. If, however, the experiment fails, the jury often greatly overemphasizes the failure, and the case may well result in a disaster. There is an old saying among lawyers that it is possible to change testimony, but it is impossible to change a physical fact. Experiments demonstrating physical facts or principles of mechanical engineering thus carry great weight, particularly when the physical facts and principles are constant. Where the case warrants it, and there is to be an experiment conducted outside the presence of the jury prior to trial, particularly if it is to be conducted by opposing counsel and his or her expert, having the experiment photographed by a motion picture camera can often be a very small but worthwhile investment.

Photographs

Ground Photographs. Photographs have come into widespread use in modern times and almost every trial lawyer uses them. Requirements in most states are simple, it being necessary only that a witness testify that the photograph fairly and accurately depicts that which it is claimed to show. Photographs are often introduced for limited purposes. Where there has been a change in the scene, such as at an intersection, and the photograph shows structures or other material not present at the time of the incident, a statement by counsel that the photograph is offered for the purpose of showing merely that which it is intended to show will render the photograph admissible for such limited purposes. Care should be taken always to offer such photographs for the explicit limited purpose so that in case an error in admissibility of the photograph is subsequently claimed, there will be an adequate record on appeal.

The Polaroid camera has definite advantages and should be available to trial lawyers or their investigators, since it develops immediately, and attorneys may quickly determine whether or not they have, in fact, obtained the desired picture for use at trial. This is especially true when the photograph is a last-minute one made either during or just prior to the trial. The Polaroid photo, when projected on the screen through the use of the opaque projector has many advantages over the large blowup. It may be produced at a minimum cost, is easily transported, and attracts attention when viewed on the projector screen.

Aerial Photographs. Aerial photographs may be obtained from many sources. One possibility, of course, is to take your own, either from an airplane or helicopter, the helicopter having the advantage of permitting the photograph to be taken from a much lower altitude than from a fixed wing aircraft. It is also possible, with a helicopter, to maneuver into just the right position to get the photograph, whereas it is sometimes impossible to do so with an airplane. Often, aerial photographs may be taken from the rooftops of buildings, from a crane extended above an intersection or other area intended to be photographed, from the top of a truck, from a tree, or from other structures.

Aerial photographs have the advantage that most jurors take a deep interest in them, since they show the scene from a different angle, one not commonly viewed by members of the jury. This explains why newspapers and news magazines make extensive use of aerial photographs. They are an attention getter.

If an aerial photograph is to be used to depict the sharpness of a curve in a road, it is important that the photograph be taken from the proper angle so that it will not portray an exaggerated curve. In order for the aerial photograph to portray, without distortion, a curve in the road, the photograph must be taken straight down the road and toward the curve rather than from the apex of the curve. If it is taken from the apex or at a ninety-degree angle to the center of the curve, the curve will appear to be much more shallow than it really is. This is, in fact, the way the curve actually looks, and a witness could legitimately testify that is a fair representation of how the curve appeared to him at the time it was taken from that angle. However, such a photograph does not give a true portrayal of the sharpness, or lack of sharpness, of the curve.

Aerial photographs may be taken with almost any kind of a camera. Perhaps the best camera for consistently good aerial photographs is the Rolleiflex, using high-speed film and developing the picture on a fine grade paper. Most photographs may be enlarged many times, and serve as a valuable persuasive aid in orienting the jury with respect to the scene of the occurrence.

Colored Photographs. Colored photographs have become commonplace in the courtroom. They have distinct advantages, such as where a collison has occurred through failure of the defendant to stop at a stop sign. If a colored photograph is taken of the road and of the stop sign from the position where the defendant should have seen the stop sign, the stop sign, being red, will stand out very clearly, whereas in the black and white photograph the stop sign is the same color as all of the other objects in the photograph. The reason that the highway commissions in the various states use red is that it is intended to attract the attention of the driver. Since little traffic on the highway is also red, the stop sign stands out very clearly.

Contrary to popular belief, colored photographs are not necessarily the most valuable photographs in depicting a scar. Black and white photographs, and use of proper shadowing, can depict a scar more realistically. The color process tends to fade or shade out the scar and makes it appear to be less obvious than it really is.

The Enlarged Photograph. The prime purpose of all photographs is to help orient the jury toward the problems at hand. The enlarged or blown-up photograph makes it possible for the entire jury to view the photograph at the same time, eliminating the necessity of passing it among the jurors. Enlarged photographs are, however, difficult to handle. They are difficult to transport and store. While they have the advantage of permitting the entire jury to view the scene at the same time, they are difficult for the witness to mark while at the same time providing testimony. Many successful trial attorneys are turning more and more to the use of the opaque or transparency projector, which permits the jury a simultaneous view while the witness can mark and illustrate the testimony he or she is giving.

Movies. In the important case where serious disabling injuries have occurred, movies taken in the injured party's home, nursing home, or hospital room, depicting her daily routine, or at least that part of her daily routine that has been changed drastically by the injury, can be very valuable. Care should be taken to exercise good taste in the production of such movies.

Display of Injuries

Some injuries are obvious, others are obscure. When an injury is obvious such as the loss of a leg, partial or complete paralysis, superficial scarring or burns that are obvious, no particular display of the injury need be made.

Where the injuries are particularly hideous to look at it is considered good policy to keep the plaintiff out of the presence of the jury, except for the brief period of time during which she makes her appearance and gives her testimony. The reason for this is that, from the psychological standpoint, people are inclined to become progressively immune or used to viewing something that is, at first, distasteful to look at. The plaintiff with disfiguring injuries is not seen constantly by any one person ordinarily, or day after day after day, and those people who do see her, such as members of her family, are not the ones who cause emotional disturbance. The disfigured plaintiff suffers injury at the hands of strangers who reject her, or are repelled by her appearance, and who refuse to give her a chance to demonstrate her value as a human being.

Where the injury is such that it is not readily observable by the jury, such as scarring on the upper thigh, a burned area on the upper thigh, the stomach, the back, or some other area of the body that is normally covered, the trial lawyer must make a decision as to whether to exhibit or ask to be permitted to exhibit the injured person's body to the jury or to photograph the injury and present the injury to the jury through photographic media. In every instance the trial lawyer must exhibit good taste and discretion lest he or she offend the jury and be accused of attempting to gain the sympathy of the jury through the exhibition.

Medical Examination in the Courtroom. One method of demonstrating to the jury a neurological deficiency or limitation of motion in joints and extremities is to have the medical witness, the doctor, at the time of his appearance on the stand, conduct an actual medical examination in the courtroom in the presence of the jury. It is one thing for the doctor to testify that the plaintiff has an absence of normal knee jerk. It is much more illustrative of the condition to ask the doctor to show the jury the actual examination and tests conducted by him upon the body of the plaintiff so that the jury may more readily understand the doctor's testimony.

To introduce such testimony, inquire of the doctor if such a demonstration will more clearly illustrate the case and render his testimony more meaningful to the jury than mere oral testimony. In most states such examination or demonstration is permissible if a doctor testifies that it is the easiest way to explain the problem to the jury.

The X-Ray. Few jurors are capable of correctly interpreting an x-ray film. Quite often the unskilled trial practitioner asks the doctor to interpret the x-ray film by merely holding it up to a light, or placing it in a view box, with the result that few of the jurors either see, understand, or correctly interpret the doctor's testimony relative to the injury as depicted or demonstrated by the x-ray film. Where the film may be readily interpreted by the jury, such as dramatic fractures, shattered bones and the like, probably prints of the film should be made and exhibited to the jury. Use the opaque projector; or, if the negative is of sufficient quality, it may be placed upon the overhead transparency projector, and flashed on the screen for the jury to view during the doctor's testimony.

The advantage of the use of the overhead projector during the doctor's testimony is that the doctor can readily mark upon the x-ray during his testimony, and the jury can readily view the x-ray and the markings of the medical witness while the testimony is given.

Appliances of Healing. A trial lawyer should approach the problem of the use of appliances of healing, such as traction apparatus, braces, lumbar corsets, and other such articles often prescribed by doctors, with caution. Very often it is wise to refrain from the use of such appliances, as jurors often get the impression that the attorney is overdramatizing his case. Always inspect such appliances prior to exhibition in the presence of the jury to make certain that they appear to have been used.

OVERHEAD TRANSPARENCY PROJECTOR

Introduction. The overhead transparency projector is in many respects a new concept in courtroom communication. It is a highly effective tool in the persuasive process, and it has been tried and proven by many successful attorneys. Most attorneys who have actually used the machine in court refuse to try a jury case without it. Judges usually regard the machine and its use with favor, since it can be easily demonstrated that it saves hours and sometimes days in trial. The value of the machine can be summed up simply: First, it is a timesaver; second, it increases jury understanding; and third, it certainly improves the powers of persuasion of the lawyer.

The machine is manufactured by the Minnesota Mining & Manufacturing Company, sometimes known as the 3M Company, and is available through its sales outlets. The 3M Company is also the manufacturer of the well-known thermofax machine. The projector may be obtained as a portable unit or as a somewhat larger upright machine with noncollapsible limbs. The device has the distinction that it can be used in normally lighted courtrooms at very close range to the screen. Since it is an inescapable fact that twelve jurors can make or break a case, it is imperative that trial lawyers use every means within their power to enhance their communication with all members of the jury.

What are its advantages over the more commonly used visual aids? The most common aid is the blackboard. The attorney customarily places rough drawings on the blackboard, and perhaps figures and computations which she calculates during the evidence. The blackboard, however, is limited to chalk and the artistic talents of the attorney using it. It also contains a limited amount of space. One problem with the use of the blackboard is that when the blackboard is used extensively it can be easily erased and the information contained on it lost as evidence.

Some attorneys use large flip charts or diagrams to explain points. These can be expensive and difficult to acquire. If they are produced spontaneously in the courtroom, here again the attorney is faced with the limitations of her artistic talents.

Documents and photographs are sometimes passed to the jury, but the problem is that each juror must examine the document individually and the attorney cannot be sure that each of the jurors examines the precise area of interest or the area which the attorney wants him to focus his attention upon.

All visual aids have advantages. The overhead transparency projector, however, combines all the best features of the others plus some new ones. The 3M Company calls the overhead projector a part of its visual communications system. It is a system that allows the attorney to convert anatomy charts, photographs, x-rays, hospital medical charts, pages from bound books, tax forms, maps, employment records, and practically everything else into a visual 60″ × 60″ picture.

When the Overhead Projector May Be Used. The overhead projector may be used in four important phases of the trial:

1. The opening statement.
2. During presentation of evidence.
3. During summation.
4. Whenever permitted by the court or statute in the jury room.

For maximum effectiveness, the projector should be placed just outside the witness box and the image cast on the wall or a screeen behind the witness and in clear view of the judge and jury. With this technique the witness can personally explain facts on the transparency being shown while facing in the direction of, and testifying to, the jury.

An important and practical application arises during the testimony of an expert witness. This is particularly true during medical testimony. A doctor testifying without diagrams is required to rely upon his medical vocabulary, which invariably is a foreign language to the jury. Some doctors are unable to reduce medical terminology effectively to lay language. Through the use of transparencies, various parts of the body (including the spinal column, which is the most common area of injury) may be flashed on the screen and are extremely helpful in furthering jury understanding.

An example of effective use of the overhead projector occurs during the testimony of the orthopedic surgeon. A series of transparencies of the spinal column and its component parts may be shown on the screen, and the witness may testify as to the injured area in its relation to the spinal column as a whole. The attorney may then, through the use of another transparency, show a more detailed close-up of the area of the spine in which the injury was observed by the doctor. With a coloring pen the doctor may wish to color in the specific area of injury as he described it to the jury. The technique is extremely effective as an attention getter, and assists the jury in understanding medical terminology and human anatomy.

Where to Obtain Transparencies. The transparencies may be easily obtained by using a thermofax machine and transparency paper, available from the 3M Company. On the other hand, the attorney may wish to take material to a local representative of the 3M Company, where transparencies may be obtained for a nominal cost. Another excellent source of medical originals is the *Medical Atlas for Attorneys*. Some thermofax machines are readily portable and may be purchased or sometimes rented from the 3M Company with the distinct advantage that transparencies may be made from material not otherwise readily accessible, such as at the County Traffic Engineer's office, and the like.

Use During Trial. During the trial an overlay of a clear transparency of a diagram may be provided, and the witness given a red marking pencil. The witness can then, in his own words and sketches, make a diagram of his version of the accident. Later, when the next witness is called, the clear transparency may be removed and the second overlay placed into position. The second witness may then use a different colored pencil, such as a green marking pencil, to demonstrate her version of the occurrence. One word of caution. The overlays should be taped to the frame so that they will return to their exact original position. This technique is an effective aid in demonstrating two versions of the same occurrence, which are permanently recorded on one transparency. Jurors often decide to take the machine to the jury room for use during discussion and re-examination of the testimony.

Transparencies of hospital records, including the emergency room admittance sheet showing the original condition of the plaintiff as described by the admitting doctor, have a tremendous effect upon the jury. Likewise, transparencies of the narcotic record, showing the pain relievers that were administered to the patient during hospitalization, are valuable in assisting the jury in understanding the extent of the pain suffered by the plaintiff. An additional advantage of the transparency projector is that the attorney may project x-ray film directly onto the screen, thus permitting the doctor, while giving testimony, to mount the x-rays and to mark in the presence of the jury, with the use of a marker pencil, the area involved, showing the fracture lines and other bony disturbances. The advantage here is that *ALL* the members of the jury see the x-ray at the same time, and are in a much better position to fully understand the doctor's testimony. The trial lawyer should always test the x-ray prior to use in trial for the reason that some x-rays, being very dense, do not project well even in the dark.

The Use of Photographs. In most accident cases actual photographs are used. Photographs may be of the cars, of the people, of the intersection where the accident occurred, or of the instruments of injury. The attorney often uses photographs to demonstrate the original injury, which has long since healed before trial.

Without the benefit of the projector, photographs are entered into evidence and then passed around to members of the jury to examine them one by one. The lawyer cannot be sure that each juror notices the specific area that is important to the case. The persuasive process demands that all jurors view at one time the specific areas of interest. The obvious advantage of a projector that projects a photograph enlarged to a $5' \times 5'$ image should be apparent. If it is necessary for the witness or counsel to point out a specific area of interest on the photograph, a simple pencil may be used as a pointer or additions and markings made with a marking pen.

Photographic transparencies may not ordinarily be made satisfactorily from a copy machine. Good photographic quality requires that the photographs be made by a qualified photographer accustomed to making regular prints. He merely puts the photograph onto a transparent rather than a paper, base.

Use During Summation. The overhead projector has tremendous use for the attorney during the summation portion of the case. She may prepare a transparency listing the individual elements of damage, and, during the summation, flash on the screen the amounts that she has claimed the evidence proves.

ADVANTAGES OF THE TRANSPARENCY PROJECTOR

Controls Attention, and Interest. Light is an attention getter. From the moment the attorney turns the projector on, all eyes focus upon the material shown and the attorney effectively captures the attention and keeps the attention while his point is developed.

Is Convenient. Through the use of the projector the attorney has complete ease of presentation and all transparencies fit readily into his brief case. The attorney needn't concern himself about large or bulky charts or photographs.

Saves Time. The projector technique eliminates the time required to pass documents among the entire jury. The old saying that a picture is worth a thousand words truly applies with the use of the overhead projector technique.

Is Flexible. During the trial, if unexpected testimony is produced by opposing counsel, the speed with which transparencies may be produced enables counsel to produce and have available a new visual aid in time for rebuttal.

May Be Used in Lighted Room. Unlike the opaque projector, the 3M transparency projector may be used in a wholly lighted room with the result that the jury and witnesses can see the material and each other at all times.

Is Inexpensive. Unlike large cardboard charts, which can be expensive, transparencies are relatively cheap. The average cost of a transparency is about thirty cents. All visual aids necessary for use in an average trial can be produced for as little as three to four dollars.

Is Versatile. The attorney can use overlays, and this revolutionary technique keeps attention on the point being made. He can also highlight the evidence with a marking pen, which makes the projector seem as spontaneous as a blackboard.

Some Suggestions for the Use of the Overhead Projector. It is considered good technique to enter the projector and transparencies in evidence as exhibits. In many instances the jury will then be able to use them during deliberation. Whether or not the machine can be sent to the jury room varies from state to state, but if an objection is raised, citation of cases involving tape recorders sent to the jury room may be useful.

One way to avoid objection is to state to the court with certainty that the visuals will be used for illustrative purposes only.

In order to secure admission of medical transparencies, the lawyer should provide the doctor in advance with copies of the drawings he will later use in transparency form. The medical witness should then be asked if the material is representative of the medical testimony he will give, and he should be told that the attorney will be using an overhead projector.

Where the attorney plans to project x-rays, it is good policy to inspect them in advance for clarity. Some x-rays are simply too dense for good projection. In some instances it will be necessary to dim the lights when working with x-rays.

It is extremely simple for a photographer to make a transparency from a photographic negative, providing she has the proper material. Ortho or THO film, or Kodak's fine grain positive works best. Be sure to ask the photographer to use 8 × 10 or 8½ × 11 size transparencies. Instruct her also to use a flat matte screen (not beaded) for maximum wide angle viewing in the courtroom. The use of projectors has become so commonplace that some courtrooms have walls specially painted to serve as a screen for projection.

A word of caution. If the attorney places the screen higher than the projector, a distorted view, known as keystoning, results. To avoid this, tilt the screen so that the screen is perpendicular to the projector.

Attention-Getting Technique. In order to use the projector with maximum effectiveness, the attorney should understand the value of light as an attention getter. He should practice with the projector, and always turn the projector light on when he wants the juror's eyes turned to the screen. The projector should be turned off when the attorney wishes attention focused on himself. Light is fascinating, and acts as a magnet to the human eye; but if it is left on all the time, it will lose its fascination, become irritating to the jury and difficult for the jury to look at.

THE OPAQUE PROJECTOR

The opaque projector has many of the same advantages and some additional advantages and disadvantages of the overhead transparency projector. The best opaque projector for all-around courtroom work appears to be the Vu-Lyte III, manufactured by Charles Beseler of East Orange, New Jersey.

The Use of the Opaque Projector. The opaque projector differs from the overhead transparency in that it requires a dimming of the lights or a darkening of the room in order to obtain the best visual image. It has the advantage that it will project anything placed upon the plate, other than transparencies. Thus, a black and white photograph or a colored photograph projects upon the screen. Many attorneys prefer to use a combination of the overhead transparency projector and the opaque projector, since hospital charts and records, photographs and other nontransparent articles may be projected without necessity of converting them to transparencies. The trial lawyer should study both machines and adapt them to his practice. The value of the use of courtroom projectors as a visual aid to assist in the persuasive process cannot be overemphasized.

9.2 CLOSING STATEMENT—YOUR LAST CHANCE

This chapter contains very few examples of jury arguments. In recent years, many good books have been written that contained excellent and inspirational examples of jury arguments. Few of the books, however, contain any analysis of why a given jury argument is effective. Here we will attempt to analyze some of the factors that make a jury argument persuasive and convincing.

No two lawyers give the same jury argument. Every lawyer must give something of himself or herself and an attempt to copy or mimic another lawyer's argument results in an appearance of insincerity and, usually, defeat.

The mere memorization of jury arguments is analogous to an engineering student who memorizes algebra formulae, as contrasted with learning the mathematical rules that support the formulae. The engineering student could, by such memorization, solve problems so long as the same problems reoccurred, but she could not readily solve new problems without knowledge of the principles involved.

Many experienced trial lawyers deliver effective jury arguments based on experience obtained in the courtroom, or based on intuitive processes. Although intuition, instinct, and feeling for the reactions of a jury will always remain the final appeal of the trial lawyer, basic knowledge of the factors involved in persuasion can greatly add to the certitude of the lawyer, and assist him or her in reaching a favorable result. The following factors and suggestions serve as examples.

9.2.1 Credibility Is the Vital Key

One of the principles affecting the acceptance by the listeners, the jurors, of a given argument is the opinion of the juror of the expertness and trustworthiness of the communicator, the lawyer. The juror should be reminded of the lawyer's role in the trial as an officer of the court. He or she must be made to understand that, as an officer of the court, the lawyer is held to certain standards of conduct and certain duties, and that her position is worthy of no less respect than that of the judge.

This factor also points up the fallibility of the premise upon which many a young lawyer proceeds when she deliberately tries to appeal to the sympathy of the jury, and asks the jury to compare her ineptness or inexperience with that of her more experienced opponent. In all probability, this comparison is harmful to the young lawyer, unless the jurors are made to feel that the more experienced lawyer was taking advantage of his expertness and was less trustworthy or reliable in his intentions than the younger lawyer.

This factor would also indicate that scrupulous fairness on the part of the trial lawyer is probably an important factor in persuasion. If the juror had an opportunity to see that one of the two lawyers in the trial never misstated or overstated a case, made no attempt to distort the facts, and framed arguments that were always consistent with an interpretation of the facts, he or she would in all probability gain higher acceptance than that of a lawyer who had in some way become suspect to the jury.

9.2.2 Remind the Juror of His Role

Scientific experiments have shown that people in our society will tend to conform to the norm of a group of which they are a part if they are reminded of the fact that they are a member of that group. For example, some interesting studies are reported in a book called, "Communication and Persuasion," by psychologists Carl Hovland, Irving L. Janie, and Harold Kelley of Yale University. A study was conducted by psychologist Kelley, utilizing as subjects Catholic students in public high schools and in nondenominational colleges. Students of other religious faiths were also included for the purpose of comparison. In the course of the experiments, some of the students received reading material intended to heighten their awareness of Catholic church membership. Others received unrelated neutral material. Students were then given statements intended to modify their opinion in a direction away from Catholic norms. Of the students involved, when their awareness of the church had been aroused, Catholics tended to show greater resistance to change than when their awareness of group membership was low. Thus, it would appear probable that an argument that reminds the juror of the significance of her role, the fact she should be an impartial arbitrator of justice, the fact that she holds significant and important factors in the scope of her decision, would be a more persuasive argument than one that failed to contain such statements.

9.2.3 The "Yes, Yes, Yes" Technique

Most trial lawyers learn early in trial practice the basic technique sometimes called the "yes, yes, yes" technique. This technique involves advancing arguments that are readily acceptable to the juror, or where the conclusions are almost inescapable and where unanimous agreement as to the conclusions may be expected. Once the juror has become conditioned to accept the first several arguments and conclusions, additional, more complex, and perhaps less conclusive, arguments can be advanced with greater probability of acceptance by the jurors.

9.2.4 Pacing the Development of Emotional Arguments

Someone has said that he who leads should be slightly ahead of his followers, but only slightly. One who leads, if he outdistances his followers too much, will lose contact with them and lose the capacity to guide them. This principle should be observed in the preparation and delivery of jury argument. Most jury trials contain elements that appeal to both the emotion and the reason of the jurors. Often the lawyer is caught up in the problems of a client and has developed empathy with the client's cause. The lawyer, however, must closely control the emotional content in the closing argument, and make certain that the emotional appeal presented is well within the range of that which the juror is ready to accept.

There is substantial evidence that when an appeal is made to fear and as a means of inducing compliance with an argument presented, the greatest amount of persuasion is produced by relatively low emotional appeals. This would suggest that when the emotional appeal of the argument is greater than that which the jury is willing to accept, the juror, probably at a subconscious level, simply "tunes out" and may not thereafter be persuaded.

9.2.5 Argue in Terms of the Already Acceptable

Psychologists are in general agreement that virtually all Americans share certain beliefs, some of which are:

1. That all people are entitled to be treated equally under the law.
2. That all people have a right to the pursuit of happiness.
3. That thrift and hard work should be rewarded, and that sloth and improvidence should not be.
4. That a man or woman should bear up under adversity to the best of his or her ability.
5. That no one should be held to a standard of perfection, and that all people are prone to err.
6. That justice should be available to everybody.
7. That if a person owes a debt he or she should pay it.

Most jurors believe in love and forgivingness, but jurors also believe in justice and in paying debts. For this reason, arguments should be couched in terms of "balancing the scales of justice," "paying the debt created by the defendant when she failed to live up to her fair standard of care," rather than in terms of retribution.

9.2.6 Aiming Your Argument at a Particular Juror

Not all jurors produce the same effect on the jury's findings. Those jurors with stronger personality characteristics will influence the ultimate outcome more than the weak or indecisive juror. Vocal jurors who are accustomed to expressing themselves will frequently affect a jury verdict more than the inarticulate. Jurors whose occupations indicate that they are accustomed to analyzing a situation and making decisions for themselves or others are more likely to strongly affect the outcome of the jury deliberations than are jurors who customarily rely on others for their decisions.

This principle is important when a study of the makeup of the jury panel indicates that the decision in the case is likely to be written largely by one or two individuals on the jury. Under such circumstances, the use of phrases and background ideas completely compatible with those familiar to, and held by, those jurors, would clearly be indicated. For example, if two of the strong-minded people of the jury happen to be electricians, it is suggested that the nerve patterns of the human body be described in terms of electrical circuits.

The deliberate phrasing of arguments to appeal to the characteristics of an individual juror must be very subtly and lightly done, however, if it is attempted at all, since if the juror feels that there is an attempt at manipulation, his or her reaction is more likely to be harmful than helpful.

9.2.7 Choice of Language May Be the Difference in Communication and Persuasion

The lawyer should use language that is familiar to the juror, but yet should use language that is admired by that juror. It is not necessary to use the precise phrases that would be used by the juror. A famous essay entitled "The Mucker Pose," explains why in a democratic country there is a tendency on the part of many people to perform to the standard of the least common denominator in society. Thus, in many instances, a person may use English that is much less correct that that of which he or she is capable, or may resort to profanity where other phrases would more adequately express the meaning. Jurors, however, usually feel that in their role as jurors they are carrying out a special function of significance to the community. Many bring to their roles as jurors almost a religious intensity. Under these circumstances, to yield to the tendencies described in "The Mucker Pose" can often be fatal. Communication may be maintained, but persuasion is lost.

9.2.8 Should You Anticipate Your Opponent's Argument?

One of the questions that frequently faces trial lawyers in the preparation of a closing argument is whether or not they should anticipate in an attempt to demolish an opponent's argument before it is raised. Although the problem must yield to the final judgment of the attorney in each case, substantial evidence exists that when argument is to be presented, and there is to be countering argument on the other side, greater opinion change in the desired direction is obtained by anticipating and forewarning the jurors of the probable arguments of the opponent.

9.2.9 Analogy as an Aid to Persuasion

Many people are unable to reason abstractly, but can competently reach conclusions that are useful by transposing experiences and conclusions drawn from analogous circumstances.

9.2.10 Using Graphic Aids in Argument

Eighty percent or more of the information received and comprehended by the human mind is visual in nature. Thus, the judge who prohibits the use of the blackboard, maps, or photographs, is to some extent putting blinders on the juror and diminishing the juror's capacity to receive and understand the information transmitted. The lawyer who ignores the use of visual aids in persuasion ignores the whole framework of human psychology. However, when a lawyer elects to use maps, photographs, or other graphic aids, he or she must be certain that the graphic aids being utilized in fact do clearly portray what the lawyer says they portray, or the lawyer will rapidly lose credibility with the jury.

9.2.11 Appeals to Fundamental Beliefs

Some appeals for opinion change may be couched in terms of fear (example: fear that justice will not be done, fear that in the event damages are not assessed there will be no deterrent for repetition of the act involved, etc.).

An effective appeal can be made to the desire for group conformity, particularly if the individual is reminded of the group of which he or she is a part—for example, as Americans we traditionally believe in equal justice for all, regardless of race, creed, or color.

Appeals may be made to the bedrock, fundamental beliefs of the individual or group involved. For example, if the plaintiff has gone back to work under adverse conditions, it can be argued that a person should not be penalized for the courage shown in attempting to work even though the activity involved in the work caused substantial discomfort. This appeal is directed to the subconscious feeling of most Americans that a person should be brave and stoical, and that work, courage, and virtue should be rewarded rather than penalized.

Peculiarly enough, some experiences show that if you state that you believe the jurors already agree with what you are about to say, you tend to induce belief in the succeeding argument.

Jurors tend to best comprehend, and thus be affected by, the first and last statements given in a particular context.

Other Factors in Persuasion

The trial lawyer must study and fully understand the principles of psychology in the mechanics of human motivation. Basic principles of psychology should be followed in presenting material; remove distracting influences, use contrast to obtain emphasis in the evidence, and use particular argument more than the ideas expressed in the body of the argument.

9.2.12 Integrating the Case in Closing Argument

Closing argument should be utilized to integrate the case, to make the case a single unit. Closing argument should remind the juror that in opening statement you had told them that certain things would be proved. Closing argument should then point out the fact that these things were proved, and you have thus kept faith with the jury. Closing argument should explicitly show the way the facts have been tied into the law as the judge gives the law. Some argument exists as to whether or not it is better to explicitly state a point upon which you hope to persuade the jury, or whether or not some inferences should be left for the jury to draw. The authors of this book believe that if the inference is plain and the jury extremely intelligent, on a few occasions the conclusion may be left for the jury to draw, but in the overwhelming majority of the cases, it is safer to explicitly state the conclusion you want the jury to draw, then point out the factors that remorselessly force you to this conclusion.

Summary

Closing argument should be carefully planned in relationship to the specific case and the specific jury. It is true that some arguments bear repetition because some situations repeat themselves from time to time. However, cases are almost never identical, and variations in the theme are almost always necessary for optimum results. The underlying psychological principles remain the same, and, if followed, permit the theme to be varied for the best result.

EXAMPLES

Parts of Closing Arguments with Analysis

There follows an example of the introductory remarks in a case in which there was a partial blinding of a little boy. A construction company left an unguarded and uncovered pit filled with partially slaked lime in an area where many small children played. The pit could have been made safe by a heavy iron grill, manufactured 10 days after the accident by the construction company involved for a cost of ten dollars. The fact of subsequent repair would not ordinarily be admissible as evidence of negligence but the cost of subsequent repair may be admissible to show the relative ease with which the condition could have been cured by the defendant and the cost thereof.

Example argument:

Ladies and gentlemen of the jury, we come now to the end of four days of trial to the point in the case where it becomes the duty of lawyers, as officers of the court, (reminding jurors of your role as a court official to add to your credibility as a source) to act as guardians of justice in this case. (reminding them of their role, the "yes, yes, yes" technique).

Before I yield to my duty as an officer of the court (again reminding them of your role) perhaps it might be well to take a few of the precious minutes allotted to me by Her Honor, the judge, (showing respect for authority), to whose jury instructions you will later listen (this makes it more difficult for the judge to unfairly cut you off), and make a few general remarks. First, on behalf of our client, we lawyers who act as officers of the court, (your role, again) and even Her Honor, the Judge, I would like to thank you for the close attention you have given us during the trial (the "yes, yes, yes" technique). All of us are aware of the sacrifices involved in serving as jurors and that the five dollars a day is far from adequate compensation (say in the beginning what is already accepted and already thought—the "yes, yes, yes" technique). Most lawyers and judges, however, feel (stealing a little of the judge's prestige) that when a citizen sits as a juror, he performs perhaps his highest civic function (appeal to pride, reminding the juror of his role, preparing him for an important decision, the question of how much a client will receive). A citizen, when he sits as a juror, sits as a final judge of the facts, cloaked with every bit of the authority and finality in this court as to the facts as is Her Honor, the Judge, as to the law (reminding the jurors of the solemnity and importance of their role). Jurors, too, have the difficult task of putting a value on intangible items of damage as well as obvious items of damage (Anticipating and preparing the juror for the difficulty that they may have in assessing the value of items such as physical pain). Any of us, regardless of lack of imagination or understanding or any of the finer feelings of humanity, can ascertain what the out-of-pocket expenses of, the economic loss to, the injured party are. The juror is often called on to do more, such as in this case in which the injuries inflicted on the little boy strike at the very roots that would have permitted the full development of his personality (appeal to pride, and the desire to protect the young). This is a more difficult task, one which the law imposes on each of you, to measure and place an economic value on what has been taken away from the plaintiff (use the little boy's first name) in this case (appealing to the subliminal feeling of the juror that debts should be paid). I am sure that each of you will recall that in the beginning of this trial (appeal to the fact that you believe the jurors agree with you), when we were selecting you as jurors (appeal to pride), that each of you swore under your oath as jurors, that if the evidence showed that my client was entitled to be paid for the damages done by the defendant (appeal to the belief that debts should be paid), you would consider and place a value on each of the separate items of damages, however difficult this may be.

Counterargument to Contributory Negligence and Its Analysis

(This is from an argument made by Craig Spangenberg, Cleveland, Ohio.)

Gentlemen of the jury. In a few moments opposing counsel will speak to you. We know from past experience from almost every other case we have ever tried against him (impugning the sincerity of opposing counsel as a source of information) that he will say that contributory negligence, however slight, is sufficient to destroy a case. I would like to say that if my client was, in fact, guilty of contributory negligence, that we *know* we are not entitled to recover (keeping attention—if we know that, then why are we here?).

It is true that contributory negligence is a bar to recovery on the part of our client. We knew that was so when we came in here, but what is contributory negligence? Contributory negligence is really composed of two things (argument must be framed in a logical way). The first of these is negligence, and the second is cause; negligence that contributes to cause; it isn't *conduct* that causes it, or *actions* that cause it, it is *negligence* that causes it that is significant. Do you understand that? There is a collision my client was involved in; there he was on the road. Now, he helped to cause it in the sense that he was there—he was driving; his conduct helped cause it, but contributory negligence to defeat his recovery must be *negligent* conduct.

Now, in a few minutes, His Honor, the Judge, will give the jury its instructions and he will say what I have already told you (appeal to authority), to the effect that my client cannot recover if there is contributory negligence, but *what is negligence?* His Honor, the judge, will also tell you that negligence is the failure to exercise ordinary care—two words. Care—what kind of care? How much care? The answer is *ordinary* care. What is ordinary? It is average, *usual.* The kind of care the average, prudent, careful person like all of you would exercise. Now, this doesn't mean the greatest care in the world. For example, it is a little like your boy going to school. When he comes home from an arithmetic examination, and is very proud because he got ninety-eight percent, what do you say to him? Do you say to him, "Son, you missed it by this little bit; you are a failure, you should be perfect"? You know what average is. Average is seventy percent. If he gets sixty percent—he's flunked, or even if he gets sixty-eight percent, he's flunked. But if he makes seventy per cent, he is average, he's passed, and he's gotten a C. That is *ordinary* ability in arithmetic classes. Ask your little boys. They will tell you they are grading on the curve. That middle block is C—that is ordinary. That is all my client was required to do, that is, to pass (effective analogy). Then when you analyze what he did in the terms of ordinary care, it can be clearly seen that he was not guilty of what the law refers to as contributory negligence.

10

How to Handle Specialized Personal Injury Cases

10.1 MEDICAL NEGLIGENCE CASES

10.1.1 The Historic Privileged Immunity of the Medical Profession

The medical profession has consistently enjoyed near immunity for its errors and omissions, from its origin in witch doctors and sorcerers to its present status of near gods enshrined in white robes in their pantheons of healing.

Why has this been so, and to what extent is it true now?

In the earliest days of the healer, knowledge was scarce regarding the actual mechanism of disease and physical malfunction. Today, knowledge is more available, but is still concealed from the uninitiated to a large degree.

The witch doctor could better withstand questions regarding his methods and results than his modern-day counterpart because no body of scientific recorded knowledge existed. The witch doctor's assertions that his "devil dance" would be helpful, if the devil were not too strong, could not be disputed—and sometimes the dance worked.

Modern medicine does not enjoy the same immunity from examination concerning the efficacy of its machinations. When the placebos of modern medicine work, no examination of the method ensues. However, when the patient dies or is maimed, questions can now often be asked and answers obtained, and responsibility for egregious error be fixed.

The medical profession in the United States still enjoys privileged immunity from legal responsibility for its errors to a degree enjoyed by no other profession.

What is the standard of care for most of society and where does it differ from that of the medical profession?

Nearly all citizens, including all professions except the medical profession, are held to a standard of reasonable care. This standard does not call for perfection. The actor simply is required to refrain from doing something that a reasonable person in the same position would not do that is likely to cause harm to another, and must do those things that a reasonable person would do.

This is not a complicated standard. It is applied every day in thousands of cases involving complex circumstances by judges and jurors. Its effectiveness is certified by time-honored efficiency and fairness.

The medical profession is not held to this standard in most jurisdictions. The doctor must merely conform to the prevailing acceptable practice in the medical profession. No matter that the standard in the profession may not be reasonable.

An analogy with the defective products cases and the responsibility of manufacturers is relevant. It is well known that whole industries have been and are negligent in the methods of manufacture or design of products, because of the failure to exercise reasonable care in adopting better procedures as they develop, or the failure to use appropriate quality control methods. In contrast, in most jurisdictions the actions of a member of the medical profession must be measured against the self-established standards of the medical profession, rather than the more objective standard of reasonable care customary in other professions.

In a few delinquent jurisdictions, the doctor is further insulated from the consequences of his or her acts by the so-called "locality rule," which holds the doctor only to the standard of care, however atrocious, said to prevail in his or her own prescribed jurisdiction, or similar jurisdictions. This rule has been seriously vitiated, however, in most jurisdictions by the advent of national specialty boards. These boards have vastly improved the overall quality of medical care and training. They do not accept a consciously lower standard of action for medical care under all of the circumstances in a small town in Iowa than in New York City. The hospital or medical facilities may not be the same, but what is available must be used with the same standard of care, regardless of locale.

The medical profession is further insulated from criticism by lack of common knowledge of medical language. There are some medical terms that cannot be readily or conveniently translated into less-specialized language, but many can be translated if desired. A "scapula" can become a "shoulder blade." A "clavicle" can become a "collar bone," etc. The lack of comprehension of medical terms keeps many patients and even sometimes their lawyers from really finding out what happened to the patient.

There is a modicum of justification for the conscious choice of specialized language. The physician is assisted in his efforts to render care by the belief of the patient in the proposed cure. If the patient really understood what was going on, his faith might be shaken. Moreover, some medical procedures and terms have evolved that have no adequate counterpart in common language. Additionally, some medical terms are "words of art" that convey in a single word a complex association of ideas.

Regardless of the justification for the arcane language, its mysteries provide freedom from care for the medical profession.

The medical profession is further protected by special statutes in some states. For example, it is not uncommon for the medical profession to enjoy a shorter period of time in the statute of limitation applicable to it than applies to other members of the public. No valid argument would seem to exist as to why such a shorter statute of limitation would not be unconstitutional when it cuts off the rights of an injured patient, but some such statutes still exist.

Attempts have been made by the medical profession, with varying degrees of success, to induce state legislatures to pass other insulating rules. Among some of these are requirements for arbitration in medical negligence cases, limitations of liability to specified amounts, requirements that verdicts above a certain level be subject to periodic payment over a period of years, etc. Many of these attempts at creating special privilege for the medical profession have been struck down as unconstitutional, but the practitioner who brings a medical negligence case must still bear their burden, as must the public, until the courts have completed the process of sweeping them away.

Three other barriers insulate the medical profession, more than other groups or professions, from the consequences of its acts.

The first of these is the great expense involved in preparing and trying a medical negligence case. Seldom can the necessary research be done, the medical testimony obtained, and the discovery accomplished without the expenditure of a number of thousands of dollars. Since this money must ordinarily be advanced by the plaintiff's attorney because of the inability of the client to do so, it becomes uneconomic to process many perfectly clear cases of medical negligence because of the limited recovery that is possible. If the damages are such that the case is unlikely to produce a substantial verdict, by the time the attorney deducts a third, or whatever the contingent fee is, and recovers the costs advanced, the result to the client is not worth the expense involved. Hence, many clear-cut cases, if they involve small or medium-level damages, must be rejected.

A second insulating factor for the medical profession is the well-recognized "conspiracy of silence" that has caused many doctors to remain silent or look the other way from even extreme examples of patient abuse or medical negligence. The welfare of the patient becomes less important than the welfare of the medical profession or the doctor. The universality of this attitude is no longer apparent. Many sensitive and responsible physicians are now recognizing an increased responsibility to their patients and the public and will now, in selected instances, testify to the truth. There is also a growing awareness that the assessment of responsibility for negligence is a powerful force directed to creating a safer society and profession.

A third factor that inhibits many patients from bringing suit is the sometimes well-grounded fear that such a suit might affect the quality of medical care that they may be able to obtain in the future from other physicians. This fear is often unfounded. Many conscientious physicians would continue to look to the welfare of the patient, even if that patient had found it necessary to assert a claim for medical negligence against a previously treating physician. However, many clients relate instances of difficulty or discourtesy from subsequently retained physicians when they learn of an existing or previous lawsuit.

10.1.2 What to Do When the Client Comes In

Instruct the client before coming in to bring all existing or available medical records. If the client has a spouse or relatives who may be familiar with the case, encourage the client to bring them. Often the spouse, friend, or relative may have observed or been told something different from or additional to what the client has seen or heard.

Instruct the client prior to your first interview to write in detail an account of his or her medical history, and particularly that part that pertains to the potential medical negligence claim. Ask for details, including dates, identity of all doctors and hospitals, including all persons who may have overheard conversations with the physicians and hospital personnel. There are often matters of great significance that may not be in the hospital records and that may even be denied by the doctor.

Look for corroboration of these details by nurses, other patients, and friends who may have visited the client.

We recall one client who told us an improbable story of an orthopedic surgeon who visited her in her room while she was asleep and who awakened her by fondling her breasts. We did not believe her. Later, we took a statement from a hospital roommate who had observed the incident with dismay and disbelief. We also had a court reporter ask not to be left alone with the doctor because of previous sexual advances from the distinguished practitioner. (He was distinguished!)

Sometimes the client's account will be such that you can identify a distinct misunderstanding on the part of the patient regarding what was told him or her, or evidence of psychotic misunderstanding of the real world. The detailed written statement is thus useful in representing the client and in deciding whether you should accept the representation.

Be alert and even be skeptical of the client who comes to you concerned about a matter of billing from the doctor. You are not in the business of resisting small claims suits or arbitrating the reasonableness of the doctor's bills. There are other means and other forums available for this.

If the case has a ring of plausibility, you will need the hospital records and all available medical records. Just because the client tells you something doesn't mean that it necessarily happened that way. The client may have misunderstood something that was said or misinterpreted some event. But listen, as intently as you ever have, to everything.

Then check it.

Explain to the client the special problems involved in medical negligence cases. It is important to preface this explanation with the statement that you are going to tell the client everything, bad things as well as good things. Otherwise, the client may misinterpret your candor and your attempt to realistically appraise the situation as negativism.

Tell the client that you take only a small percentage of the medical negligence cases offered you, and that should be the truth.

Tell the client you will not accept his or her case without investigation and research, and that you will accept a contract subject only to your right to tell the client subsequently that you do not think the case should be processed for his sake and yours.

We try to get the client to advance the first small amount of money necessary to obtain the hospital and medical records. If you take the case, you will be advancing a much greater sum. The requirement that the client put up some money will make him or her realize the seriousness of bringing a claim of medical negligence and will help to eliminate his desire, if any, to take a "cheap shot" at the doctor.

10.1.3 Evaluating the Medical Negligence Claim

When you have all the information available, undertake a careful study of the medical records and the medical literature if you are not already familiar with the condition or procedure involved.

Many medical negligence cases should be eliminated from consideration at this level.

Do not confuse a "bad" or "unfortunate" result with a deviation from the standard of acceptable medical care. An unfortunate result may still represent medical care of the highest quality.

Do not forget what you learned in law school about proximate cause. Terrible medical errors may not have caused an injury, or the condition may not have been avoidable or improvable, with the best of care. A typical example would be one of late diagnosis of cancer, when it is not possible to prove by a preponderance of the evidence that the cancer had not already metastasized at the time of the first opportunity to diagnose. Remember that the burden of proof is on the plaintiff.

10.1.4 Deciding Whom to Sue

If there are several possible defendants whose negligence contributed to the injury of your client, you should sue them all. If you leave out one of them, thinking that you will sue only the most strongly negligent of those possibly negligent, it will come home to haunt you. The defendants included in the suit will point the finger at the absent defendant as the offending culprit and may thus confuse or mislead the jury.

In general, we do not recommend suing nurses, orderlies, interns, residents, or other employees of a health care provider if the employer is legally answerable for their conduct. Exceptions exist where, for example, an emergency room physician may be employed by a professional group or corporation that provides emergency service to the hospital. Peculiarities in insurance coverage alone would probably dictate that he or she be individually included in the suit. Similarly, when the employee's actions are so outrageous or offensive that they possibly invoke in the jury a desire to punish, the jury should not be denied the opportunity to state such an emotion by expressing it in a verdict.

Do not overlook the possibility of negligence on the part of medical suppliers of drugs or equipment. Often there have been warranties and representations made to physicians by such suppliers in an effort to sell the items in question on which the doctor may have relied to the detriment of your client.

Consideration must always be given, before accepting a medical negligence case, to the welfare of existing clients. If you have an existing case in your office in which the testimony of the prospective defendant doctor is involved, you probably could not take the medical negligence case.

Once you make a preliminary determination that a medical negligence case exists, that the damages are sufficient to make it economically practical to handle it, and that you have no conflicts of interest that would prevent your handling the case, what do you do next?

10.1.5 How to Determine if Medical Negligence Exists

First, you begin the search for medical proof and then, ordinarily, you begin the search for medical testimony. (There are a very few cases that would not require medical testimony in which the circumstances speak for themselves. For example, when various items of surgical hardware are left strewn in the patient's anatomy, or where the wrong kidney is removed, or the wrong leg is parted from its owner. Honestly, these things happen! But not often.)

Where do you begin? Your own library, first. You should establish a basic medical library. Suggested medical negligence references are:

1. A good medical dictionary—*Stedman's* is a good one.
2. A good medical atlas of anatomy.
3. An excellent textbook on general medicine, such as *Textbook of Medicine* by Beeson and McDermott.
4. A good textbook of anesthesia, such as *Techniques and Procedures of Anesthesia* by Adriana.
5. The *Directory of Medical Specialists* published by Marquis Who's Who, Inc., Chicago, Illinois.
6. *The Intervertebral Disc* by Spurling.
7. *Textbook of Clinical Neurology* by Wechsler.
8. *Campbell's Operative Orthopedics* published by Mosby.
9. *Glossary of Hospital Terms* by the American Medical Record Association.
10. *Surgical Errors and Safeguards* by Thorek.

Other texts can be added on a case-by-case basis as new problems arise. Eventually, you will have a truly formidable medical library.

Second, if possible, establish a relationship with some doctor who is willing to review cases for you and to express opinions, even if he or she is not willing to testify. The few thousand dollars you will have to pay the doctor each year will soon justify themselves, if you are kept from accepting even one case that is fatally flawed for some reason that you have overlooked. A little experience will soon permit you to tell if the advice you are getting is sincere and sound, or if it is being slanted to protect medical cronies and fellow practitioners.

Establish a private file in your office as you gain experience, containing information as to doctors who have testified for you and others. Obtain and retain curriculum vitae. Accumulate information as to which doctors are able witnesses who can express themselves lucidly and persuasively. Some of the better qualified doctors can be terrible witnesses, either because they come across as arrogant and unlikeable or because they fail to prepare themselves for testimony in a given case, preferring to rely on general knowledge. One of the most dangerous witnesses you can put on for your client is a doctor on whom you have relied who believes his superior knowledge will permit him to deal with effective defense counsel when he has not prepared himself in cooperation with you on your particular case.

Electronic research is dealt with elsewhere in this book in greater depth than in this chapter. However, in locating experts, the computer finds one of its greatest uses. It is possible to determine quickly and easily what articles have been published in nearly all technical journals of general circulation on virtually any subject; the names, addresses, and backgrounds of the authors; and to obtain copies of the articles and thus know the opinions already expressed by the authors in these articles on the subject matter in question.

If you approach a doctor with articles in hand and mind on a given subject that he or she has already written about, the chance of obtaining the doctor's agreement to testify is vastly enhanced.

Expect to be billed generously by the doctors who help you analyze your case or who testify. Be prepared to pay promptly when billed. The payment must not be contingent on the outcome of the case or contingent on the size of the verdict. The doctor should not have to wait on payment for services any longer than it takes you to write the check and deliver it.

Do you always file suit when you are satisfied you have a case? Usually, but not invariably.

If you have a case in which the liability is clear, a "lay-down," and if the damages are readily determined, we suggest that you give the doctor and his or her carrier a short period of time to settle without suit, perhaps thirty to ninety days. Your courtesy will rarely be appreciated, but at least you will have conformed to a high standard of responsible practice.

Do you settle with some of the defendants and continue the suit against others? Sometimes, but not usually.

An excellent technique is to settle with one defendant, with the agreement that he or she must continue in the suit until the jury goes out, and that then the settlement will be announced to the judge and that defendant dismissed from the suit.

It is hazardous to agree with a defendant that he will combine his efforts with yours to fix the blame on another defendant. In many jurisdictions, such an agreement is discoverable and may be disclosed to the jury, and in some jurisdictions, such agreements may be disapproved by the court.

Your discovery must be complete and continuing in medical negligence suits, particularly in reference to prospective experts and witnesses to be used by the defendant. It is so much easier for the defendant doctor to obtain expert witnesses than the plaintiff that it is easy, in football parlance, to be "blind-sided" by an unexpected and undiscovered expert. You must diligently discover—and then seek the court's assistance in setting a reasonable time for witness disclosure that would still permit discovery to be made.

Medical negligence cases involve a high element of teaching skill. The jury usually will have little knowledge of medical terms or anatomy. Medical negligence, consequently, will usually call for more than usual use of demonstrative evidence and teaching aids. The jury can find a medical negligence case a fascinating journey into new fields of knowledge, but you must prepare the road maps and translate the foreign language for them. The jury must be made to understand what the client's condition was when the doctor was retained for treatment, what was expected of the doctor if he or she conformed to an acceptable standard of medical care, what the doctor actually did, wherein the treatment did not conform to the acceptable standard, and what was the resulting harm to the plaintiff. If you fail to satisfy the jury as to any of these factors, the result will probably be no verdict for your client, or at least an inadequate verdict.

Summary

The experienced personal injury trial lawyer should accept some medical negligence cases on a highly selective basis. They present special problems of proof and presentation. The societal results are needed and serve not only as a vehicle to secure justice for your client, but also serve as a goad to the medical profession to eliminate or prevent negligent acts or conditions of practice. In addition to the techniques of evaluation and proof, particularly applicable to medical negligence, apply the general client and trial techniques given in Chapters 3 through 8 of this book.

10.2 DEFECTIVE PRODUCTS LITIGATION

The field of defective products litigation is largely new and is as comprehensive and dynamic as our complex society.

It has expanded in direct proportion to the changes occurring in our society and must continue to expand, if the rights and duties of the public are to be given expression in the courts.

The field challenges us to keep pace with change, and can only be coped with if we utilize all of the facilities available to seek information and organize it.

When one realizes that in the memory of many persons now living, refrigeration, air conditioning, electricity, radio, television, automobile, and airplanes have first appeared, and that new products are still appearing and being employed in our society at an ever-increasing rate, it is obvious why the field of defective products is as pervasive as it is in every segment of society.

The identification, comprehension, and proof of defective products cases involve nearly every area of specialized knowledge and its interface with society.

A topic this broad cannot be covered in a single chapter of a single book. However, some basic suggestions can be offered that will assist in the approach to defective products litigation.

10.2.1 Building a Technical Library—Some Suggested Books

The first basic suggestion is to ensure access to an adequate legal and technical library, and then use it.

For your convenience, if you desire to build a technical library in a subject area, a list of books and sets of books that are useful is appended.

1. *Products Liability* by Frumer and Friedman
2. *A Lawyer's Desk Reference* by Harry Philo
3. *Manual of Accident Prevention and Construction* by the Associated General Contractors of America

4. *SAE Handbooks* for successive years
5. *Guide to Hazardous Materials* by National Fire Protection Association
6. All of the National Fire Protection Codes
7. The Standard Building Codes for your section of the country, such as *The Southern Standard Building Code*
8. Catalogue of the American Standard Codes
9. Any local building codes, such as plumbing, mechanical, etc.
10. *Products Liability of Manufacturers* by PLI

It should be apparent that this is by no means a complete or even adequate list of what your safety library should include. Each case brings its own research problem, but also presents the opportunity and necessity of adding to your library.

10.2.2 How to Analyze the Liability Problems

Realize that nearly any lawyer can learn to research the law and the facts. The art lies in learning to think in terms of areas of possible negligence on the part of designers, manufacturers, assemblers, sellers, and maintainers of products.

In analyzing liability problems in your case, apply the principles of hazard and risk analysis (safety engineering) discussed in Chapter V.

Use the methods of research discussed in Chapter VI dealing with electronic research.

Early in the investigation and development of your case, retain the most knowledgeable and reputable expert you can find and consult him or her.

However, in many cases you may become your own "best expert" in that you must perceive the theory of liability, research it, and then investigate it with the help of your expert. Many specialized and highly knowledgeable individuals are not accustomed to thinking in terms of risk recognition, and eliminating or minimizing the hazard and risk.

10.2.3 How to Plead a Defective Products Case

When you plead your case, plead broadly on all theories of the case such as strict liability, design negligence, manufacturing negligence, breach of implied warranty, breach of specific warranty, failure to warn, etc. Often in the development of the case, by discovery, acts and areas of negligence become apparent that could not be discerned prior to the discovery process.

10.2.4 Proving a Defective Products Case

Keep an expert witness file and exchange information freely with other trial lawyers. Often experts can be obtained by the methods described in the material on electronic research.

If your damages justify it and the liability looks promising, do not be afraid to spend money in research and case development.

The proper handling of defective products cases involves the acquisition of the proper research tools and the application of the necessary imagination and diligence to perceive and develop the case, in addition to the use of the general client and trial techniques given in Chapters 3 through 8 of this book.

If all of the above is to daunting or too expensive, pick the best lawyer-specialist in the field and refer the case. You can always ask for copies of all pleadings and correspondence, attend the hearings and depositions, and fully participate. You do not have to "invent the wheel." Why not watch one being built and then copy the methods used?

10.3 HIGHWAY ENVIRONMENT CASES

10.3.1 The Controlling Agency as a Possible Defendant

An often overlooked defendant is the governmental agency that owns and controls the highway and its right-of-way. Most such agencies enjoyed governmental immunity until the collapse of the principle in the 1960s.

All highways and streets are under the control of the governmental agency that owns, and has assumed by law, the right of control and the duty to build and maintain the facility. With the obligation to maintain the street or highway, there exists a concurrent and very important duty to provide a facility that is reasonably safe for use by the public. This necessarily implies that the governmental agency will and must maintain the roadway and the roadside area free of hazardous conditions that may cause injury or death to the traveler. Normally this responsibility extends to the entire right-of-way, but in all cases includes any hazard on or adjacent to the roadway.

When the controlling agency fails in its duty to provide a reasonably safe roadway and roadside environment, and injury occurs, that agency, without governmental immunity insulating it from suit may be required to respond in damages if it can be shown that the hazardous condition was a part of the proximate cause of the injury.

10.3.2 Safety Engineering Principles Applied to Environmental Cases

As a prelude to understanding the responsibility of those who own the roadway and its environment and the duty to provide a hazard-free environment, the attorney should understand some of the basic principles of safety engineering and the descending scale of reasonableness that provides the basis for establishment of liability in the environment case.

Accept first the following definitions:

1. Hazard: "A hazard is an existing condition that, when coupled with human activity, can produce injury or death."
2. Risk: "The risk is the chance that a hazard will produce injury or death."

Any good highway engineer, traffic engineer, or other person charged with the responsibility of affording a safe environment for vehicles using the roadway will agree that a *condition* which, when coupled with the human activity of vehicles being driven in close proximity to it, over, or around it that can produce injury or death, is, in fact, a hazard. Such person will also agree that the risk of injury or death is directly affected by exposure to the hazard, in direct ratio to the exposure factor.

Example of Hazard

Every motorist has encountered a railroad crossing at grade, that is to say, a railroad crossing that crosses the highway at the same level. Any reasonable person will agree that a railroad crossing at grade constitutes a hazard and that if there is one car a day crossing the railroad track and one train per day crossing the roadway, the hazard exists and the risk that a collision will occur is present, though minimal. In the business of safety engineering, the first objective should be to *eliminate the hazard,* if possible or economically feasible. This is the reason we see in high-exposure areas railroad crossings that are elevated over roadways or tunneled under the roadway, thus eliminating the *hazard* of the railroad crossing and the *risk* of a collision between the two vehicles.

It is not feasible to overpass or underpass every railroad crossing with a vehicular street or highway. So in the descending scale of reasonableness, where it is impossible to eliminate the hazard and thus the risk, the next reasonable activity must be to minimize the hazard and the risk and to instruct and warn as to the remaining hazard and risk. The example of minimizing the hazard and risk is the installation of road-crossing gates, which to a large extent inhibit the traffic from encroaching upon the railroad track at and before the time of the train approach, and it is axiomatic that where such a condition exists, advance warning of the presence of the track must be installed, as well as warning of the location of the track in the form of a crossbuck—also a gate, and warning of the approach of the train through the use of flashing lights, bells, or horns.

If, for some reason, be it economic or otherwise (it is usually based upon exposure established by traffic counts), it is not considered reasonable to minimize the hazard and risk and instruct and warn as to the remaining hazard and risk, then in the interest of safety, the least that must be done is to instruct and warn the traveler upon the roadway of the presence of a railroad crossing ahead, of the location of the crossing, and of the approach of the train through the use of bells and horns on the train to afford some opportunity to the motorist to protect himself from injury or death.

These principles must be understood by the attorney who seeks to analyze, prepare, and prosecute a case against a governmental agency for failure to eliminate the hazard or instruct and warn as to the hazard and risk. Thus, they are repeated as follows:

In the exercise of reasonableness, if a hazard exists, the responsible party must do the following in the descending scale of reasonableness:

1. Eliminate the hazard
2. Minimize the hazard and instruct and warn as to the remaining hazard and risk
3. Instruct and warn as to the hazard and risk
4. Warn as to the hazard and risk
5. Do nothing

Where a duty exists to protect travelers on the public thoroughfares, a do-nothing posture on the part of the governmental agency should mandate a recovery to the aggrieved party.

Roadway and Roadside Hazards

It is almost universal law that a governmental agency that owns the roadway and is charged with the duty of maintaining it in a reasonably safe condition is liable for damages caused because of the maintenance of a hazard in or adjacent to the roadway absent a fair and adequate warning of the presence of the hazard. Nor is it necessarily a defense that the hazardous condition was open and obvious. The maintenance of a hazard on or adjacent to the roadway for an unreasonable length of time under conditions of repeated exposure can form the basis for liability on the part of the governmental agency, even though minimal warnings of the presence of the hazard may have been installed.

What is a hazard? A hazard is any existing condition that, when coupled with the human activity of traveling upon the roadway, can produce injury or death. A twelve-inch drop-off from the edge of the roadway to the adjoining shoulder is an obvious hazard and one that cannot be justified under any circumstances and under almost any method of warning. Indeed, the maximum allowable depression from roadway to shoulder, as established by the Federal Standard Specifications for Construction of Roads and Streets, is three inches and in most instances, such a condition cannot by specification or in reasonableness be permitted to remain overnight.

An intersection—four-legged, "T," or "Y" constitutes a hazard that warrants fair and adequate signing to alert the motorist to its presence and with sufficient advance notice to afford the motorist an opportunity to see and react to the hazardous condition. It is not our purpose to provide a laundry list of hazards that can and do exist on and adjacent to roadways and it is strongly recommended that every attorney who aspires to successfully prosecute a roadside environment case acquire, study, and understand all of the minimum requirements contained in the *Uniform Manual on Traffic Control Devices for Streets and Highways.*

10.3.3 Provisions of State Motor Vehicle Manual

Most states have adopted a uniform manual and have incorporated it as a part of the body of law for the state. It must be emphasized that the provisions of the manual are minimum standards and many conditions warrant additional study and signs that, in the exercise of reasonableness, are intended to assist the motorist in avoiding injury because of conflict with the hazardous condition. The manual repeatedly admonishes the governmental personnel to conduct engineering studies to determine if additional signing is required and to analyze the condition for the purpose of affording the optimum in instructions and warnings to the motorist to assist the motorist in avoiding injury or death.

10.3.4 Standards in Road Construction and Maintenance

From the advent of the first automobile and first motor vehicular roadway constructed until approximately the 1960 decade—since the governmental agencies that owned the roadway and right-of-ways were absolutely insulated from suit by the principle of governmental immunity—the state highway officials and others, with unbridled dexterity, established standard after standard in the design, method of construction, construction, and maintenance of the nation's roadways. Up until the 1930s, little effort was made to standardize roadway signs and each state and governmental agency was at liberty to develop signs or no signs almost at will. In the 1930s and forward, the National Association of State Highway Officials and others saw the need for establishing standardized signs as to shape, color, and placement.

10.3.5 Types of Highway Signs and Their Importance

There are three basic types of signs:

1. The guide sign
2. The warning sign
3. The regulatory sign

The primary purpose of the guide sign is to assist the motorist in finding his way, the sole function of the warning sign is to warn the motorist of hazards on and adjacent to the roadway, and the function of the regulatory sign is to mandate conduct on the part of the motorist. A stop sign is a regulatory sign and has a distinctive octagonal shape. It is red with white letters and in the western world contains the word "Stop." Warning signs, with some exceptions, are diamond shaped, are yellow with black letters, and contain words or symbols intended to alert the motorist to the nature of the hazard to be encountered. Guide signs are variable in shape and color and function only to assist the motorist in finding his route or identifying the location of his destination.

The Importance of Warning Signs

Since warning signs are used to alert the motorist to hazards on and adjacent to the roadway and since a failure to adequately warn the motorist of such hazards can be the basis for liability, the warning sign is of utmost importance to the negligence lawyer seeking to establish liability on the part of the responsible agency.

A warning sign must be placed sufficiently in advance of the hazard to afford the motorist time to see it, understand it, and react.

Warning signs for construction and maintenance projects are used to notify drivers of *specific hazards* that may be encountered when those operations are underway. Failure to provide warnings as to *specific hazards* is a direct violation of the manual and is evidence of negligence.

The manual says, "No one standard sequence of signs or other control devices can be set up as an inflexible arrangement for all situations due to the variety of conditions encountered." It goes on to say, "Minimum standards of application are prescribed for typical situations." If it is not practical to prescribe detailed standards of application for all the situations that may conceivably arise, minimum standards are presented in the manual for the most common situations. The manual states, "It is emphasized that these are minimum desirable standards for normal situations and that additional protection may be provided when special complexities and hazards prevail." The manual also contains this interesting observation. "In particular situations not adequately covered by the provisions of this manual, the protection of the traveling public... will dictate the measures to be taken . . ."

It is strongly recommended that the attorney carefully review in detail all of the provisions of the manual, particularly with respect to warning signs, and continue his or her education and research by acquiring and reviewing the volumes of literature generated by the Highway Research Board, the National Association of State Highway Transportation Officials and its publications. Of particular value are the "Blue Book," published in 1965 and entitled *A Policy of Design for Rural Highways,* and the "Yellow Book," first published in 1967, entitled, *Highway Design and Operational Practices as Related to Highway Safety,* published by AASHO. The attorney should also review the highway safety literature abstracts published by the federal government, should have in his library *Highway Engineering* by Oglesby, *Highway Engineering* by Ritter, Volumes 12–13 of the *Highway Safety Program Manual,* published by the Federal Highway Administration, a publication known as *Traffic Reviews for Operational Safety,* and *Positive Guidance in Traffic Control,* published by the United States Department of Transportation.

Other Warning Methods and Delineators

Roadway markings are essential to safety. Continuous edge-line markings should be placed on all roads more than twenty-two feet in width where traffic volumes justify the expenditure. It is particularly important where shoulders are bad. So says the publication entitled *Roadway Delineation Systems,* NCHRP Report No. 130, nor is it appropriate in most circumstances for a highway authority to fail to provide edge-line markings when indeed the average cost is little more than ten cents per foot for continuous white edge-line markings.

Many drivers feel that the view of the roadway surface ahead is their principal source of information for safe driving. View of the roadway is especially important on a two-lane highway where drivers are more dependent on road geometry for guidance. The effectiveness of edge lines has been suggested repeatedly by team members on all types of highway facilities. Despite a high contrast between the shoulder and through lanes, drivers are benefited by the presence of an edge line. Edge lines apparently give the driver a greater sense of security in operating a vehicle and if this is in fact the case, edge lines should be provided in order to allow the driver to perform the driving task under more nearly optimum conditions. Rural two-lane highways present the driver with the task of tracking and thus attention is focused on the pavement. Under these conditions, the pavement marking message can be very effective.

10.3.6 The Highway Shoulder: A Bad One Can Kill

It is desirable that a highway shoulder be flush and level at the through-lane edge to permit pull-over at highway speed without major steering effort to regain control. A flush, smooth shoulder area also is valuable when a driver unintentionally edges off the traveled lane; in effect, it is an auxiliary lane on which a driver corrects his or her path. The shoulder is the most useful part of a clear roadside area on which a driver of an out-of-control vehicle has a chance to begin to regain control. Edge-striping is useful to help regain traffic in the pavement area. (See *Current Practices in Shoulder Design, Construction, Maintenance and Operation,* Research Board Circular No. 142, April 1973.)

Roadside Hazards

An intensive crash program to remove roadside hazards on existing streets and highways and to engineer the roadsides of new facilities with safety as a major criterion should be paramount to the highway department of each state. Only in this way will the motorist who inadvertently leaves the traveled way have adequate protection against death or injury. The shoulder should be flush with adjoining through lanes. Even the most superficial study of traffic accident experience shows that a substantial number of vehicles leave the traveled way, inadvertently or otherwise. Because this is true, every reasonable effort should be made to design the roadsides for this eventuality. The motorist must be given as safe a roadside situation as is practical to provide. The value of edge lines in enhancing safe travel and extending night visibility is universally accepted. Paint is inexpensive and edge lines and lane lines should be applied and maintained as needed in construction areas and on detours to assist traffic flow. Construction and maintenance operations should include adequate advance warnings for all unexpected conditions.

So states *Highway Design and Operational Practices Related to Highway Safety,* published by the American Association of State Highway Officials in 1966.

It should be remembered that approximately thirty-five percent of all injury-producing and death-dealing motor vehicular incidents are single-vehicle accidents involving "run-off-the-road" occurrences.

This being true, it should be apparent that every single-car accident warrants a thorough investigation of the highway environment and the roadside hazard picture.

10.3.7 A Minimum Technical Library for Highway Environment Cases

The following is a partial list of documents and material that should be reviewed by the lawyer in analyzing, accepting, preparing, and trying a roadside environment case:

CHECKLIST FOR DETERMINING LIABILITY OF CONTROLLING AGENCY IN HIGHWAY ENVIRONMENT CASE

1. Accident report
2. *Manual on Traffic Control Devices for Streets and Highways*
3. Construction contracts (if incident occurred in a construction area). All supplemental specifications referred to in the contract
4. *Standard Specifications for Construction on Primary, Farm-to-market, Secondary, State Park, and Institutional Roads and Maintenance Works on the Primary Road System*
5. Project plans
6. District Engineer's file
7. Job descriptions for Department of Transportation personnel involved
8. Highway safety literature
9. *Highway Engineering,* by Herves & Oglesby
10. *Highway Engineering,* by Ritter
11. *Highway Design & Construction,* by Bruce Clarkson
12. *Highway Design & Operational Practices Related to Highway Safety,* AASHO Report, 1967
13. *Highway Safety Program Manual,* Volumes 12–13, by Federal Highway Administration
14. *Traffic Engineering,* by Institute of Traffic Engineers
15. *Roads & Streets*
16. *American Road Builder*
17. Highway Specifications for Construction & Maintenance

18. Publications of the Highway Research Board

19. Safety manual of the Department of Transportation, Highway Division of your state

20. Annual speed checks at selected primary road locations, performed by the Highway Division

21. Traffic Reviews for Operational Safety

22. Highway sufficiency ratings, prepared by state Department of Transportation personnel

23. *Positive Guidance in Traffic Control,* published by the United States Department of Transportation

24. *Current Practices in Shoulder Design, Construction, Maintenance & Operations,* published by the Highway Research Board, April 1973

25. *Traffic Control Devices,* by the United States Department of Transportation

26. Your state highway division maintenance manual, policies, and procedures, published by your state Department of Transportation

---

Care should be taken to research and review all available material on the suspected cause of the injury-producing accident. The library at a state university is a good place to start. Many universities have excellent Transportation libraries, such as the one at the University of Michigan at Ann Arbor.

Summary

The analysis, review, preparation, and trial of a highway environment case requires extraordinary judgment, diligence, imagination, and foresight.

A study of the history of highway construction, maintenance, and signing is strongly recommended. Always go to the accident scene and view the highway environment and the adjoining structures. Ask yourself the following question. What was the real cause of the injury? Would the injury have occurred but for the drop-off from the roadway to the shoulder, or the roadside hazard with which the vehicle impacted? Use the definition of hazard, that being "an existing condition that, when coupled with human activity, can produce injury or death," and identify the condition that contributed to either the cause of the accident or the cause of the injury or both. Review the signing to determine whether adequate warning was provided the driver of the existence of the hazard involved. Never assume that a single-car accident is the sole fault of the driver. It may be the result of a systems failure involving the person (the driver), the machine (the vehicle), or the environment (the roadway or roadside environment).

10.4 AIRCRAFT CRASH LITIGATION

Some lawyers spend a professional lifetime specializing in the preparation and trial of aviation-related cases.

There are strong arguments to be made supporting the position that the average lawyer should never attempt to undertake the handling of an aviation-related accident unassisted. The purpose of this discussion is not to attempt in any way to turn you into an expert on the subject, but to alert you to the subject in a general way and to warn you of the problems you may expect to encounter.

10.4.1 The Causes of Air Crashes

Air crashes are caused by a failure of the overall system in one or more of the following activities:

The Pilot

The National Transportation Safety Board statistics indicate that more than eighty percent of all air crashes are attributable in some way to pilot error or failure. It must be borne in mind that these statistics are generated from the "probable cause" findings of the National Transportation Safety Board and do not necessarily reflect the real cause of an airplane crash. You should understand that the National Transportation Safety Board's activities are concerned solely with an attempt to fix probable cause and not to determine who was legally responsible for the crash. This is a trap that very commonly causes the inexperienced lawyer to fail in pursuit of damages. The National Transportation Safety Board and its activities will be discussed later in this chapter, but you should be warned that it is foolhardy indeed to expect that the board, through its investigative process, will in effect do your investigation for you and hand you the liability on a platter. This just plain does not happen.

The conduct of the pilot is governed by the Federal Air Regulations (FAR), for the most part covered in Part 91 of said regulations. (See C.F.R., Title 14, Part 91.)

The pilot is charged with the responsibility of determining that the aircraft is in an airworthy condition, and is at all times during the flight responsible for the safety of the flight.

The pilot is justified in relying upon those who have special expertise in the design, manufacture, and maintenance of the aircraft to accept the certification by such parties that the aircraft is in an airworthy condition. The pilot is responsible for, amongst other things, determining that the aircraft is airworthy within the limits of his or her expertise. The pilot must know of the performance characteristics of the aircraft, as well as its limitations. The pilot must ascertain that the aircraft is properly fueled, contains enough fuel for the projected trip, is loaded properly within the weight-balance envelope, that the projected trip will be made in weather conditions that do not exceed his or her capability as a pilot, and that there is nothing about the aircraft that renders the aircraft unairworthy within his or her knowledge.

The careful pilot must have available to him or her and refer to the Airmen's Information Manual (AIM), understand the appropriate air traffic procedures, and how to manipulate the controls in the aircraft in an appropriate manner so as to avoid structural damage to the aircraft, and otherwise assure its safety in flight. The pilot of the aircraft has been held to be negligent in failing to assure that the aircraft maintains flying speed, thus control of the aircraft, in failing to assure that the aircraft contains sufficient fuel to reach its destination, in flying the aircraft into weather that exceeds his or her capability, in failing to abort a take-off when in the exercise of reasonableness he or she should have done so, in executing an approach to landing in an unsafe manner, and a host of other incidents of unsafe, thus negligent, conduct.

If you are a nonpilot attorney, you should early on employ the services of an expert airman to advise you regarding the standard and safe procedures to be used under the circumstances of the flight.

The Machine Manufacturer

Contrary to popular opinion, all aircraft are not airworthy when delivered by the manufacturer. Some are unairworthy or defective in design, some are unairworthy or defective in fabrication.

The manufacturer of a general aviation aircraft is governed by the provisions of Part 23 of the Federal Air Regulations (See C.F.R. Title 14, Part 23), and the manufacturer of an air carrier aircraft is controlled by the provisions of Part 25 of the Federal Air Regulations (See C.F.R., Title 14, Part 25).

A reading of Part 23 and Part 25 should convince you that such requirements are minimum in nature, often vague, and capable of multiple interpretations.

The Federal Aviation Administration, because of its lack of personnel, has in many instances opted to permit the design and manufacture of general aviation aircraft to be performed under a system known as the Delegation Option Authority (DOA), which, for practical purposes, permits the manufacturer to design, test, and certify the product as airworthy with a minimum of interference from personnel employed by the Federal Aviation Administration. Does this come as a shock to you? It does to most inexperienced persons, both lay and professional. It is another valid reason why you should seek expert help where a suspected design defect is present and suspected as a cause of the crash.

The manufacturer of general aviation and carrier aircraft is unique in that, though the federal government prescribes certain minimum requirements that must be met in order to obtain from the government a Type Certificate and a Production Certificate, many aircraft at some time during their history develop or demonstrate defects that affect safety in flight. Most aircraft manufacturers have a system of communicating with the owner/operator of the machine known as a *service bulletin, service letter,* or *service instruction.* The bulletin is normally the document that affects safety in flight. The usual procedure is for the manufacturer, upon identifying a safety-in-flight defect or problem, to issue a service bulletin to all owners and operators of the make and model advising the owner/operator of the problem and suggesting a method by which a remedy may be obtained.

Where the problem is of a nature that it becomes apparent to the Federal Aviation Administration that the owner/operators of the aircraft should be required to comply with the service bulletin of the manufacturer, the federal government, through regional counsel for the Federal Aviation Administration, and the Engineering and Manufacturing Branch, now known as the Airworthiness Certification Division, causes to be issued and published an airworthiness directive, sometimes known as an AD Note, which has the force of law and which mandates that the fix be performed by a certain established time in order to continue the airworthiness of the aircraft. Since no aircraft may be legally operated without a valid and current airworthiness certificate, the owner/operator has no choice but to comply, or in the alternative, run the risk of a charge of operating an aircraft while in an unairworthy condition.

It should be emphasized that *aircraft don't just crash. Someone makes them crash.* That someone may be the person (pilot) or the machine (the aircraft) through a defect in design, manufacture, or maintenance.

Maintenance

Another important aspect of air crash litigation and one that requires careful review is the maintenance of the aircraft by repair stations and other maintenance facilities that are authorized by the Federal Aviation Administration to perform repair and alteration work upon the aircraft. Every aircraft has, as part of its documentation when delivered, an airframe or aircraft log book, and an engine or engines log book. If you expect to successfully prosecute an aircraft-related injury case, you should obtain, *without fail,* copies of such log books and at an early date. You should also seek out and copy or obtain the originals of all work orders and invoices that describe the maintenance activities relative to the crashed aircraft. A failure to do so can result in a disastrous failure to obtain important and vital evidence.

Those facilities that maintain aircraft and perform repair, alteration, and maintenance are normally authorized by the Federal Aviation Administration to do so. Every mechanic or repair station facility that performs maintenance, alteration, or repair on an aircraft is required by law to describe the activities in the aircraft or engine log and to identify the repair station or mechanic, together with the license number of the person or facility that performed the function. Normally the aircraft logs contain only a brief description of the activities performed and it is necessary and vital that all work orders and invoices relating to the activity be procured so that you may know, understand, and identify all such activity that relates to the cause or suspected cause of the crash.

It is imperative that you employ the services of an expert maintenance person to review the documentation, including log books, work orders, invoices, service bulletins, and airworthiness directives that are applicable to the aircraft. An important reminder: When aircraft salvage is sold, the logs go with the wreckage. They are sometimes lost or destroyed. Delay in acquiring the logs can be disastrous. Get them, even if you have to purchase the wreckage to acquire them.

It is not uncommon for an aircraft manufacturer to take the position that because an airworthiness directive or service bulletin was not complied with, the manufacturer bears no responsibility for the resulting crash and injuries. Such is not the case. An aircraft manufacturer who was fully aware that the wing spars on his product were developing cracks, and who attempted a "cheap fix" by securing the issuance of an airworthiness directive requiring the owner/operators to have the wing spar examined on a periodic basis, was nevertheless found guilty of negligence when the wing of an aircraft failed in flight, causing death to its occupants.

As in most fields of law, it should be emphasized that the nonspecialist should and must obtain the services of experts in the field of piloting, manufacturing, and maintenance of the aircraft. Failure to do so can result in a failure to recognize a valid claim to the detriment of the client.

Summary

Aircraft crash litigation is a sophisticated business. It is particularly sophisticated because of the many interrelated facets and activities that can join to cause a catastrophic crash. Flying an aircraft in terms of manipulating the controls is a relatively simple endeavor. The judgment that is required of a careful and prudent pilot often spells the difference between a successful flight and one that ends in the death or injury of the aircraft occupants. Both of the authors are experienced fixed-wing pilots and have handled many aircraft crash litigation cases. One author is a rotor-wing pilot and learned to fly helicopters specifically as a preliminary to the handling of helicopter litigation, taking the position that it is unreasonable to believe that a lawyer who does not drive as simple a machine as an automobile could be expected to effectively, consistently, and successfully handle automobile crash litigation. It may sound ludicrous because almost every lawyer drives an automobile, but consider for a moment the handicaps that would ensue if a nonautomobile-driver laywer attempted to handle motor vehicle crash litigation with no real understanding of the requirements of safe operation and the rules of the road.

11

Making Your Mark in the Field

11.1 ACQUIRING THE NECESSARY SKILLS

The chicken comes before the egg—or does it?

Is it necessary to bungle your way through a few clients' cases—and lives—before you can competently handle a personal injury lawsuit? Not if you follow the suggestions of this book.

Methods of acquiring skills: (Take your pick of three.)

1. Go to work for an existing firm, oriented either to plaintiff or to defense, for the period of time necessary to learn.

2. Associate an experienced personal injury trial lawyer in your first few cases. Tell the lawyer frankly that you wish to acquire skills in the personal injury field. Request that he or she furnish you with copies of all pleadings and correspondence. Attend the depositions, hearings, and the trial. Be present at client conferences. At the end of three or four cases,you will be ready to begin handling some of your own cases if you still want to. (Many lawyers find it more profitable and fun to stop at this stage and specialize in other fields. No lawyer can be an expert in all fields.)

3. Attend some of the many seminars provided by trial lawyers. At many of these, you will find some of the most distinguished members of the trial bar sharing and exchanging secrets and skills.

4. We do not recommend this last method! You can blunder your way through a few cases against skilled insurance adjusters and experienced defense counsel, settling for tender largess or the bounty of juries.

There are no other ways!

11.2 HOW TO BUILD A PROFITABLE REFERRAL PRACTICE

If you acquire skills, and if you become a lawyer to whom cases are referred, what rules do you follow with your referral lawyers?

1. Always treat them respectfully. The chances are they know much more about many subjects than you do, and may be making more money.

2. Always consult with them, particularly in the presence of their clients. Send them copies of everything.

3. Always return their clients to them after the completion of the referred case. Never accept another case from the referred client without reassociating the referral attorney.

4. Have a complete and fair agreement about referral fees at the beginning of the case, including the responsibility to be assumed by the referring lawyer. Keep in mind the fact that a lawyer may ethically share a fee only with an attorney who assumes a proportion of the responsibility. The client must be fully informed of the shared fee.

5. Use standardized representation contracts and forms and make sure the referral lawyer and the client understand them.

11.3 THE FINE ART OF ESTABLISHING PERSONAL CONTACTS AND RELATIONSHIPS

Lawyers refer cases for several reasons. The most important is concern for the client and the recognition that in our complex modern world, no lawyer is at his or her best in every field of practice. Some lawyers may refer cases as part of a learning process.

Some cases are referred because of the great expense of preparing them and the fact that the necessary costs and expenses must be advanced by the lawyer in most instances. This is particularly true in medical negligence cases and defective products cases. The lawyer nearly always has invested not only his or her time and skill, but large amounts of money in these two types of cases. The belief of some physicians that lawyers will consider taking a case that they do not believe has merit is naive and inaccurate. No lawyer with common sense who expects to stay in practice would consider investing the thousands of dollars in cash and valued time in a claim without merit. This is not to say that meritless cases are not taken and prosecuted by some lawyers. However, this is nearly always the result of an inaccurate appraisal of the facts or erroneous conclusions drawn from them. An important principle—never underestimate a nuisance case.

And—not to be forgotten—some lawyers refer cases for the additional reason that they like the lawyer to whom they are referring the case and enjoy working with that lawyer. Arrogance or disrespect to the referring attorney is one of the quickest ways to induce him or her to take clients elsewhere.

Despite lowered standards of practice encouraged by United States Supreme Court decisions regarding advertising and solicitation of business, we believe that active solicitation and contacts, even with other lawyers, reflect on the integrity of the solicitor and demean the bar.

However, it never hurts to be friendly—especially to other members of the bar. It is much easier for lawyers to refer a case to someone they know and like than it is to refer to a stranger.

Contacts with non-bar members in civic groups, church, and community activities will produce a certain amount of personal injury business, if the image presented is one to engender respect and confidence. However, this type of contact is less likely to build a practice concentrated in the personal injury field than it is in the field of general practice.

11.4 THE LESS OBVIOUS BENEFITS OF BAR AFFILIATIONS AND SERVICE

This can be one of the most effective means of adding to a personal injury practice, especially if the activity is in any of the specialized bars that are concerned with personal injury practice.

There are three reasons for this.

First, members of the specialized bars tend to respect other bar members for their activity. It is taken as an expression of desire to continue to develop and improve skills.

Second, cases will often come to a lawyer's office that he or she cannot handle for geographical reasons. When this happens, he or she will usually aid the client in finding skilled representation in the proper geographical area. What is more natural than to refer the case to a colleague, known and respected from bar work?

Third, knowledge rapidly becomes common in the trial lawyers' associations as to the skills and areas of specialization of other lawyers. This leads to referrals of cases to those lawyers who have developed such skills and specialized knowledge.

11.5 LIMITING YOUR PRACTICE

Limiting your practice is closely related to the degree that the lawyer has developed specialized skills. It would make little sense to limit your practice to, let us say, medical negligence, if you had not developed skills and a volume of practice in the chosen area. However, once the skills and volume of practice are developed, the limitation of practice to the chosen area tends to be self-reinforcing. It also permits the practitioner to select cases with greater care.

11.6 PREPAID LEGAL SERVICES

Prepaid legal services plans exclude contingency fee contracts in personal injury cases from the coverage of the plan. Hence, such a plan does not usually represent a method of developing a specialized personal injury practice.

However, because of the high volume of general practice clients that potentially can result from such a plan, a significant number of personal injury cases can be a byproduct of such representation. One possible solution is the specialization within a firm, thus permitting one or more firm members to handle the personal injury practice generated by the prepaid legal services. Another solution is for the participating lawyer in the prepaid legal services plan to refer the cases to other specialists. If the requisite continuing responsibility and activity is maintained, there is no ethical or practical reason that a substantial volume of referral fees cannot result from such relationship.

11.7 ADVERTISING: WHEN, WHERE, AND HOW

Despite United States Supreme Court decisions, most lawyers continue to feel that better lawyers do not advertise except perhaps in a few very specialized fields, such as patent law. Few lawyers accept the rationale of the Supreme Court decision to the effect that lower-cost legal fees are likely to result from advertising, except in a few areas of practice.

We feel that advertising in the legal profession, in most instances, has resulted in lower quality of legal services to those who responded to the advertising, and has lessened to a substantial extent the effectivenss of the control by peer group appraisal of the quality of services offered by the legal practitioner. At least in the field of personal injury law, the net effect of advertising has been to permit largely inexperienced and unqualified practitioners to intercept cases that would normally have been referred within the profession to recognized and skilled practitioners. A few of the lawyers who advertise have stumbled their way through a sufficient number of cases acquired by advertising to develop competence, largely at the cost of the first quantum of clients acquired by advertising.

If we are correct in our belief that advertising has not had a good effect on the quality of services to the public or on the legal profession, eventually the harm being done may cause the error of the Supreme Court to be corrected. In the meantime, it will cost the practitioner who advertises the respect and friendship of much of the bar.

11.8 FORMER CLIENTS ARE YOUR BEST ADVERTISING

Former clients produce an astonishingly high percentage of continuing legal representation if the services have been satisfactory and if the client has fully understood the billing process.

One of the ways *not* to enjoy this continuing source of clients is to fail to furnish a written disbursement sheet with full explanation to the client of every expenditure and deduction. It is also important that the client be informed at the beginning of the representation what to expect in this regard, preferably in writing. Client's memories are sometimes short.

It is also wise to inquire carefully and sincerely at the close of the representation regarding any questions that the client has and if he or she is fully satisfied. If the client does not understand it, furnish the necessary information or explanation. If he or she is dissatisifed, unless the client is wholly unreasonable—make him or her satisfied. One particular case is only part of a flow of cases. If the lawyer makes a little less money in one case in an effort to be sure that the client is fully satisfied, he or she is likely to make it up in the long run.

11.9 COMMUNITY REPUTATION: HOW TO GET IT

The public will often acquire a surprising amount of information about lawyers in their area of practice over a period of time. Most trial lawyers have a fairly high profile in their community. The lawyer may acquire the reputation of a "fighter," or a "crook," or of being "above reproach." It is all up to the lawyer; personality, life style, and community reputation have a substantial effect on the capacity of the lawyer to attract practice.

11.10 THE OPPORTUNITIES AND PITFALLS OF MEDIA PUBLICITY

This has been one of the most troublesome areas for the personal injury practitioner. There is no doubt that media reports of a signal victory will cause other clients to seek out the lawyer's office. There is also no doubt that the deliberate seeking of unwarranted publicity is frowned upon by the overwhelming majority of the bar. The personal injury lawyer must walk the delicate and narrow line between responding courteously to the press and its legitimate right to inquire as to newsworthy items, and the deliberate courting of the press for the purpose of creating publicity.

Strong ethical questions exist when the lawyer releases to the press the details of a client's settlement, particularly without the client's permission. The potential invasion of privacy and conflict of interest in the pursuit of the publicity gives the ethical lawyer more than pause. In recent years, "structured settlements" that involve payments to clients over a long period of time have become common. In the context of media publicity, however, the discussion of these has been particularly noxious. The total pay-out to a client over a period of thirty years can be several million dollars, while the present value of the settlement may be a much lesser sum. If the personal injury lawyer reports this to the press as a settlement for the amount of the total pay-out, without reporting the present money value, it constitutes a deceptive kind of publicity seeking that is particularly demeaning.

CONCLUSION

The preparation for trial, and the actual trial of a case, requires an artful blend of skill, imagination, and ethical sensitivity; a surgical precision in the recognition of the significance of specific facts as they relate to each other; a warm concern for the client's interest constrained by social responsibility; and recognition of the limits of legal propriety.

The preparation and trial of a lawsuit is not unlike the attempt to present a New York play with dramatic effect, and social consequences, but you are limited in your selection of the theme. The facts are not chosen by you and, in some instances, are inflexible in that your cast must be chosen from limited and untrained personnel, and the audience reaction may often have permanent impact on the life of your client, sometimes with almost life-and-death effect.

Insomnia and hypertension are the natural lot of the trial lawyer. The failure of a trial lawyer who has a seriously injured plaintiff as a client can cast the dark shadow of poverty over the remainder of the client's life, can limit the client's capacity to obtain adequate medical attention, and can lessen the educational opportunities of the client's children. Success in the trial, however, can illumine the remainder of the client's life and partially recompense the victim of injustice for the damages that have been inflicted.

The greatest reward for the trial lawyer should not be money. It should be genuine feeling that he or she has been able to make a substantial contribution to the intangible quantum of justice in the world.

Index

E

I

J

L